# THE ORIGINAL SIN

# THE ORIGINAL SIN
# A SELF-PORTRAIT BY
# ANTHONY QUINN

**W H Allen.**
London and New York.
A division of Howard and Wyndham Ltd.
1973.

Printed and bound in Great Britain by Butler and
Tanner Ltd, London and Frome for the publishers
W H Allen & Co Ltd, 43 Essex Street,
London WC2R 3JG.

ISBN 0 491 01250 0

*To Mama,*
*who forgave me the day I was born*

*A section of illustrations follows page 152*

# THE ORIGINAL SIN

I WAS LIVING IN NEW YORK, surrounded by possessions, family and position. I had three pictures running simultaneously on Times Square and I was appearing in a play at the same time. Everywhere you looked on Broadway you saw my name in lights.

Some lovely ladies from a drama society gave a luncheon for me. They invited prominent personalities from many fields to pay me homage.

When I was called upon, I tried to thank them. I started haltingly. I looked out at the sea of friendly faces before me, waiting expectantly. Then I heard myself mumbling that I felt like a total failure. I can still recall the shock and dismay that greeted my words. Everyone wanted a light, gracious talk and there I stood declaring that success to me did not mean a thing.

When I finished, my hosts applauded politely, but I had hurt them. I had made a resounding *faux pas,* using their forum as a confessional.

On the way out, I was stopped by a young actor. I thought he of all people would understand. Instead he was furious.

"You shit! I have never been so ashamed of anyone as I was of you today. I have never heard such phony humility. If you're not a success, who is?"

The poor guy had once starred in a picture, but his career had come to a halt. He was trying to climb back up and was having a tough time. I suppose he identified with me, and wished he could have the seemingly enviable stature I had attained.

He left me there alone on the street, and marched angrily away.

I started for the town house I owned on Seventieth and Park Avenue. I had paid a fortune for it. It was six stories high, and each floor was filled with fine period furniture, with paintings, sculptures, and rare books. The thought of these possessions gave me no comfort. As I walked down Fifth Avenue, the towering buildings seemed to be falling in on me. I crossed over to Central Park. I began running. With each step my panic increased. I ran until I thought my lungs would burst. Exhausted, I fell down on a grassy mound overlooking the reservoir.

I longed to cry, but my throat wouldn't respond. I felt the greatest sorrow I had ever known, but I couldn't produce a tear. On my knees I called to God for help. There was no answer. I waited with my eyes closed. I waited but He must have been busy elsewhere.

When I opened my eyes the lights of the city were blinking on all around me.

It was then that I saw "the boy." He was under a tree. I got up and struggled toward him. He turned and ran.

"You little sonofabitch, you made me do it! If I ever catch you. . . ." But he was gone.

That night when I went to the theater, my voice was gone. I couldn't speak above a whisper. We sent for a doctor. He hurried to the theater and examined my throat. He said there was nothing physically wrong.

"Then why the hell can't I speak?"

"I don't know," he said. "Either you have a growth on your cords which I can't see, or you have a lie caught in your throat."

A lie caught in my throat!!!

There were a thousand lies caught in my throat! Which was the one that was crippling me?

Somehow I managed to get through the performance that night. I tried to deal with the truth, the whole truth of my life, though the audience heard only a man rasping awkwardly on the stage. They couldn't know with how much pain.

I had watched the clouds gather, ever more menacing, and now the storm was fast upon me. I was out in the wilderness alone, and there was no place to hide.

"What profit hath a man of all the work which he taketh under the sun?"

I saw that all the work that I had done was vanity and vexation of spirit.

Why couldn't I find rest in the night?

Now, when I should be enjoying the summer of my life, why could I find no purpose?

I was drowning.

Lost.

"Kid, help me," I cried. "Help me or we'll both drown."

# 1

THE OFFICE looked like a million others, all cut from the same mold. The desk was neatly equipped with the usual twin pens that never worked, the fake leather blotter, the marine brass clock, the rotating calendar.

The big, expansive man behind the desk wore a well-advertised brand of tweed suit. The only personal thing in the room was his smile. Sitting opposite him, I tried to define it, but the effort failed. Nothing of importance, beyond the usual pleasantries, had been exchanged since I had entered his office. Finally, I asked him if I should lie down on the couch.

"Why?" the doctor smiled. "Are you tired?"

"No," I said, "I only thought. . . ."

"You don't look very sick to me, Mr. Quinn. Let's sit and talk."

It wasn't at all as I had imagined.

"A few days ago I saw you in an Italian movie. That last scene of you crying on the beach was moving as hell."

Shit! Here I was paying this sonofabitch fifty dollars an hour and he was just another fan.

"I'm very ignorant about movies," he continued. "You're the first actor I've ever met professionally, so forgive me if I ask stupid questions. But in that last scene, were those real tears or were they induced by smelling onions or something like that?"

Fifteen minutes of the precious hour had passed and we were discussing movies!

"No, Doctor. They were real."

"You mean you really cried?"

So he's going to be one of those? "Yes, I cried."

"How does an actor cry? I mean you must have to remember painful things in your life to induce real tears."

Christ!

"It must be a form of self-analysis, isn't it?"

7

Don't worry, I thought, there is plenty of pain in my life to draw from.

"I guess so," I shrugged.

"Were you thinking of anything in particular that time on the beach?"

"Yes."

"What?"

"Well, first of all, I was thinking of the poor bastard I was playing. He had lived a rough, meaningless life. He had never felt love. When he had finally found it, he hadn't known what to do — except destroy it. There on the beach, he felt the immensity of space. The eternity which he would have to face alone. It was probably the first time he had ever really seen the stars, and what they represented to him was an eternity of loneliness."

I couldn't avoid a catch in my throat as I recalled the scene.

"You feel very close to the character, don't you?"

"I have to feel close to all the characters I play. I don't always succeed."

Suddenly I realized that the doctor was not merely a movie fan.

"Do you believe in love, Mr. Quinn?"

The question stunned me. I wanted to get up and go. The whole thought of analysis was painful and embarrassing. I felt boxed in, claustrophobic. I wasn't at all sure I was going to like this man. He was too ruddy, too healthy-looking. Probably a square.

"Do you believe in love?"

That's what it was all about.

That was why I was sitting there like an idiot.

If he'd asked me, "Do you believe in God?" I could have dug into my bag of theological arguments and substantiated them with my reading and personal experiences. I had dabbled enough in the subject to run that obstacle course. But "Do you believe in *love?*" — that was the big one. The biggest.

I thought, yes . . .

> I love the first days of spring when new leaves appear.
> I love the sun and the sea.
> I love the sound of children's laughter.
> I love the rustle of trees.

8

I love the pungent smell of earth after rain.
I love the innocence of the first snow.
I love Mexican music.
I love Puccini.
I love learning.
I love a good night's sleep.
I love discovery.
I love the smell of incense in church.
I love Thomas Wolfe.
I love Rouault.
I love Michelangelo.
I love my children.

Of course I believed in love, the kind Jesus was talking about, or Gandhi. But had I ever been able to love unconditionally? I certainly loved my children, and yet, I had imposed laws even on them.

With women I had failed utterly. There, my conditions were unbending and archaic, the result of my religious training and heredity. The Indian blood in my veins was too strong to allow for any jazzy modern concepts. With women no flexibility was possible.

"Whither thou goest, I will go; and where thou lodgest, I will lodge; thy people shall be my people, and thy God my God."

The doctor had waited patiently for my answer.

"The kind of love I believe in is too complex to answer with just a yes or a no," I said. "But for the moment, let's say yes, I do believe in love."

"Then don't worry. Everything is going to be fine."

He tried to make a joke. "Any man who believes in love can't be too sick."

I smiled feebly at the feeble joke.

"When you called me the other day, I must admit I was thrown for a loop," he continued. "My wife and I have seen you in a lot of pictures. I did a bit of homework on you before you arrived today."

He brought out a manila folder. There was a bunch of newspaper clippings. He leafed through them and found one he was looking for.

9

"Here it is. It tells about your being born in Mexico during the revolution."

"Yes. April twenty-first, 1915."

"It goes on to say that your mother and father both fought on the side of Pancho Villa. Correct?"

"Yes, I suppose so."

"Why do you say it like that?"

"I mean the period is all mixed up. I'm sorry. Yes, they did fight with Pancho Villa."

The doctor nodded. "I'm afraid all I know about the Mexican Revolution is what I saw in the picture *Viva Villa,* with Wallace Beery. Was Villa like that?"

"I thought Beery was great in the part, but I don't think he caught the burning intensity of Villa."

"What do you mean?"

Then I told him an anecdote related to me by my father, about when Villa rode to the top of the hill and saw the Pacific Ocean for the first time. He had stared at the ocean's immensity for many minutes without saying a word. Then he'd reined his horse and started back down the hill.

His lieutenant, riding behind him, said, "Quite a sight, eh, Jefe?"

"It's too small to quench my thirst," Pancho had said over his shoulder.

"That's quite a remark," said the doctor. "When did your father tell it to you?"

"When I was a kid."

"And it stayed with you all these years?"

"Yes."

"Do you feel the ocean is too small to quench your thirst, Mr. Quinn?"

"Yes."

If there had been any doubt in the doctor's mind about my being sick, I felt it had been dispelled by my answer.

To hell with him. Let him earn his money, I thought.

The man had a good poker face, however, and went on examining the clippings.

"It goes on to say here that your father was an Irish adventurer and your mother an Aztec princess."

I had to laugh out loud.

He looked up. "Why do you laugh? Isn't it true?"

"My father was part Irish, that part is true. But I was laughing at the Indian princess crap."

"My wife and I thought it was very romantic when we read it."

"I guess that's what Paramount Pictures publicity wanted you to feel. They didn't think it was romantic enough for my mother to be plain Mexican."

"Why was that?"

"What the hell, Doc, you live in Los Angeles. You know what most people here feel about Mexicans."

"I don't. I've only been here a couple of years, Tony. May I call you Tony?"

The question about Mexicans irritated me. He had begun to look like a red-necked Texan already.

"Sure, if I can call you by your first name."

He roared with laughter. "You can call me anything you want — and that isn't all you're going to call me before you're through."

"Well, being a Mexican in southern California is not exactly an open sesame. For years they used to have signs at dance halls and restaurants: 'No Mexicans allowed.' Mexicans were lazy, thieves, greasy; they were either zoot-suiters or Pachucos, marijuana smokers."

"Did you ever smoke marijuana, Tony?"

"No, I never did."

He made some marks on a piece of paper. I wondered what the hell he was putting down.

Across the way in another office building I could look into a dentist's office. A guy in a white coat was staring down an old lady's throat.

"What was your mother like when she was young?"

I could see the man in white start to drill on the old lady.

The doctor saw me looking out the window and got up and pulled down the blinds. I was glad I wouldn't have to follow *that* operation.

"I was asking you, Tony, what your mother was like when she was young."

I had heard the question but I was desperately trying to avoid the answer.

The doctor smiled understandingly.

Christ! What was my mother like? Was she ever young?

If I start telling the sonofabitch the truth he'll probably say I'm one of those guys with a mother complex. That's too simple. Even I don't have to be a psychiatrist to understand that. What do I tell him? That my mother made the best chili con carne in the world? Do I tell him about the hunger, the pain? Do I tell him the truth?

Yes, she was young back there in Juárez. We were both young back there, when we were alone. We really didn't need anybody else. We had each other. Maybe that's where the trouble started. That again is too simple. There is no denying that it became complicated when he came back.

I was three years old and I knew that I had more than met my match. I knew I would lose out to my father. He was too damned big for me to compete with, so I fell in love with him instead. But he took my place and maybe that's why I spent the rest of my life trying to be like him.

What was my mother like? Just a few days ago I had asked her. I knew the answer might be back there somewhere.

"Mama, remember the time when I was walking along the roof of an adobe hut somewhere in El Paso, or maybe it was Juárez? I remember a hut and a ladder and you down below calling to me, asking me to be careful and not to move. You got some man to climb the ladder and get me. I remember that I almost enjoyed your fear. I kind of enjoyed taunting you. I could feel through your fear and concern that you really loved me. The more concerned you became the happier I was. And finally, this man climbed up and he brought me down, and you caught me in your arms and you kissed me as if I had come back from the dead. When was that, Mama?"

"You couldn't possibly remember that, my son. I must have told you about it."

"No, Mama. I remember it very well. When was it?"

"That happened when you were about a year and a half old."

"I remember it, Mama. I can still see your face. I can still see that man's face who came up to get me, and that ladder. I can almost touch it even now."

"Why are you trying to go back to the past, son?"

"Mama, wasn't that about the time you worked for a blond

12

woman? I remember playing in her yard when you did the laundry and cooked for her."

"What about her, son?"

"Didn't she want to adopt me once, or something?"

"But son, you were only a year and a half. How can you possibly . . . ?"

"Mama, I remember."

"So what about that woman? You say you heard us talk?"

"Yes, I heard this woman offer you some money for me. She said she wanted to adopt me and take me to school, and then you said, 'I'll think about it.' "

"Oh no, son. You're not going to tell me that you really thought I was going to sell you, or give you away. I was insulted, but I couldn't say to the woman, 'Who do you think you are talking to?' Maybe you're right. Maybe I should have slapped her or something, but I was embarrassed. After all, I was working for her. She seemed like a very intelligent lady and she had talked about it and said, 'After all, Nellie, he's a lovely boy and I've never had any children and my husband and I are in love with him.' And we had had a very difficult time, as you know, and sometimes I hadn't been able to give you food. I didn't like to see you hungry and I thought maybe it would be a wonderful opportunity. They were very rich people, a nice American couple, and I did so want you to grow up in America. I lived in constant fear that they would send me back to Mexico. I wasn't doing it for myself, Tony. I was doing it for you. I wondered if I wasn't being selfish in keeping you. Yes, I did say I'd think about it. I thought, am I not being selfish in keeping this boy? You were a very intelligent boy, a beautiful boy. Everybody was in love with you, and I kept saying to myself, maybe they're right, maybe I don't deserve such a boy. You were very much like your father. And I thought, maybe I couldn't provide for you, maybe you would end up being just another Mexican fruit-picker if you lived with me. I did think about it. I thought about it a long time. I used to go to sleep crying every night at the thought of giving you up. But I have to confess that I did think about it, son. Why, is that bad?"

"No, Mama, it wasn't bad, now that you explain it to me. But back there I don't think I understood. After all, I was an infant and to think that you were even considering letting me go . . . I mean, now that you explain it, of course. You say that it was for my own good, but I think that must have hurt me a lot, Mama. I guess I thought that you were selling me to those people."

"Oh my God, you couldn't have thought that. There wasn't to be an exchange of money, Tony. The blond woman, she was merely saying that she wanted you to go and live with her. She wanted to take you to Kansas City, or some place like that, and she said she would give you everything in the world, and that her husband wasn't a young man and when he died he would leave everything to you. Of course, I wasn't ever to see you again. I wondered if I wasn't passing up a good opportunity for you, but there was never any thought of exchanging money. Oh God! You couldn't have thought that all these years."

"I don't know whether I thought about the exchange of money, Mama, but I guess I thought that even if you were considering giving me up that maybe you didn't care enough about me."

"Tony, you were my first child. You were the only person I had in the world. Your father was off somewhere; I hadn't seen him in almost a year. My mother had thrown me out of the house. I had nobody in the world but you. How could you even think that there was anything else in the world for me? We had been through so much — the trip we had made from Chihuahua to Juárez together. Of course, you were just an infant then, but later, when you first began to walk, we used to have so much fun. I used to love to be with you and I took you every place I went, and sometimes I lost jobs because they didn't want me to bring you around because they thought I couldn't do my work as well, and I would quit. I only went to work where they would accept you because I never wanted to be away from you for one single instant. How can you think I didn't love you?"

"Anyway, Mama, that's when the doubts began."

"That's silly. I won't even listen to that kind of talk, Tony. You can't possibly think that I didn't love you."

"Did it ever occur to you, Tony," the doctor was saying, "that your mother really thought that she was doing you an injustice by not giving you to that family? After all, it had been a tough life for her. She was just a young girl, wasn't she, and in a strange

*14*

country, lugging you around, not being able to feed you some-times. And when this woman suggested that she would like to adopt you it certainly would have crossed your mother's mind that maybe it was the best thing to do. Now, in retrospect, can't you see your mother's viewpoint?"

The man was digging into places where it hurt.

"Hello, Elephant," I heard a deep voice say.

At that time we lived on the banks of a stench-drenched canal in a shack made of discarded crates and odd pieces of tin.

It had rained all night and my mother and I had huddled in our blanket by the stove trying to avoid the water pouring down through the perforated roof.

Now it was morning and the sun was finally coming through. My mother told me I could go outside and play if I wanted.

"Váyase a jugar," she said.

She always addressed me in the polite form as if she were speaking to a superior. Only years later, when I was a grown man, did she begin to address me as "tú."

I took my only toy — a red cast-iron streetcar — and went outside.

The puddles in the red clay road reflected the fleeting clouds. Over to the left I could see the huge gas tanks that glistened in the sun.

As I was taking my streetcar on its perilous voyage across the pool of water, I saw his shadow. I turned around and saw a pair of shoes. It seemed to me that my eyes kept going up forever as I looked and saw silhouetted against the sky and the turbulent clouds a face I knew was my father's.

"And you'd never seen him before?" asked the doctor.

"Not that I could remember. My mother tells me I had seen him last when I was eight months old. She had carried me in her arms all across the northern Chihuahua desert in search of him. Finally, she had found him and his mother at a train station, having breakfast in a restaurant.

"Another two years were to go before my father and I were to meet again."

"Hello, Elephant."

"Hello, Papa," I said.

"Where's your mother?"

He reached out for my hand and I led him to the shack across the street.

"Do you know where we found you, Elephant?" my father was saying. "In a pigsty. Didn't we, Nellie? We found you among some pigs, and your mother and I took pity on you and took you home with us, didn't we, Nellie?"

I wonder if he knew that a three-year-old boy might seriously consider that he didn't belong to anyone, that maybe he was a stranger who had been picked up somewhere and that the blond girl he thought was his mother, was not his mother, and that this big giant of a man was not his father.

That night as I lay by the stove, rolled up in the blanket on the floor, I could hear my father and mother. I wondered if they were giggling about me. I wondered if they were really my father and mother. I sobbed in the dark.

Next morning when I woke up I had a fever. My "father" had gone off to look for work with one of the neighbors. My "mother" was fixing some gruel for me. I refused to eat it. I kept pushing the spoon away. Finally, I spilled it all over her dress.

"What's the matter with you, son? What's the matter with you?"

Suddenly it poured out of me. "You're not my mother and he's not my father. He said you found me in a pigsty."

She threw her arms around me and hugged me tight.

"Is that what's been bothering you, son? Is that why you're sick? It was a stupid joke of your father. It was a stupid joke, son."

She began kissing me like she always had. She kissed me until I went back to sleep.

Half asleep, I heard my father enter the shack and I heard my mother whispering.

"You know why the boy was sick? Because of that stupid joke of yours that we'd found him in a pigsty. He's a very sensitive boy. You mustn't say those things around him."

The big man came and peered down at me as I lay on the blanket. I smiled feebly hoping to be reassured. The big man started to laugh.

"Is that why you're sick? Because of what I said?"

I was hoping he'd take me in his arms; instead he laughed harder and said, "I wasn't kidding; we did find you in a pigsty."

My mother became angry and started punching him. "Don't talk to him like that. Leave him alone. Don't believe him, son. It's just a bad joke."

The big man became furious. "Don't mollycoddle him," he said. "I want to be able to joke with my son. He can't be so sensitive that I can't joke with him."

Strangely enough, the fact that the man had called me his son — even in anger — satisfied me. The big man had called me his son. I *was* my father's son. It had been a joke.

The mark and the scars disappeared as I grew. I learned by looking into the mirror that I was made in the likeness of my father. That it had been a joke.

The doctor was scratching away on his piece of paper.

"I wonder why he said that?"

I defended my father. "The poor bastard had his own problems. He had been working in Pennsylvania in a foundry. A piece of steel had lodged in his left eye. It was beginning to turn gray. The doctor had told him he'd eventually lose his sight. There was so much left to see. God knows, two eyes were not enough for him, and here he was about to be left a 'one-eyer.'"

"You really loved him, didn't you?"

"Yes. I guess he and the kids come closest to what I call love."

I saw the doctor glance at the clock on his desk. My hour was up. It was a gesture that was to drive me crazy later on.

I learned after a while not to start on any important subject late in the sessions. In the middle of some emotional discovery, the doctor would begin putting the manila folder away and I'd know that he had stopped listening.

As I walked out to the elevator that first day I saw a young, attractive girl get out and head for the doctor's office. She was fidgeting in her purse.

What the hell was she looking for? What answers did she hope to find there?

I didn't think I would go back next day.

# 2

I GOT OUT of the car and looked around. Down below, the lake glistened in the sun, not much different than it had been when I was a kid wandering around the neighborhood. Almost the only sign I had that life had changed was the Lincoln Continental I had arrived in, with its custom leather upholstery and its special stereophonic sound.

As I walked down the path to my mother's house, I turned back and saw "the boy." He was standing near the car, staring at it. I thought, that'll show you, you sonofabitch, I made it!

He walked around the sleek, black convertible, but was unimpressed.

Screw you, I thought. Nothing ever pleases you, you bastard!

He stood there watching me go to the front door of the house. As my mother opened it, I looked back. He was still standing there, wearing that taunting smile I'd learned to dread.

I bent over and kissed my mother.

"Hijito!" She used the diminutive. To her I'd always be a little boy.

I looked around the living room. The picture of an Indian sitting on his white horse still hung on the wall. He hadn't changed expression in thirty years. He had really come to the end of the trail. One of the few new things in the room was a painting of me by my friend John Decker. I'd given it to my mother one Christmas. Another addition was the television set. Otherwise, everything was much the same. Time, like the lake down below, hadn't moved in the intervening years.

My mother brought me a cup of coffee. The house was quiet. We were by ourselves, except for all the ghosts.

"Why are you going to the doctor, son? What can it lead to, all these questions?"

"The truth, Mama. There is something bothering me and I've got to find out what it is." I already had a suspicion.

"What's back there that you can possibly want to see again?" she asked. "Is it only pain and hunger that illuminate the truth? Your first words were, 'I'm hungry.' A mother wants to give her firstborn the stars and the moon. I had nothing to give you except a dried tortilla. Life gave us reality. I could only give you dreams. Was that wrong? Was I wrong, son?"

"No, Mama. You weren't wrong. It's just that life isn't working out the way I want, and I want to find out why."

"Do you feel sick, son?"

"I'm just not happy, Mama."

"But that's your nature. Your father was not a happy man. Your uncles were not happy men. Of course, they would go out now and then and get drunk, and go to bad women and think they were happy. And anyway, who says we were put here on earth to be happy?"

I tried to make a joke — "Television."

She didn't laugh. "Seriously, son, you are rich, you have wonderful children, you're a success — of course you should be happy."

"But I'm not," I almost shouted.

I got up and stared out the window.

"Son, what is that doctor doing to you? Is he hypnotizing you, or something?"

I was sorry I had blown up. I put my arm around her. "No, he doesn't hypnotize me."

"Does he give you drugs?"

"No."

"Then what do you do in that office?"

"We just talk."

"And for that you pay him all that money?"

"Yes."

"Why don't you go and talk to a priest, someone who is close to God? And it costs much less."

"Maybe that will come later."

I went back to the cup of coffee. I dreaded hurting this lovely, kind woman. But she had to carry me back. We had to go back together.

She began —

"Your great-grandparents on my side were Indians, Juan Pallares and Pilar Cano. The Pallares had seven children: the boys were Pedro, Hipólito, Paulino and Braulio; the daughters were Guadalupe, Petra and María."

I had to smile. "Mama, please let's cut out the begats."

"The what?"

"Mama, I want to know about you and me, Papa, Grandma and Stella."

"Don't you want to know about my uncles and aunts?"

"Yes, Mama, but another time."

"All right, your great-grandparents had three girls: Guadalupe, Petra and María. María became my mother, your grandmother. She was put to work at the age of seven for a woman named Oaxaca. She came from a family that owned a lot of mines and land around Chihuahua. This lady had a nephew who naturally came to visit very often. It was God's will that at the age of fourteen my mother became pregnant from this nephew."

" 'We make guilty of our disasters, the sun, the moon and the stars — an admirable evasion of whose master man to lay —.' "

"What?"

"I was quoting, Mama."

"Aren't you listening to my story?"

"I'm sorry. Please go on."

"My mother used to tell me that the first labor pains began behind the millstone while she was grinding corn. When the Oaxaca lady became aware that my mother was in labor, she kindly assisted in bringing the infant to life. The infant was me."

My mother got up and poured herself more coffee.

"Oh, Tony, why do I have to tell you all this? What good is it going to do?"

"There's nothing wrong in what you're telling me, Mama. I just want to see it the way it was."

"Don't you hate me for telling you I was born behind a kitchen stove?"

"No, Mama."

"I wish I could tell you I was born in a big canopy bed, surrounded by beautiful nurses dressed in white, and my father there taking me in his arms and smiling at me."

"I like the real story better, Mama. That pink-cloud kind of dreaming is what got me into trouble. I want to see it all again. I want to touch it and smell it."

"You think the stench is beautiful?"

"It's part of life. A flower cannot exist without fertilizer."

"But promise you won't hate me after I tell it all to you?"

"I promise."

"The Oaxaca lady, of course, asked María who the father was and my mother had to confess it was José, the lady's nephew. When José's family heard about it, they sent him to the United States to study engineering."

I had to laugh at the incongruity. I wanted to ask why not horticulture or husbandry, but decided to let her continue her own way.

"The Pallares family, on the other hand, went and took María away from the Oaxacas and put her to work with another family."

"Where there were no nephews, I trust!"

"Don't be sarcastic, son. My poor mother suffered enough shame being disowned by her own family. The only one who took pity on us was my uncle, the priest. He took us into the Sierras to live with the Indians, the Taraumares. Sometimes I think those seven years were the happiest of my life. We spent our days hunting and fishing. People only spoke when necessary. Nobody thought he was better than the other. When there was no meat, we all ate beans from the same pot.

"Because I was blond and had green eyes, the village all treated me like something special. I really felt loved by them.

"If it hadn't been for the fact that I caught smallpox we might have lived there all our lives. I never saw my mother happy after my uncle came and took us back to Chihuahua. She had become accustomed to the Indian ways and found city life very difficult. Besides, my uncle died soon after and we were on our own.

"We always lived on the outskirts of the city, as my mother felt more at home there. It reminded her of the mountain life. Sometimes she spoke of going back, but we never did. We found life very different from what we had known in the Sierras. We spoke in the Indian dialect and the city people thought it was funny. In those days Indians were looked down upon. Most Mexicans talked proudly of their Indian blood but secretly wanted to be Spanish. Only the revolution changed that."

"Had the revolution begun then?"

"No, that was later. Oh, people grumbled, but overthrowing Díaz was unthinkable. He had led the country so long that everybody had come to accept him as one of the family. He was like some rich uncle. If anyone thought of a father of the country, it was Benito Juárez. But that was because he was like one of us."

"How did you and Grandmother manage to stay alive?"

"The only thing Mother knew how to do was washing and ironing clothes. It became my duty to go from door to door asking if they had any laundry they wanted done. I liked it best when we worked in homes. I enjoyed being with people.

"When I was fourteen or fifteen we were working for a woman named Conchita. She taught me to read by making me embroider the letters of the alphabet on a pillow cover. At first, my mother was very upset at the thought of my learning to read. She taught me books were evil. But after a while, when I was able to read 'Cinderella' aloud to her, she forgave me. 'Cinderella' was her favorite story.

"I can't tell you how happy I was years later that I had learned to read. Books became my best friends and kept me from complete desperation. That was one thing your father and I had in common — we loved books. You inherited your love of books from us. My God, you have so many. Do you read them all?"

"Most of them, Mama."

"Yes, I love books, but most of all I love people. I love to talk to people. From books you get knowledge, but from people you get wisdom. I love to hear people laugh. If I had been a man I would have joined a circus and become a clown. Do you like clowns, son?"

"I feel sorry for them because I know how much they have to suffer to make people laugh."

"Why do you always have to see the negative side? Why not just think of the laughter they create?"

"Because there can't be a positive if there isn't a negative."

"That's too deep for me. I just like the happy side of things. My mother used to say that if ever I got lost she'd know where to find me. She would just look for a crowd laughing and I would be in the center making a fool of myself.

"Anyway, this lady, Conchita, had a cousin named Victorio who fell in love with me. . . ."

My mother must have caught a sign of annoyance on my face.

"You don't like to hear that other boys besides your father found me attractive, do you?"

"No. I hate it."

"But, darling, that's not normal."

"Mama, if I was what you call normal I wouldn't be here making you go through all this and I wouldn't have to be going to a doctor. I believe in one man for one woman, and vice versa. But because no one in the world lives by that concept, least of all myself, I can't feel love — and I want to."

"But love is not a fairy-tale existence, son."

"Mama, just tell me the story and let me come to my own conclusions."

"Where was I?"

"You were with Victorio, but you can skip that. Tell me about the revolution."

"You're just like your father. He romanticized the revolution. He thought the revolution would make it paradise on earth. To me it was just the smell of gunpowder and the crying of the wounded. I saw no romance in it. We were just poor people fighting for our stomachs. The talk of brotherhood and the flag-waving came later from people who had profited from our suffering.

"Around 1910 we began hearing the talk of overthrowing Díaz. Names like Orozco, Pancho Villa and Francisco Madero were cropping up. No one knew anything about Madero, but if he had the courage to stand up against Díaz we thought he must be very 'macho.'

"There was talk that Madero was up north in Juárez and that he didn't accept the results of some elections. I don't know if he was right or wrong, because none of my people ever voted. That was something only big landowners or people in important positions did. That was the way of life and we accepted it.

"I know that around that time a lot of Federal soldiers began arriving in Chihuahua. The city was full of talk and confusion.

"We heard that Pancho Villa and a small band had attacked

23

a trainful of Federales who were headed north to arrest Madero. Pancho Villa had defeated them, and he became a hero right away. You could see things change in the city. Everybody felt courage now. All the resentment they had been swallowing for years now came out. Things could be different. Maybe it wasn't God's law that some people should starve while others had plenty. Maybe the man who plants the lettuce can also eat the salad.

"Many men left and went to join Pancho Villa. It became the 'macho' thing to do.

"My mother, who was most definitely against the rich people because of her own personal experience, said, 'Now they will see. Now he will put them in their place.'

"We waited for things to change. I guess we all imagined that the wealth was going to be distributed all around. But nothing happened, except that now there was more excitement.

"There was talk that Orozco and Villa were not very friendly with each other. The men were confused because to them the revolution was all one. But it seemed that inside the revolution there was another revolution.

"The one thing I will say about that time is that the music became more lively. There seemed to be more singing. Each side had its songs; I have to be truthful and say that Pancho Villa's people had the best.

"Then a new name was being heard of — Zapata. He was from the state of Morelos. People spoke well of him and for a while they thought maybe he would be the leader. What will happen when he and Pancho Villa meet? Maybe they will hate each other and we will have to fight Emiliano Zapata. In 1913, after that poor man Madero was assassinated, Villa and Zapata finally met in Mexico City. To everybody's surprise they liked each other. Neither one could read, so neither one felt superior or inferior to the other.

"But things changed again. Now we heard there was a new enemy, Victoriano Huerta. There was more confusion. But that was what the revolution was — confusion.

"One of my father's brothers, David, believed very much in the revolution. Even though the Oaxacas had lost most of their lands and mines, he was a fair man and loved the people. He joined up with Pancho Villa.

"In Villa's camp one day someone introduced him to Pancho, and said, 'Chief, here is one of those rich ones who believes in the revolution. He is of the Oaxaca family.'

"He thought he was doing something nice for David.

"Pancho spat on the ground, and said, 'I don't· trust the sons of whores. Shoot him.'

"They shot him there and then.

"Though my mother had suffered because of the Oaxacas, I couldn't gloat at their tribulations. In the eyes of God, *that* man was my father. I felt sorry for the change that fate had dealt him. Now he had escaped to America and the house was full of 'revolutionaries.'

"I was about fifteen when I heard that a new family had moved into one of the better 'barrios' up near the cathedral. I went up to ask them if they had any washing to be done. I had heard that the new family was well-off. Their name was Quinn.

"When I knocked on the door, a very good-looking woman answered. You could see by the way she dressed and carried herself that she was a great lady. Standing behind her was a tall, good-looking boy. He must have been about seventeen. He towered over his mother.

" 'Yes?' the woman asked.

" 'Do you have any laundry you want done?' I asked.

" 'No, we have a maid who does all our washing.' She started to close the door.

" 'I iron shirts better than anyone else. Won't you please try me?'     ·

" 'No, thank you. Our maid irons well enough to suit us.'

"The young boy turned to his mother. 'Why don't you give her some of my shirts to do?'

"You could see that the woman didn't like the boy interfering and she closed the door. I could hear them arguing as I walked away.

"A few days later, as I was walking by their house, the young man came out of the house and followed me down the street. I pretended I didn't see him. Finally he caught up with me in front of a bakery shop.

" 'Listen, I'm sorry about the other day.'

" 'That's all right,' I said.

25

" 'Do you really iron shirts well?'

" 'So they say.'

" 'Maybe I can still talk my mother into giving you our laundry.'

" 'No, thank you. I don't mind asking for work, but I won't beg for it.' And I walked away.

"After that, I used to see him standing on street corners. You couldn't miss him, he was so tall. But I hardly ever saw him with anyone else. He always seemed to be alone.

"I had learned from some of their neighbors that they were from Parral. Doña Sabina, the boy's mother, had been married to a railroad engineer whose name was Frank Quinn. He had been killed in a train accident three or four years before. God only knows how neighbors find out so many things, but they even knew that Doña Sabina had been left quite a bit of money and that the railroad company gave her a pension every month. They said that Mr. Quinn had been a very handsome blond man and that he had come from Ireland. The son must have looked very much like his father, because he didn't look like the rest of us. You couldn't see any Indian in him.

"One day the boy, his name was Francisco, came up to me. It was a Saturday afternoon, and he said, 'I am going to join the army and I want you to be my soldadera.'

"Of course I was astounded. Imagine the nerve! 'Why?' I asked.

" 'Because I believe in the revolution and Pancho Villa.'

" 'No,' I said. 'Why do you want me to be your soldadera? You hardly know me.'

" 'I've seen you around, and I like you, and well. . . .' He looked off into space as if he was annoyed that I wanted any explanation. 'Anyway, I decided that if I went off to fight I would like you beside me, that's all.'

"Funny, but something about the way he said it, seemed to say so much more — and he was handsome. 'I'll think about it,' I said. And I walked away.

"That night I couldn't get that boy out of my mind. There was something lonely, wild and strange about him. A few days later, when I was coming out of the bakery, he was standing there, as if he was still waiting for my answer.

" 'Well?' he said.

" 'I can't just decide like this; we have to talk,' I said. I wanted him to say why he had chosen me. I wanted to hear him say a lot of things.

" 'Look,' he said, as if he'd guessed. 'Don't expect pretty speeches from me. I hate to make speeches.'

"I hesitated for a long time. I wanted to run away from him, but I felt all bound up. I couldn't have taken a step if I'd wanted to.

" 'A train is leaving tomorrow to join Villa down south. I'm going to be on it. They say it leaves at dawn.' And he walked away.

"That night I bundled a few of my things.

"At dawn I left the house.

"The station was filled with young men and women. There was almost a festive air, as if we were all going to a picnic instead of a war.

"I looked around for Francisco. Finally, I saw him in his big sombrero and with bandoleros across his chest. He towered over the rest. I ran toward him. I had hoped my appearance would finally make him break down and say something nice, something romantic. Instead he said, 'So you decided to come?'

"What could I say, but 'Yes, I want to fight for the revolution.'

"He smiled as if one excuse was as good as the other. 'Okay, come on.'

"He led me to one of the freight cars that were to carry us south to Durango. I followed him as if I'd been walking behind him forever. We'd never even held hands.

"As the train chugged through the brown countryside, everyone in the freight car was singing songs. Men sat in groups around other men playing their guitars. The women sat around cleaning guns or sewing. Francisco and I sat against the front end of the car. We were more protected there from the wind that came through the wide-open slats.

"We hadn't spoken much. He stared out at the speeding countryside most of the time.

"Around noon the train came to a halt in the middle of the desert. We were all ordered to get off the train. The women were told to feed their men. All the women made a dash for the fields, where we gathered dried mesquite to build our fires. Thank God my mother had taught me to cook, so I didn't disgrace myself among the other women.

"Francisco said the tacos were very good. He even invited a couple of the other men who didn't have their women with them. They all complimented him on his woman's cooking. He just nodded.

"After a while we were speeding south again. The sun was going down behind the mountains and the air was getting cold. People started covering themselves with their rebozos and serapes. A few lit kerosene lamps. In the car someone was singing softly and other people were preparing to go to sleep.

"It occurred to me that soon I would have to do the same. I would have to go to sleep near this boy whom I hardly knew, this boy who had never said pretty things to me and who just took me for granted.

"He saw me shivering there in the cold. 'Come on, get under the blanket.'

"I said, 'I can't sleep with you.'

"'That's crazy. I'm not going to touch you. Just get under the covers. It's cold.'

"I shook my head.

"'You think people can only sleep together when they are married?' he laughed.

"'Of course,' I said, knowing that it wasn't true.

"At the other end of the car was a priest.

"Francisco called to him, 'Father, come over here. This girl and I want to be married.'

"The priest was a very young man. I don't think he'd ever performed the marriage ceremony before.

"'Well, I don't know . . . ,' he said.

"Francisco became annoyed. 'Look, we're in a war and this train could be dynamited any second. This girl and I want to be married before we die.''

"The first thing Francisco said after the simple rites was, 'All right, get under the blanket.'

"A few days later we reached Durango and got off the train and made camp.

"Next day a sergeant came up and ordered all the men to pick

28

up their guns and follow him. Francisco picked up his gear with all the rest and they started up a hill where we could hear shooting.

"We women just stood there and watched our men march off to their first battle. Many of the men looked back and waved to their women. Francisco never did.

"The horror of the war for me was the waiting. We women waited there all night, listening to the shooting. I found myself kneeling. I prayed he would come through that first battle.

"Next morning at dawn a horseman came and told us to pick up our blankets and food and go and cook for our men.

"From the top of the hill I saw what a battle meant. There were bodies all over the plain. Some were dead, some were wounded. Many were asleep, exhausted from the fighting of the night before.

"You could hear the screams of women as they discovered their men dead or wounded.

"Finally, I heard a voice: 'Manuela!' There he was sitting behind a rock. That was the first time he'd called me by name.

"As I walked toward him I could see a new look in his eyes. 'Manuela, it was great. It was better than I had expected. I was afraid I'd be scared, but when the shooting started I wasn't afraid at all.' He didn't say he was glad to see me.

"I knelt beside him and cooked him his breakfast. He could hardly eat, he was so excited at what had happened the night before.

"I understood so much about him that day. He was different from the rest of the men. To them he was a 'gringo' — his name was Quinn. He was always trying to prove that he was as Mexican as they were. Later I saw him get in many fights in camp because someone would make the mistake of calling him 'gringo.' Here he was fighting for the revolution, and his own comrades would not accept him as one of them.

"After that first battle, one was like the other. The same smell of gunpowder, the same sounds of the bugle, the shooting and the cries of the wounded. The same fears at the end of each battle that he would not return.

"I don't know if I was in love with him. One didn't have time to ask such questions.

"Those first few battles had changed all my girlish ideas of love. We were not characters in a fairy tale. I wasn't waiting for my knight to come on a white charger. I was constantly afraid that the next charger would be black and that he would take my man.

"Love was ugly hours of waiting and fears. Love was cooking for your man as he went off to battle, mending his clothes when he returned. Love was giving thanks to God that your man was still alive.

"One night, a few months later while we were all packed down on the train — this time shuttled farther south to Zacatecas — I told him I had felt the first stirrings of you in my belly. He laughed.

"A few days later, we women were washing clothes on a river-bank when a sergeant rode up. 'Any of you women pregnant?'

"A few of us held up our hands, and we were told to go to camp and gather up our belongings. We were being sent back to our homes because they felt the men didn't fight as well when they had to worry about their pregnant women.

"We begged the sergeant to let us say good-bye to our men. He refused. Some of us were carried bodily and put on the train leaving for Chihuahua. I cried for the first time at being separated from Francisco. I realized that I *was* his woman. I wondered who would feed him, who would take care of him.

"In Chihuahua I went to see my mother right away. I was told she'd moved away. No one knew where she had gone.

"I went to Doña Sabina's house. I tried to tell her not to worry about her son, that he was fine. But when she saw me with a belly, she couldn't get rid of me fast enough.

"One of the neighbors offered me a small room where she said I could have my child. There was only a small mat on the hard earthen floor. She occasionally brought me sewing to do so that I could earn our bread while I awaited my child's birth. I wanted a man-child. After all my mother had suffered and I myself had experienced, I decided a man-child was better off. I begged God each night to make it a man-child.

"One day a poor mad woman came to see me. Most people treated her with disrespect and called her a witch, but I had always felt sorry for her and had been nice to her.

"Now she brought me a geranium plant to keep me company. She asked me if I wanted a boy or a girl.

"I said, 'I would like it to be a boy.'

"She said, 'It's all there,' and pointed to the flower. I didn't understand.

"She explained that one day the geranium bud would open. If the child inside my belly was a girl, the bud would be white; if a boy, it would be red.

"I watered the plant every day, hoping to hurry it along.

"My belly was now growing huge and I could feel the impatience inside.

"The first huge pain awoke me during the night. I knew the time had come. Out in the street it was dead still. I was afraid the pains would become unbearable and that I would scream and wake up the whole neighborhood. I leaned over and lit the candle. I waited to see if the geranium had blossomed yet.

"It was still closed up tight.

"The first pain had passed. I lay there in the candlelight waiting for the next contortion inside of me to begin. When it came I bit my hand to stifle a scream.

"I prayed to God that my child would not be born in the middle of the night. I wanted a child to be born with the sun in the sky. I wanted a child of hope, not darkness.

"Outside I could see the dawn beginning to appear. I relaxed finally. Now my child could be born if God wished. He must have heard me, because I felt a huge wrench inside of me. I couldn't stand it any longer. I reached over to open the stubborn plant. I wanted to see if the flower inside was white or red.

"While I had my hand on the flower, I felt like all the rivers inside of me burst. I screamed. I clutched at the bud in my hand. It was blood red.

"When I woke up, our neighbor was holding you in her arms. You were a huge child, son. From the beginning you looked like a Quinn. You were so white. Only with time you became dark.

"When you were two months old, Francisco came back. His turn had come up to leave the lines. He arrived injured, poor boy. He had been wounded in the arm in the last battle in the hills of Santa Rosa, near a cemetery. As soon as he got back he came to see me.

"I was living in an old neighborhood where I had found a room.

"All of us who had fought with Villa were given bilinbiques — money coupons. It was Villa's money. We didn't get much — about twenty pesos — and even with that it was difficult to find something to eat. You had to line up on Via Yuma, where they passed out the food. Sometimes I would stand until four or five in the morning for a few ounces of cornmeal and beans.

"To help me out, a lady gave me some washing to do. It was fine ladies' clothes. I later found out that they were from the local bordello. When your father came to see me and he saw the pile of fine clothes, he asked me what I was doing. I explained to him that I was doing the clothes for the local bordello. He was furious. He said, 'You mean you're washing clothes for a whorehouse?'

"I said, 'Please don't call them names: After all, it's wartime and they are doing their service as well.'

"Francisco wouldn't listen to reason. He began to throw all my washing and ironing across the room. He said he wouldn't have me working for any whores.

"As you can see, our first meeting after his return was not a romantic success.

"He went to live with his mother again.

"When he had recovered from his injury, he went to work in a local foundry. The only times I got to see him were when I took him his lunch and in the evening when he'd stop by to see his son, who never ceased to be a joy to him.

"But one day he said that I must stop bringing him food, that his mother didn't want me to and that she would send food with the maid. But he would still arrive in the evening and play with you. He would lie beside you and talk to you as if you understood, as if you were already a grown man. I had to laugh at the long conversations that you had together, ignoring the fact that I was in the room.

"How he loved to play with you. I remember once he came in and told me to dress you in your best clothes. You couldn't have been more than a few months old.

" 'I'm taking him to see a bullfight,' he said.

32

"I remember I followed the two of you as Francisco carried you on his shoulders.

"That afternoon we watched the bullfights for the first time as a family. He held you in his arms all afternoon. That was the first time that I really felt that I had a family.

"When we got back to my room, he said, 'Manuela, I'll be back in a few minutes. I don't care what my mother says, I am going to introduce my son to her. If she hits me, she'll have to hit both of us.' He laughed his big laugh. 'Don't worry, if she starts shooting, I'll protect my son. She'll have to kill me first.'

"Well, it had been such a nice afternoon and I had enjoyed seeing both my men happy, and I let him take you with him. I went into my room to wait. An hour went by, then two, then three. I began to get worried. I began to think all sorts of terrible things. The more I thought, the more desperation took hold of me.

"I was afraid to leave in case he came back and found me gone. I didn't know what to do. I sat there on the doorstep, looking up and down the street. I sat for hours praying, 'Please, God, don't take my son away. Anything, anything, but not my son. Don't let them steal my son.'

"Finally I saw the big form of your father coming down the street, holding you fast asleep in his arms.

"He didn't say a word and went quietly into the room and laid you down on the pad on the floor. He knelt there on the floor looking at you sleeping.

"When he turned I saw that his eyes were swollen. He had been crying. That was the first and the last time I ever saw tears in his eyes. He had beautiful eyes. It was painful to see them swollen with tears.

" 'My mother refuses to accept you,' he said. 'She absolutely refuses. What can I do? She keeps telling me that she is my mother and that my first responsibility is to her, not you.'

"I said, 'She is right. She came before me. She does come first.'

"He went away that night. There was no more to say.

"Next day his mother sent her maid, María, with some food. No money, just some food. It was already cooked. She would send food once a day — soup, a pot of beans, tortillas. Whatever they ate at the house, she would send at the same time.

33

"One day, María arrived and said, 'Manuela, I hate to bring you such news, but Doña Sabina and Francisco have left for the United States. She has sold everything and they have gone north.'

"The revolution had taken a bad turn and Doña Sabina was afraid the Federales would conscript your father into their army.

" 'Where did they go?' I asked.

"She hesitated. She had been told by Doña Sabina not to tell me, but she finally saw you and couldn't keep the secret from me. 'Juárez,' she said. Then she left.

"When I was alone I felt that the walls would crumble on me. I felt as though the earth held me in a vise. It was the end of the world, but then and there I made up my mind that my son would not be without his father.

"I was able to sell some rags, my mattress, table, and a figure of a saint. I didn't get much money, but I collected enough to leave.

"I went to the depot. The trains were mostly full of soldiers or cattle. I waited in that cold station three days and three nights.

"A man had been standing on the platform when I first arrived. I caught him looking at me many times. He never took a step toward me, never tried to speak. At first I thought that he was someone I had known when I was a soldadera, so I asked him: 'Señor, why do you look at me so much? Have we known each other?'

"He said, 'No, but I was wondering about you. I am waiting for a train I am supposed to take north. I'm an engineer.'

" 'What kind of engineer?' I asked.

"He laughed. 'I drive trains.'

" 'Oh,' I said, 'maybe you could help me. I, too, am going north, but I don't have enough money for the passage. The only thing I have are some bilinbiques. I could give you those.'

"He waved them away. 'Those pieces of paper are worthless.'

" 'It's all I have,' I said.

"He thought for a long time. 'Tomorrow I'm taking a troop train north. We could be attacked on the way. We might have to fight. There is great danger. Would you take such a chance?'

"I must admit, the thought crossed my mind that dying might be the solution to all my problems. My only concern was my son. What was to become of him? That I decided to leave in God's hands.

34

"When the train arrived, this kind man sneaked us into the coal-wagon near the engine. He hid us under the coal so that the sergeant wouldn't see. Oh my . . . was it hot in there! The only light at night was from the fire as they stoked the engine. The rest of the train was in darkness, except for the occasional matches as the soldiers lit their cigarettes.

"The train traveled slowly as it made its way north through the enemy lines. The trip seemed to take forever. I woke up during the night and the engineer was eating a tortilla. He caught me looking at him and offered me a bite. Then you woke up and began crying. It was so hot near the engine, you couldn't get back to sleep. I took out my breast and fed you.

"By train the trip to Juárez from Chihuahua usually takes many hours. It took days.

"One night we were surrounded by horseback riders shooting at the train. We could hear the riders yelling, 'Viva Orozco!'

"The engineer turned to me and said, 'I told you, lady, it might get rough.'

"I thought to myself, if it's to be it's to be. Maybe death is the only answer for my son and myself.

"The soldiers on the train started firing back. Soon we heard a yell from the raiders: 'Don't shoot. We're only fooling. We don't care if you are Villistas or Orozquistas — you are sons of whores.'

"I guess people were getting tired of the revolution.

"We finally reached Juárez. I didn't know anyone there, not a soul. We arrived at dawn. It was an ugly day in an ugly town.

"The troops started jumping off the train as we pulled into the station. The engineer told me to wait. He jumped out and went to talk to someone. After a while he came back and told me to climb down. He looked around the station as if he were afraid. He told me I had better get away before anyone saw me. He handed me my blankets with our belongings wrapped up inside, and said, 'Hurry, and good luck! I wish I could help you more, but I can't. I hope you find your man.'

"I hurried away, sensing that if anybody saw me he'd get in trouble. He was the nicest man I ever met in my life, truly a noble man. I have never forgotten him, yet I never knew his name.

"I wandered around those dirty streets of Juárez not knowing what to do. Then I suddenly remembered that my Uncle Braulio had moved up north. I thought perhaps he was in Juárez.

"I made no move to contact him. I don't know why. It wasn't that I was shy or independent. I guess it was just pride. I don't like to bother people with my problems. I don't like to ask help from people. It obligates you. A favor is the most difficult thing to pay back.

"I had been walking with you and my roll for hours. I was afraid I'd faint. My head began to spin and I knocked on a door. A lady answered. She had a very charitable face.

"I told her I had just gotten off the train. I must have looked a sight, for I could see that you were all black from the coal. The woman looked at us and her face shone with understanding. She invited us in.

"I told her my story. She listened and sighed. She told one of her daughters to get me something to eat, and offered me her house.

"I thanked her, but said that I had to look for Francisco. I asked her permission to leave my roll with her, and went out to continue my search. She sent Che Che, her young son, to lead me through the town. He took me to several small dismal hotels. I inquired at each one if Sabina and Frank Quinn were living there. They all said no. Then the boy took me to a marketplace where he said everybody went to drink lemonade or pulque. It was a sad and very poor marketplace, but there were many people wandering around.

"I kept looking and hoping I'd see Francisco and Sabina; I didn't. So I returned to Señora Florencia — that was the nice lady's name. I asked her how one crossed into El Paso. I had a feeling that was where I would find Francisco.

"She said, 'All you need is two cents to cross the bridge. Do you have money?'

" 'No, but I have some bilinbiques.'

" 'They're no good here, much less in America. I will give you two pennies.'

"She sent her little boy with me to show me the way to the bridge. When we got there, I took the roll from Che Che and told him to thank his mother for me. I went across to El Paso. No one asked me

36

any questions on the American side. The man took my two pennies and waved me into the United States. That's all there was to getting into America — no questions like What's your name? What do you want? Nothing. Just as long as you had two pennies, you could cross into America.

"Thank God I had been able to wash. My boy and I looked very clean as we walked into America. That was on the second of August, 1915. You were not yet four months old.

"El Paso seemed to me the biggest city in the world. I couldn't imagine anything being bigger.

"The first thing that occurred to me as I crossed the border was to go to church. I wanted to thank God for having brought my son and me safely this far. I also wanted to ask Him to help me find Francisco.

"I walked around until I found a church. I was very lucky to find it empty. The priest was fixing some candles on the altar. I went up to him and asked if I could talk to him. He took me into his chambers. He took the roll from me and put it on the floor. I was ashamed of my roll because I hadn't had time to wash it. He didn't seem to mind. He listened to my long story very patiently.

"When I finished, he said, 'Don't worry, my daughter. God will help you. In the meantime, I will ask Doña Julia if she can use you in the kitchen to cook for the students here in the seminary. She is very strange and doesn't like many people, but I think she will like you. In any case, I'm sure she will like your little boy.'

"During my story he had taken you on his lap, Tony. You had fallen asleep in his arms. He seemed to like holding a child in his arms.

"We crossed the courtyard to the kitchen and he introduced me to Doña Julia. She was a very tall woman and kind of fat. He told her I was willing to work for something to eat and a place to sleep. He left us there.

"The woman didn't say anything. She went to the stove and started ladling out some food on a plate. She nodded for me to sit down at the table. It was the first meal you and I had had in days. Thank God my breasts still had enough milk for you, but you were getting to the age when you needed more than milk. You

37

were a huge boy. Everyone thought you were six or seven months old. You had the appetite of a year-old child.

"When I finished eating I got up and washed my dishes and helped her clean up the kitchen. I told her that if she had any laundry I'd be glad to do that too. She said no, that I should get some sleep.

"I spread my blanket near the stove and lay down beside you. We were so tired we went right to sleep. I hadn't felt so safe for a long, long time. It had been a good day and God was just a few yards away.

"At dawn I woke up to feed you. When you'd had enough, I bundled you up and put you down, back to sleep. I got up and found a broom. I swept out the kitchen and put everything in order. Then I swept the courtyard. It was a beautiful day and it all looked so pretty and peaceful there. I would have loved to stay there forever. How wonderful, I thought, if my son could grow up in a peaceful atmosphere like this.

"When Doña Julia showed up to start fixing breakfast she was surprised to see how clean everything looked. She didn't say anything but I could tell she wasn't used to having people work as hard as I did, but I always liked work and I loved to surprise people.

"She fixed me coffee and some refried beans. I was still hungry and I ate it all too fast.

"Then she said, 'I think you'd better gather up your things and get out of here.'

" 'Have I done something wrong?'

" 'No. You are a hard worker and a good girl. I can see that. But you are very young. We have many young men here studying for the priesthood. I think having you around will disturb them.'

"She walked across the courtyard to the church where the priest lived. A few moments later, they came back together. He seemed sad. I was still sitting at the table. I hadn't moved since the woman had spoken. I was so stunned.

"The priest told me to take my roll and my child and follow him. At the church he reached into his pocket and pulled out a fifty-cent coin.

" 'I'm sorry, my daughter — perhaps Doña Julia is right. Take this and may God bless you. You will always find me here if you need me.'

"There I was on the street again. But this time I didn't feel so lost — I had fifty cents in my hand. At least we could eat.

"I wandered about the city looking into stores. I didn't know there could be so many different things — clothes, medicines, bottles, machinery, candies. I had never imagined there could be so many different things in the world.

"I stopped to buy some candy from a woman who was pushing a cart down the street. I asked her, 'How much does a room cost?'

" 'It depends what kind you want.'

" 'I want a room for my son and myself.'

" 'How much can you pay?'

" 'Not much. Where do the poorer people live? My son and I only need a room where we can sleep and rest.'

"She gave me directions: 'Go down the street till you come to a canal, then turn to the right. Go along the canal till you come to some huts. You'll know when you get there. There are many poor people living there who will gladly take you and your son in for a few pennies a day.'

"When I got to the canal I asked if they had rooms for rent. But they were all very expensive. As I proceeded up the canal the houses got worse and worse. I finally came to a neighborhood that looked miserable. I asked a woman how much the rooms were, and she said that they had nothing for less than one dollar a month.

"All I had was forty-nine cents. I had spent one cent for candy, like a fool. I told her I was sure to find work and I could pay her the rest in a few days. She was very understanding. She said I didn't have to pay anything in advance, that I would probably need the money to feed my child.

"She took us to our room. It wasn't very much, but it was a roof and it would keep us out of the wind. The floor was earth, but it was swept clean. It was nice to have a home of our own finally.

"Next day I asked around the neighborhood if there was any work. Some kind people gave me clothes to wash. I took them to the canal where the other women went. I started to earn twenty and thirty cents a day.

"Whenever I had a chance and finished my work early, I'd dress you and head for Juárez to look for Francisco. We must have gone across that bridge fifteen or twenty times. Even the men who took the two pennies on the bridge got to know us. They would greet us like old friends. A couple of times they even let us cross without paying.

"One morning, after I'd crossed the bridge heading for Doña Florencia's house, I saw them in a restaurant. There they were! Francisco and Sabina sitting near a window eating!

"But we talked about that the other day, Tony."

"I know, Mama. But tell me again how you remember it."

"Well, I felt the clouds break and the sun burst through for me. I went into the restaurant and walked up to their table. They didn't see me until we were standing beside them. They were both very well dressed. Sabina was a very elegant woman. Francisco looked so handsome in his dark suit and white shirt. He looked thinner, I thought, but I had never seen him so handsome.

"He was the first to notice us. You should have seen his face when he saw you. He stood up and took you in his arms. He hugged you so hard I thought he'd break your little back. But you didn't seem to mind. You were certainly a pair; you both seemed to be made of the same material. That is why I went through so much to get you together again — you belonged to each other.

"Francisco turned to me and asked how I had gotten there. I told him only the important things. I didn't bother with the small details. Sabina never spoke; she hardly looked at us.

" 'Do you live here in Juárez?' Francisco asked.

" 'No, El Paso,' I answered. 'I thought I'd find you here. I've been looking for you everywhere.'

" 'You came all this way from Chihuahua? Just you and he?' he asked, pointing to you.

"He never asked me to sit down. He even seemed to forget his mother. All he could think of was the toy in his arms. He asked me in what part of El Paso we lived. I told him.

" 'I'd never find it,' he said. 'When will you be coming back this way?'

" 'Any time you tell me, I'll be here.'

"I spoke right out. I really was telling him I belonged to him as much as his son. It was for him to make the decisions. He was the man. Whatever he said, I would do. It took a lot of nerve for me to say it in front of his mother; but I wanted her to know how it was with me.

" 'My mother and I are going to look at a house right now. But if you could come here tomorrow, I will go to El Paso with you. Then thereafter I will know the way.'

"I said, 'Fine.'

"I took you from his arms and left.

"Next day I went and bought you some new clothes. I was at the store waiting for it to open up. It was a humble little suit, but it was the best thing they had. It was for a year-old child. The storekeeper didn't believe you were only six months old.

"I dressed you all in white. I looked fairly well myself. I chose a dress that only had a very small patch. You could hardly see it; it was under the armpit.

"When we crossed the bridge into Juárez, Francisco was already there waiting for us. He ran to take you in his arms. When we crossed the bridge back to El Paso he carried you on his shoulders. I started to pay — from habit, I guess — but Francisco pushed my hand away."

"We finally got to our house. I wasn't ashamed of it. It was very clean. I even had a geranium in a flowerpot beside my bed. It was in bloom and made the house very pleasant. He looked around. I don't know what he was thinking.

" 'Where does the Elephant sleep?'

"That was the first time he called you Elephant. He was very proud that he had a big son. Your father himself was over six feet tall, but he always said, 'The Elephant is going to be bigger than me.' He wanted his son to be bigger, stronger and handsomer than he. I used to worry about putting such a responsibility on an infant. But that is the way men are. They want so much from their sons.

"Anyway, I said, 'He sleeps right here, next to me.'

" 'On the floor?'

" 'We're used to it.'

"He didn't say anything. Maybe he took it as a reproach.

" 'Are there many men in this neighborhood?'

" 'Yes. There are also a lot of women and a lot of children. Why do you ask?'

" 'Nothing — no reason.'

"But I knew he had a reason. He was an extremely jealous man.

"He didn't say anything more. He was not one for speaking very much. At least not to me. He stayed there in the room and played with you for a long time. He tickled you and told you stories. I had to laugh because Francisco was such an idiot to talk so adult to an infant, and yet you looked like a bigger idiot pretending you understood. But when you two got together you had a language all of your own and nobody else existed.

"When it started to get dark he got up to go. 'I will come back soon. You mustn't come looking for me anymore. I will come on my own.'

"He forbade me to go to Juárez anymore and I obeyed him. He was the man and he had given me orders.

"One day you and I were sitting in a restaurant eating when I felt a man standing behind me. I turned and saw my Uncle Braulio. He looked at me for a long time.

" 'I didn't know you had a child.'

" 'Yes, this is my son.'

" 'What are you doing here in Juárez, so far away from home?'

" 'I live in El Paso,' I said. 'I come to this restaurant because I like the way they make the tripe.'

" 'Where is the boy's father?'

" 'Here in Juárez.'

" 'Where does he live?'

" 'Why?'

" 'Never mind. Where does he live?' he insisted.

"I told him. He was a very energetic, educated man. He had a great dignity also. He said no word of reproach to me. He left the restaurant and went to look for Francisco.

"I later learned that he had gone to Doña Sabina's house and found Francisco at home. He asked him to step outside. Sabina wanted to know who he was and what he wanted with her son. Francisco apparently sensed something, for he told his mother not to interfere. He went out into the street with my uncle.

"Those two had a great deal in common. They were both over

six feet tall and carried their bodies the same way — proudly. They even had the same way of speaking.

"When they got out into the street Francisco was prepared for anything. He probably expected the man to challenge him to a fight. Instead, Braulio put his arm on Francisco's shoulder and said, 'Do you love your son?'

"Francisco was angered by the question, but nodded that he did.

" 'Why aren't you with him, then?'

"Francisco resented questions. He would have preferred the man to hit him rather than pry into his personal life.

" 'It's a long story.'

" 'Where can you and I meet to talk? I think we have to have a talk.'

"They made a date to meet later that day. Braulio came back to the restaurant and told me he had spoken to Francisco.

" 'Please . . . ,' I started to say.

" 'Don't worry, I didn't scold him. I am a man — I understand. But he too must learn to be a man. We'll talk. Now you must come home and meet your aunt.'

"That was the first time any of my mother's family had acknowledged me. I was very glad to find I had a family. We went to his house and I met his wife, Otila. Then he went out. A few minutes later he returned with Francisco!

"Now I must make a cónfession: I have left something out. I didn't think it important to tell you before. I was just telling you certain events. But you must understand that I considered your father my husband and my man. One doesn't recount the times one makes love. That is only for love stories, not telling your life.

"We had been together as man and wife. That is all. And now I was pregnant again. It was starting to show on my body. So my uncle said to your father, 'Well, Mr. Quinn, you have a beautiful son and apparently another one on the way. My wife and I will be delighted to walk to church with you right now and be your best man and bridesmaid.'

"He said it in such a decent tone that Francisco couldn't get angry.

" 'But we're already married,' he protested.

"Braulio nodded. 'But this time you'll have witnesses.'

"So we walked to the church with you in your father's arms and we were married again.

"After the quick ceremony, Francisco went back to his mother. I went with Otila and my uncle to their house. I felt very comfortable knowing that I was really married. I could breathe easier. If he didn't want to see me again, that was up to him. At least my children were now legally his, too.

"I went back to El Paso and I made up my mind it was my destiny to live alone. I didn't mind working for you and the child growing inside me. Now I had an added purpose. My family was getting bigger. Those two beings became my whole life now. When Francisco failed to show up for weeks, I decided to forget him.

"After a month or so, he arrived one day when I least expected him. He had come to see his son and to check how the one in my stomach was coming along.

" 'It's beginning to move inside me,' I told him.

" 'You can feel it move? How does it feel? Does it hurt you?'

" 'Only when it kicks or changes position. It is very restless.'

"He laughed, but said seriously, 'You don't have to be inside a belly to be restless.'

"He asked me at what time the baby moved inside of me. 'It's moving now,' I said, and took his hand and put it on my belly.

"You began to think it was some kind of game and you put your little hand on my stomach, too. There we sat, the three of us, waiting for the child inside my belly to kick.

"I felt sorry for Francisco. He didn't have the capacity to just live simply. I understood why he had said that about being restless. I learned to watch for that look on his face. It was a look of panic that came over him, like someone caught in an elevator or a room with a locked door. He'd get up and start pacing.

"He was always looking for some miracle to happen. It was always out there in some tomorrow.

"Sometimes he'd come and live with us for days. I hoped he had come to stay. He had begun to talk to me. He'd tell me all sorts of plans and dreams he had for his children and me. I'd go to sleep feeling so happy that he had decided to make a family, but in the morning he'd wake up with that look. The look of the man who has to start running again.

44

" 'I have to go.'

" 'Where?' I'd ask.

" 'I don't know. I can't stay.'

"Then he'd be gone. But when he was happy, he could change a leopard's spots. How he loved to sing. As a matter of fact, he forgot that we had no food to eat. He thought we could all live on songs. Then he'd get spurts of energy and go to the marketplace and unload the wagons. He was a big man and could carry huge sacks of rice, sugar and beans on his back. He'd work like a demon for a few days, bring me some money, then spend the rest of the week playing with his son and singing all day long.

And the women, they were all in love with him. They all envied me. He wasn't someone that one could see on the street every day, I have to say that. Oh, he had a pretty mouth. His lips were so beautiful that they almost looked like they belonged on a painting. But I never heard those lips say 'I love you.' It pains me to tell you, his own son, but that is the truth. I never heard those words from your father's lips. The only time he said 'I love you' was in the beginning when he wrote me a love note. That was the first and the last time.

"Your father was a very strange man. One day he brought home a steak. We had moved by then and we were living a few blocks down the street. It was still on the same canal but it was a better neighborhood.

"Your sister, Stella, had already been born. He had been away when I gave birth to her. I hardly had enough money to buy cotton to wrap her in when she was born. I had to give the midwife my last three dollars to help deliver her.

"Anyway, this night he arrived with the meat wrapped up and I cooked it while he played with you children. When the steak was done I cut it up in three pieces. A piece for him, one for you, and one for myself.

"We had barely taken a few bites of the steak when you, poor child, who never seemed to get enough to eat, said, 'I want some more meat.'

" 'You have a big piece on your plate yet,' said Francisco.

" 'I want some more,' you insisted.

"With that, Francisco grabbed my plate and his and dumped all the meat onto your plate.

*45*

" 'All right, you eat it all.'

"You didn't understand. You were happy to see all the food on your plate and began to eat. Francisco drank his coffee slowly.

"After a while, you'd had enough and pushed your plate away. Most of the meat was still on it.

"Francisco shoved it back under your chin, and said, 'You're going to eat it all, Elephant.'

" 'I'm not hungry anymore,' you cried.

" 'I don't care,' insisted Francisco. 'You said you wanted it all and you are going to eat it all.'

"You started to cry, but tried to force the meat down. You took a couple of bites and then started to gag. You clutched your throat. I reached out to help you but Francisco stopped me. He sat there drinking his coffee while you were choking to death. You were beginning to turn blue. Your breath had been cut off by the piece of meat caught in your windpipe. I begged Francisco to do something. He finally got up very slowly, picked you up, turned you upside down, and shook you like an old sack of flour. You disgorged the piece of meat and all the rest of your dinner with it. You had been a few seconds from dying.

"Francisco seemed to be unperturbed. He sat you back on the chair and asked if you still wanted some more to eat. You were sick with terror by now.

" 'No, Papa.'

" 'Next time, be sure you have room for what you want, son.'

" 'Yes, Papa.'

" 'Don't cry. Take your lesson like a man. Be grateful you've learned something. Here, have some coffee, Elephant.'

"Imagine — his son almost dies and he gives him a lecture that he should be grateful!

"I never understood that kind of logic. But that was Francisco. A very strange man. I never knew how to behave around him. If I sang, he would tell me to keep quiet, that he wanted to think. If I was quiet, he said I depressed him because I was always sad. I guess we were just not in tune.

"Funny thing, son, you remember the incident of the meat and you have a different viewpoint of it. You still think your father was right. But then you are like your father. You don't remember

46

that you were sick for days after that. You don't remember that you were one step from death.

"You might get the impression that I don't speak well of your father, that I have painted a poor picture of him. That would certainly be wrong. When your sister was born he was very proud. As a father, he loved his children to a point of delirium. If he'd only once said to me 'I love you,' it would have meant the world to me. But I am grateful for the two children he gave me, and he was the only man I ever loved.

"Besides other qualities my children inherited from their father, some good and some bad, they did inherit the quality of being good to their mother. For that I am very grateful. I can die in peace knowing my children have been good to me. The only thing I've never understood about my children is why they should not feel the greatest and most fortunate in the world. They both have money, they both are healthy, they both are intelligent and know how to read and write — what more could any sane person want?

"After your father and I married, I was no longer afraid of Doña Sabina. I took you and your sister to meet her. She was quite surprised. You looked so much like her son. You both were obviously Quinns. By that time you walked like your father and already had that Quinn scowl.

"She said very little to me but couldn't keep her hands off you children. I could see she loved you very much.

"She was a great lady and I respected her, although she was cold to me. Later I learned to love her. She became closer to me than my own mother. That was after she had moved to El Paso. She lost all her money, and had to go to work. She found a job in a delicatessen. Imagine that proud lady who had never lifted a finger going to work in a place selling sausages and pickles. But even then she kept her pride.

"One day, when it was snowing, she came and asked if she could take you to work with her. She said there were all sorts of good things for you to eat there. I bundled you up and she carried you off.

"At that time I was working for a woman named Carmen. I would wash the clothes for her and do the ironing too. I would take you and Stella with me. She fed us very well. She was a generous lady.

"Your father was not around at the time. I hate to keep repeating myself, but it was hard to keep track of his comings and goings. But at that time he was not around. He had joined the American army and was sent to a training camp in Pennsylvania.

"Doña Sabina would often come and have dinner with me and on Sundays she'd take you away all day to movies and things. It would give me a chance to put my room in order. We still lived all in one room.

"My uncle too used to come and visit me. One day he told me he was very proud of me, that he thought I was a very good wife and a good mother. That was the nicest thing anyone had ever said to me. The rest of the family treated me like I had brought disgrace to them. So coming from the most educated member of the family, it moved me very much. He made me cry. I had tried so hard to please them and now my uncle was giving me his blessings.

"That was a very happy time for me. The only dark spot was that your father was not around.

"The army had sent him to work in this ammunition factory in Pennsylvania. While he was there, his left eye became infected. I guess that gunpowder got into it, poor boy, and they sent him to a hospital. He was there for a whole month and never wrote one word to anyone about it. He hated to admit to anyone that he was sick.

"When he got out of the hospital, they discharged him from the army. He didn't return to El Paso for three months. God knows where he'd been or what he'd been doing all that time. He never said. Later I found a picture in his wallet. A picture of him under some huge trees. It looked like a lumber camp.

"One day, there he was. You led him into the house as if he'd never been away. Your sister was sleeping in a trunk. I'd gotten this trunk and made it into a bed for her. The tall sides kept her warm. She was always catching colds or measles or whooping cough or something, so I invented this bed for her with the high sides that kept out the cold.

"There he was suddenly, standing in the doorway. Oh, he looked handsome that day, so tall and strong-looking. He looked like he would go through the ceiling.

"He picked up your sister and started to dance around the

room. 'This is my doll,' he said happily. Then he grabbed you and danced around with both of you.

" 'How are you, Elephant? My big Elephant.'

"He kissed and kissed the two of you. Finally he turned to me and he said, 'Nellie, dress up. We are going out.'

"He hadn't been to see his mother yet. That was the first time he'd come to us before going to her first.

"I told him we should stop to see her. It was early afternoon and she'd probably still be working. He agreed and we went by the delicatessen. She was thrilled to see him, naturally. The funny thing was, they didn't hug or kiss each other. Neither one was very demonstrative. And yet Sabina and Francisco loved each other very much. They were certainly different from me. When I love someone I have to show it. Sometimes I realize that I show my affections too much. I know I must embarrass you children because I can't keep my hands off you. But that's the way I am.

"Sabina invited us to sit down and have dinner there in the delicatessen but Francisco refused. He said he was taking his family out to a restaurant and would see her later. I think Doña Sabina was a bit surprised at his new independence.

"He took us to a nice little restaurant with clean tablecloths. He put you next to him. You sat there like a little man beside your father. I held Stella in my arms. All through dinner he teased me about what he had done while he'd been away. He told me he'd met a very beautiful girl in Pennsylvania.

"I listened to him. I never knew when he was teasing. He'd been away for a long time and he was bound to find other women. Women were easy for him. All the young girls in the neighborhood had their eye on him whenever he came to visit me.

"I didn't understand why he wanted to impress me by telling me about this woman. He knew what I thought of him. For me there was no better man alive. He didn't have to prove it to me. Besides, it was his life and I knew he had to live it the way he saw it. I was not going to change him.

" 'Anyway,' he said, 'I started thinking about you and the children and I thought — what the hell, I already have a family.'

"He looked at you and Stella and laughed. 'They're even prettier than I had remembered them.'

"That's the way we spent all dinner — his teasing me and telling me about his adventures. He didn't mention the army, or his eye, or the hospital. Maybe that was too personal. He did tell me that he was going away again.

"I asked him when he would be back. He looked at me very seriously and said, 'I don't know if I'll come back, but if I do I'll stay for good.'

"What could I say? I just nodded my head.

"A few days later some inspectors came to the neighborhood and started boarding up a lot of the shacks as unsanitary and unsafe. The women and children began crying as they were literally put out on the streets, but the inspectors said there was a terrible epidemic of smallpox further up the canal and all the area had to be cleaned up or burned down. Actually, the authorities had certainly been patient enough with us. I mean, letting us all cross the border to escape the revolution and letting us set up those huts next to the canal. I do think we'd imposed on their hospitality, but we were very poor people. We barely had enough to eat. They could hardly expect us to pave the streets and put in sewers and electricity. We were forced to drink that dirty water from the canal. Of course we had to boil it first, but the inspectors were right; many people were getting sick.

"The block we were living in was condemned.

"There was no house to be had anywhere. Everyone in El Paso was afraid to take in anyone from the contaminated neighborhood. I took you children and went to live under a tree in the outskirts of town. It was nice weather at the time. Thank God there were a lot of trees around because other people got the same idea. Families just went out and found a tree to live under.

"I would say we lived there three or four months. When it started to cool off at nights I went looking for a new place for us to live. Eventually I found a nice room. God has always looked after me. I'm not a religious person but I believe in God. He is very good and all-powerful. I know He looks after me. That's why life has never frightened me. I can walk unafraid because God is with me, but I am not religious.

"A life isn't exactly like a story. It's never 'once upon a time.' In life, time gets all mixed up. No sooner does one thing happen than something else comes in. My own life, even though I lived it, it's hard to say it happened like this and like that. Only death and births are remembered with such exactness, and even those are sometimes forgotten.

"I never knew where your father was. He'd disappeared. I suppose I saw Sabina during that time. She must have known I was living under that tree. I'm sure I saw her. Why didn't I go live with her? I don't know. My pride, maybe. She had her life, I wanted to live mine. I didn't like to admit I needed help from anyone, including your grandmother and your father.

"Anyway, I found a nice clean place and it didn't cost too much. Three dollars a month. A few doors down the street was a bakery. Don Fernando used to save the day-old bread for us. I'd wet and reheat it and it was better than the fresh.

"Somewhere about that time your father showed up. He found work here and there. One night he said Doña Sabina's younger sister Inez and her husband Glafiro were coming to El Paso. He said that his mother had invited them over.

"I had seen Inez once or twice in Chihuahua. She and Glafiro had two children — young Glafiro and Socorro. Socorro was your age, Glafiro four years older.

"Francisco said Inez and her family had arrived and couldn't find a place. Could they come and stay with me? Imagine all that tribe in one room! But I could never say no to Francisco, so I agreed.

"Poor Glafiro had a hard time finding work. Inez could have taken in washing but she wouldn't think of it. I don't think she had ever worked until that time. She did offer occasionally to look after you children while I went to work, but I never left you in her care. I didn't like anyone to look after my children. Where I went, you went. My life was your life and yours was mine.

"One day Francisco came to the house very excited. He said to Glafiro, 'Have you found any work?'

"Glafiro said, 'No.'

"'There is a train leaving in a few days for Glamis. They are taking a lot of people. Will you go? It will mean working on the railroads.'

"'I'm not afraid of hard work, but what about our families?'

"'My woman and children go where I go,' your father said. He turned to Inez. 'Will you go with him?'

"'Where?'

" 'My woman doesn't ask where. It's better than you all living here in one room like pigs.'

"Finally Inez agreed to go. I hate to tell you about that trip. It embarrasses me to remember.

"Down at the freight yards, there were hundreds of people yelling and screaming to get on the trains. Glamis sounded like paradise to them. Even though we were all being pushed into dirty cattle-cars, everyone was begging to go. Francisco and Glafiro had these papers and we were allowed on. There were people there who were willing to buy those pieces of paper.

"The trip was worse than any we'd ever made in the army. Half of the trainload was young children, screaming and crying. You can imagine the smells and the filth on that train. The thing that kept running through my mind was that perhaps Francisco had finally come to stay.

"I don't remember how many days and nights we traveled. The trip seemed to take forever. Once we got to the end, however, it was worse. They dumped us all at a siding. There was no town or anything. Two or three buildings, that was all. I heard we were in California.

"A man came along and pointed to some old boxcars and said for us to go there. Those were to be our homes. Your father and Glafiro ran to choose one for our two families. Inez and I gathered up the children and our belongings and crossed the tracks. Your grandmother also helped carry things.

"Inside the boxcar it was like an oven. Outside it was hot enough, but inside was hotter than any hell I can imagine.

"That was around 1918.

"Who would have thought years back that the great Doña Sabina and her family would find themselves on the same cattle car with me and my children?

"Still, it was nice seeing a new land. We watched the 'Great America' outside our window. True, it was only desert land, but still we had to admit it was the American desert. Beyond that desert was wealth and happiness.

"Francisco was in all his glory in Glamis. I'd never realized how well he spoke English. There in Glamis I heard him for the first time. We had gone to the little grocery store by the side of the tracks and he began to talk to the man behind the counter.

The man was obviously surprised too, because he said, 'Oh, you speak English?'

"Francisco said, 'Yes, what's so funny?'

" 'Nothing, except that most of these people who work on the railroads are Mexicans.'

" 'I'm Mexican too,' said Francisco.

" 'Oh, well . . .' The man got nervous and didn't know what to say. I didn't understand too well why Francisco had gotten angry. He handed the man a piece of the paper that entitled him to groceries from the railroad company. The man took the paper and filled up a bag with groceries. As we were going out, he called Francisco back. He put out his hand.

" 'No offense was meant. If you care to, you are welcome to come and work for me anytime you want. I could use somebody that understands these people's lingo.' Francisco shook his hand and said he'd think about it.

"They became very good friends after that. I told Francisco to accept the man's offer. Somehow I couldn't imagine that beautiful man, your father, working like an ox on the railroad.

"He said no, that he had talked Glafiro into coming to work on the railroad and that he would work beside him.

"It used to break my heart to see those men go out into that broiling sun each morning. Their job was to fix the railroad bed and lay new tracks.

"At the end of a few weeks, most of the men gave up. They said that there was too much work and too little pay. Many went back to El Paso and some of them just headed across the desert for Los Angeles. Finally, Glafiro and your father were the only ones left. I suppose the reason they were still there was because neither one would admit to the other he couldn't take it.

"Even the inspector who came by one day wondered how they had gone on doing the work by themselves. They needed one man to hold the spikes on the railroad ties while the other two men hammered them in. Otherwise, it slowed them down terribly. It wasn't a very difficult job, but very important.

"The inspector said he'd bring a man to hold the spikes. Francisco asked him how much the job would pay.

" 'Same as you get.'

" 'Just for holding a spike?' asked Francisco, surprised.

53

" 'It's still work.'

" 'Never mind getting another man,' said Francisco. 'I have a friend who will do the job.'

" 'That's okay with me,' said the inspector. 'Just so the job is done.'

"That night Francisco said to me, 'Nellie, how would you like to ride with me to work tomorrow morning?'

"The men used to go to work on this handcart that they put on the rails. They made it go by pumping handles up and down. Often you and young Glafiro would get on it and Francisco would let you ride for a mile or so, then you'd walk back. I liked the idea of riding the handcart.

"Next morning I left with Glafiro and Francisco. They both pumped the handle and we rolled down the rails very fast. It took us about an hour to get to where they were working. I had thought I was just going along for the ride, but when we got there Francisco handed me some long pincers and told me to hold the spike in place while he and Glafiro hammered it into the railroad tie.

"I helped the men all that morning until we stopped for lunch. I had prepared Francisco's basket early that morning. Glafiro had his own. We all went and sat under the shade of a scraggly tree and had our lunch. It was almost like a picnic.

"Then Francisco asked me if I thought I'd like to come to work with him every day. 'All you have to do is hold the spikes while Glafiro and I hammer them in. You will get the same money we're getting.'

"I hadn't thought of it as a job. I thought we were just out on a picnic, but the work wasn't hard and I knew we could use the money, so I agreed.

"I had been working with the men for a week or so when the inspector came around unexpectedly. He was surprised so much work had been done. Even though we were alone — the three of us — we worked a full day.

" 'You boys are doing a very nice job. Where's the other man you hired?'

" 'He couldn't take it out here so I got her to help us.' He pointed.

"The inspector looked at me. He thought it was some trick, I guess, to collect the extra wages.

" 'You mean this girl is doing a man's work?'

" 'She's as good as any man around,' said Francisco. 'Come on,' he said to me, 'let's show him.'

"The two men and I nailed down about ten ties. The inspector shook his head.

" 'I wouldn't have believed it. Who is she?'

"Francisco hesitated for a little bit, then he said, 'She's my wife.'

" 'Well, it's your business. I don't care who does the job as long as it gets done.'

"He gave the two men their salaries, then he handed me fourteen dollars! That was the most money I'd ever had at one time in my life. I offered it to Francisco; after all, he was the head of the family. But he pushed it back to me.

" 'You've worked hard for it. It's yours, keep it.'

" 'All I need money for is the family. I have no use for money for myself.'

"With that he handed me ten dollars from his salary and told me I was to keep the money from then on to run the house.

"We were really getting to be husband and wife by then. That night when we got back to our boxcar, Francisco told his mother that now that I was working on the railroad with him it would be her job to do the cooking and that she would have to watch the children. The way he said it, he wasn't asking her as a favor, he was telling her. She agreed.

"A few weeks later we had laid so much rail that it was now taking us longer to reach the end of the line. The inspector said we'd have to move our wagons closer to the work. Shortly after that an engine arrived. They hooked the wagons to the engine and we moved further down the line.

"I suppose nowadays all this sounds unbelievable. It might even sound strange, a young girl working on the railroad, but we Mexican women were used to it. We fought beside our men and found it only normal to work beside them. I loved working hard beside Francisco. When we came home at night we were both tired and hot. We understood each other's pains. That is almost more important than sharing each other's happiness.

"Sometimes it was so hot out there in the sun that the barrel of water we brought out in the mornings would be boiling hot. We tried everything; we even buried it in the sand. Nothing helped.

55

"You know, they make fun of Mexicans sleeping, I mean taking the siesta, but let anyone who laughs go out and work from six o'clock in the morning until twelve in that hot sun and see how long they last on their feet. No human could stand working in that fire between twelve and two-thirty. There was nothing else to do but find some shade and wait for the heat to pass.

"Nobody was there checking on us. We were on our honor. We never cheated the railroad company of one second of their time. We gave them a full eight hours' labor for their dollar a day.

"I learned a lot about your father at that time. Don't forget he was still a young boy. He was only twenty-one or twenty-two. He was not afraid of hard work. As a matter of fact, he enjoyed it. But, more than that, he took pride in his work. He wanted to do his best.

"Once he found two ties that were just a little bit crooked. Nobody would have noticed and it certainly didn't affect the safety of the trains, but he said it looked bad. Glafiro and I argued with him for an hour. He wanted to take up fifty feet of rails and straighten out the railroad ties. It meant losing a whole day's work, but we helped him. If we hadn't, he would have done it himself.

"Next day, when we were finished, he looked over the work and said, 'There, doesn't that look better?'

"Yes, it did, I had to admit — but was it worth all that work and sweat? To him it was. Imagine working overtime with nobody paying you just to make it a little bit better!

"One day, a very hot day, I almost fainted in the sun. During the lunch break I wasn't able to eat a bite. Up till then I'd always been able to keep up with the men, but that day my womanhood showed up. I fell fast asleep during lunch. Francisco tried to wake me up around three but I couldn't make it. He and Glafiro went back to work by themselves. With one hand Francisco tried to hold the pincers that held the spike and with the other hand he swung the hammer. It was almost impossible to do it. The hammer was very heavy. You needed two hands to lift it. Even then after a few minutes it weighed a ton.

"He worked like that for an hour or so, then I guess his arm got tired. He reached down to straighten out the spike with his

56

hand. Glafiro couldn't stop the swing of the hammer and drove the spike into Francisco's hand.

"The quiet had awakened me. I saw Glafiro bending over Francisco. His hand was a mass of blood. I let out a scream and ran to him. We put him on the handcart and started pumping our way home.

"His hand was still bleeding quite badly. I tore off part of the hem of my dress and bandaged it the best I could. The blood still gushed out. He told me to tie his arm tight above the elbow.

"When we got to our boxcar, everybody rushed to see what had happened. Francisco was very pale by then. Doña Sabina started screaming and crying. Francisco was furious.

" 'It's nothing. Shut up! You'll only scare the children.'

"All night we bathed Francisco's hand in hot water and salt. About midnight I heard his moaning. I woke up and took his hand out of the basin of water. It was turning dark blue.

"Sabina became terrified: 'Gangrene is setting in.'

"In the distance I heard a train whistle. I ran out into the night. There was no stop there. The trains just went by us. The nearest station was about twenty or twenty-five miles west.

"I stood in the middle of the tracks and tried to flag the train. It was coming very fast. I hoped that the engineer was looking out and would see me, otherwise he was going to kill me, but I wouldn't leave the tracks.

"God was with me. The engineer put on the brakes and the train pulled to a stop. I ran up and told him my husband was dying, that he had to go to a doctor. Two men ran over to our boxcar. Francisco already had a very high fever and was delirious. One of the men looked at his hand and told the other to help him pick up Francisco. He was such a big man we all had to help carry him to the train.

"I wanted to go along with Francisco; I didn't want to leave him alone, but the engineer said I'd only be in the way. He said they would see he got to a good doctor.

"The train pulled away. We all stood there by the rails long after it had disappeared around the bend.

"Later I learned that the engineer had stayed with Francisco until he got him to a hospital in Los Angeles. They had stopped in some small town to see a doctor, who said he could only give momentary relief. Francisco would lose his hand unless he had the best medical attention. Since Los Angeles was the nearest place where a top doctor could be found, the engineer had taken Francisco to Los Angeles the same night.

"He left him at the hospital and disappeared. We never knew his name.

"We suffered, Doña Sabina and I, not having any news of Francisco. Three whole days passed before a note tied around a piece of coal was thrown from a speeding train.

" 'Your husband is doing fine. He is in a hospital in Los Angeles. It is on Washington Street and Central Avenue.'

"That's all it said. No name or anything. But Sabina and I were relieved and happy. We didn't know how to write Francisco. We would just have to wait for him to come back. We had spent so much of our life waiting for him, we were used to it.

"We were afraid that the inspector would take our jobs away so Sabina, Inez and I went to work every morning with Glafiro. Sabina and Inez took turns swinging the other hammer. Poor fine ladies. The revolution had certainly not made their life better; I suppose that is what is meant by equality.

"One day the inspector came and caught us working. He had already heard from someone about Francisco. He told us that he would be back in a few weeks. He made no comment about the fact that we women were doing the work of men. He paid us each a man's salary. He was a good man.

"A week or so later the man who ran the little grocery store back in Glamis came with a letter for me. It was from Francisco:

Nellie —

I am not coming back to Glamis. Tell my mother she can do what she wants. She can go back to El Paso or come to Los Angeles with you and the children.

Tell the inspector I have already talked to the railroad people and they are willing to give my family passage to Los Angeles. I signed some paper saying my accident was not their fault, and they are giving me the tickets for signing.

The inspector will put you on the train and tell you where I am in Los Angeles.

Francisco Quinn

"Doña Sabina, of course, decided to go to Los Angeles with us.

"Inez broke down in tears the day we left. She thought it was some kind of trick to get away from her. She was furious at Doña Sabina for abandoning her. She felt that since she was the younger sister of Doña Sabina she should stay with her.

" 'My place is with my son and his family,' said Sabina, as we boarded the train. Inez walked off and never bothered to wave to us as we pulled away. Glafiro and his children did.

"If El Paso had seemed to me the biggest city in the world, you can imagine what Los Angeles looked like. When we got out of the station and saw the miles and miles of buildings, I thought to myself, 'Well, here we are, on another new adventure.'

"The minute I saw Los Angeles I fell in love with it. I knew I wanted my family to grow up in that city.

"We went out into the street. We had never seen such traffic. All the noise, automobiles backfiring, streetcars clanging, fire engines screaming down the street. It was like a huge sideshow! We stopped and asked some people where Washington Street was. It was about twelve long blocks from the train station.

"What with you two children in tow and all our belongings on our back, it took us forever to walk those twelve blocks.

"Almost everybody we met in Los Angeles spoke Spanish, especially on Grand Avenue. That was the street where most of the Negroes and the Mexican people lived.

"At the hospital, I found a nurse who spoke Spanish. I told her I was looking for my husband, Francisco Quinn. She smiled when she heard his name. She told me to go up by myself, that children were not allowed to go into the patients' rooms.

"Francisco was in a room with another man who had his legs all bandaged up. Later, I found he had third-degree burns. He was from Canada.

"When I walked in, Francisco and the man had been laughing. Francisco had a tube stuck in his bandaged hand. The tube emptied into a bottle by the side of the bed. I had been so anxious to see him that I had forgotten about my appearance. I had been up all night. My dress was the same one I had left Glamis in. I guess I didn't look my best.

"We just stood there looking at one another.

" 'How do you feel?' I asked.

" 'Better. Where are the children?'

"I explained to him that they were downstairs, that they weren't allowed in.

"He made me tell him everything that had happened since he had left. Then he introduced me to the man in the other bed: 'This is Nellie.'

"He didn't say, 'This is my wife' or 'This is Mrs. Quinn.'

"The man in the other bed said, 'How do you do, Mrs. Quinn? Have you found a place to live?'

"He spoke Spanish with a very big accent, but I understood what he was saying.

" 'No, we just arrived and we don't know anyone in Los Angeles.'

"He took a pencil and paper and wrote down an address. He said the woman there would help me find a place, and to mention his name.

"After a while, I said good-bye to Francisco and left to look up the woman. Sabina and I walked down Main Street, each one carrying a child and a roll. We found the lady. I didn't know what her relationship was to the Canadian, but she moved very fast and found us a house on Clover Street, right off Main.

"When I saw the house I was sure it must be some kind of mistake. It was a palace. It had one big room and two small ones. The rooms were painted in a very pretty blue color. It even had a basement downstairs and, Tony, electric lights!

"Oh, Tony, I wanted that house so much but I knew there was some kind of mistake.

" 'How much does this cost?' I asked her.

" 'Do you like it?'

" 'I love it. But we have very little money. There must be something cheaper.'

" 'Don't you worry about it. You move in, we'll straighten it out later.'

"I never knew what arrangements had been made. Maybe it was one of Francisco's secrets. He always had secrets from me. Nevertheless, we moved in.

"That first night, Sabina and I didn't know where to sleep. We were so used to living in one room. We became hysterical with laughter because we couldn't decide where to sleep. Imagine having such a problem!''

# 3

IT WAS DARK OUTSIDE when I left my mother's house. Poor woman, I had made her dig deep. I knew it had been painful for her. It was up to the doctor to help me put it together now. God knows I'd tried for years. But I knew that I had developed blind spots. I needed someone to help me look at it.

When I reached the top of the steps, "the boy" was still there. Christ! The last person I wanted to see at that moment was that little bastard.

As I got into the car and turned the key the motor responded immediately. I could hear the three hundred horses heaving under the hood, waiting to be unleashed.

I had turned on the lights and put the car in gear, when "the boy" walked up. I could almost reach out and touch him.

He had that familiar grin on his face.

"Like the story, mister?" he said mockingly.

I could have gotten out of the car and killed the brat.

As it was, I revved up the engine and almost hit him as I sped away, but he was too fast for me and sidestepped nimbly.

I could still hear him laughing when I reached the boulevard below.

On the right, the lake shimmered from the lights on the hill. Beyond, I could see Angelus Temple, where I had dreamt of becoming a great preacher.

I decelerated the engine and knew I couldn't continue. I parked by the side of the road, got out of the car, and headed for the park.

"Hey, Sid. Come on, I'll race you to the lamppost!"
"Willy, you going to the dance tonight?"

"Brother, when the guy had you in the corner I saw your knees buckle. Did he hurt you, Brother?"

"Danny, Danny, why didn't you invite me to that party that Saturday night? Danny, you were like my own family. Were you ashamed of me?"

"No, Tony, I just wanted to go it alone — once. It wasn't even a good party. I just wanted to see if I could cross on my own!"

Suddenly it was a bright Saturday afternoon and the five of us were walking around the park.

"Hey, there's a Spencer Tracy picture down on Temple Street. How about going down?"

"Naw, who wants to see a movie?" Brother shrugged.

"Tracy is great. He stares everybody down. He ain't afraid of nobody," insisted Sid.

"Naw. . . ."

Just then a red streetcar was clanging by and Willy started stuttering that we sh-should hop it a-and s-s-see how f-far we cou-could all get. But by the time he'd said it the streetcar was way down the block, and we all laughed.

He smiled too, realizing his stuttering was funny. The only thing he never stuttered with were his hands and feet.

"You could have been a great painter. You could have been, you could have been, Willy."

"Hey, let's walk up to Belmont High. The track team is working out."

Nobody said yes or no, but we all started sauntering in the direction of the red brick high school on the hill.

Now and then Willy would run out and catch an imaginary football thrown by Dan.

"Danny, what happened to all those books you read? Did you put them to use? Do you still dream of D'Artagnan? Do you still recite *Cyrano*? Did you find it, Dan?"

Brother had me in an imaginary corner and was throwing punches at me. He kept bobbing and weaving. I kept my left up, covering the left hooks, and tried to get under his guard.

"Brother, your dark skin glistened in the sun. You had it all — speed, power, body, brains. Who got to you, Brother? Couldn't you take it? You could have been the Lightweight Champion of the World! Why didn't you get the crown?"

The boys in their green and white uniforms were going through their paces on the other side of the fence. We watched them for a while. We five kids on the wrong side of the fence felt as one about those young blond knights. They represented all that we could never be.

It was Sidney who started goading the boys as they ran down the cinder track. He began yelling obscenities at them. Sidney was the smallest of us and we told him to stop because we would have a fight on our hands.

But his frustration and anger at seeing those young Adonises would not be stilled.

"Fuck them, who the hell do they think they are? Hey, you," he yelled at one tall gangling boy as he sprinted by. "I'll wipe the floor with you."

The boy turned around and walked slowly toward the fence. Soon three or four other trackmen joined him.

The kid stared at Sidney. "What did you say?"

"I said you are all shits and you all run like fairies."

The tall boy turned pale with fury.

"You wait there, you lousy kike, and I'll come and take care of you."

The boy started for the gate at the far end of the field. His teammates went up and stopped him. Sidney hadn't moved.

"That's it, hold him. He is scaring me to death."

Finally, the whole team had become aware of the fracas and headed for us.

The track coach came to see what the shouting was about.

"Look, kids, we don't want any trouble. Why don't you boys just vamoose?"

Willy spoke up. "A-a-ain't this a-a-a fr-free c-country? We c-can stay h-here and w-w-watch if we w-want."

The coach seemed like a nice guy. He said, "You can watch all you want. But I don't want any trouble."

"From what I can see," said Sid, "you are going to have a lot of trouble with that fairy team of yours. They couldn't run downhill if you had pitchforks up their asses."

"You think you could do better?" asked the man.

"I can outrun anybody on your team. As a matter of fact, any one of us can."

The rest of us looked at Sidney in surprise. None of us shared his sentiments.

"I'll tell you what we're going to do, boys," said the coach. "We're going to have our own private track meet. You boys come in and run against our team."

Our bluff had been called. Only Sidney responded to the challenge.

"Come on, you guys, let's go and run their asses off."

The four of us followed him halfheartedly. The coach offered to loan us some track shoes, but Sidney waved his generosity aside.

"We'll run as we are."

So there on a lonely Saturday afternoon, with no one watching, one of the great events of my life took place.

Sidney decided that he would be our representative in the hundred-yard dash, as well as the two-twenty. Brother was to race the four-forty and I the eight-eighty. Willy and Danny were to share the mile race, high jump and shotput. By that time, Sidney expected to have recuperated enough to take the high school team on at the broad jump, and the pole vault and hurdles.

"Sidney, tell me the truth. You wanted to beat them all by yourself, didn't you?"

"Line up for the hundred-yard dash," the coach called out.

Sidney lined up against the four boys in their uniforms. They crouched in their starting boxes like trained hounds. Sidney looked ridiculous beside them. He refused to take the classical position of the dashmen.

"On your marks — get set —"

The gun went off.

You'd think the gun had fired Sidney out of a barrel. His chubby legs raced down the cinder track like loose pistons. His face was contorted in anger and determination to win. There was no style, just guts racing down to the finish line. He beat their best runner by half a yard.

The coach called for the two-twenty.

Willy tried to take Sidney's place but Sidney wouldn't hear of it.

"I'll beat these bastards alone."

Bang! The gun went off and Sidney was zooming down the track. His legs seemed to be saying, "I'm a Jew — I'm a Jew — I'm a Jew — I have to run faster than you." Again he won.

He fell on the grass by the side of the track in exhaustion. Between breaths he told Brother to run his ass off in the four-forty.

"Brother, you looked like a beautiful glistening black cat running around that track. The first two hundred yards you were way ahead of the pack. But you didn't pace yourself. We were all running in anger that afternoon. We were all slugging it out. In the ring you would have known better. You would have saved yourself for the rounds to come. But we wanted to win by a wide margin — by a knockout. We wanted no leftovers — no doubts. We all started too fast. But you did come in second, Brother. It took the City Champ to beat you."

And now it was my turn. Eight hundred and eighty yards to run. One half mile of fright lay ahead of me.

I found myself lined up against those three fellows with their shining spiked shoes. There I was in my dirty tennis shoes daring to compete with those blond heroes.

I would have given anything not to run that afternoon.

"Mephistopheles, you could have claimed my soul for nothing!"

Sidney stood beside me while we were lining up. He sensed my fear.

"Tony, the only difference between them and you is that they are wearing fancy suits. Just put one foot in front of the other and stay with it. You've got to win!"

The gun went off and all I saw was a blur as the red earth passed beneath me. Ahead I saw a pair of heels kicking up the cinder. All I had to do was to keep up with those moving heels.

I seemed to have been running forever when I became aware of someone pacing beside me on the inside of the track. I heard Sid's voice.

"You're doing great, Tony. Only six hundred more yards to go."

Six hundred? Christ! My lungs seemed about to burst and I had only run one-fourth of the distance!

I kept watching those heels in front of me. Tchn-gug — tchn-gug — tchn-gug. Those long strides of the boy in front of me represented everything I wanted to be — assured, controlled, and measured.

When I came around the turn the second time I knew I couldn't make it. My feet felt like I was wearing weights and my lungs

65

refused to respond. I could feel the vomit gathering in my throat

Sidney was running beside me and talking to me.

"Tony, I know it's tough. I know you're feeling sick, but stick with it. In a few seconds you'll get your second wind. Nobody is better than us, Tony. We don't need no goddamned spiked shoes and pretty uniforms to show these bastards we're as good as they are."

"Christ, Sidney! Is that all the damn race has been about? To prove to people we're as good as they are? Sidney, even now my lungs are bursting. I need you. Where the hell are you?"

"Tony, the guy in front of you is a phony. He is just a pacer for the guy behind you. In a few seconds the guy behind you is going to pass you. Let him get just one stride ahead of you, let him lead you until the last hundred yards — then open up."

"That's what I mean, Sid. Have we been pacing ourselves behind the wrong guy, behind the wrong values? Isn't the real runner always the guy behind us?"

The boy behind me, sure enough, passed me. I could hear his breath smooth and even as he pulled up alongside me. He seemed to be miles tall.

"Don't worry," Sidney was shouting. "He's feeling just as sick as you are. They're not supermen — the goyisha bastards. Keep up with him."

I kept running, struggling for air. I tried desperately to ignore the huge pain in my chest. I felt that I was going to explode and my guts were going to spill onto the track.

"One hundred more yards — let it all out —"

Let what all out? There wasn't a breath left inside me. The world was spinning. I could feel the blood pounding in my head. I knew that in two more steps I'd turn into a fountain of gore.

"Tony, there is just one man between you and the finish line. Run your ass off."

God, how easy it would have been to quit. How simple. One can always find an excuse. However, I knew deep down that to fall meant never to rise again.

Next thing I knew I was lying on the grass vomiting. I looked up and saw the faces of my four pals. They were smiling.

"Hey, boys, did I faint or something?" I managed to ask.

"You — you w-w-won," said Willy.

I felt my stomach turn over and emptied it out on the grass once more.

So that's what it feels like to be number one — to be surrounded by puke and smiling faces, I thought. To feel yourself painfully gasping for air.

Yet how often have I longed to know that feeling once more — to be number one!

That need was to torment me and haunt me for the rest of my life.

But how does one determine one's number in life? One's number in love? Where is the finish line and who are the other runners? Who are the ghosts you are running against?

How the hell do you determine where you stand with a woman? How do you know you haven't been given the trophy merely by default?

The doctor said, "Christ, Tony, you certainly must have truly felt number one at times?"

I told him about the panther.

"On Saturday afternoons, my cousin and I would go over to the zoo, where my father worked, and help him feed the cats. Among the animals was a small black panther, a female, with which I was madly in love. Of course, we were warned by my father not to get too near her. I had to spear a piece of meat and chuck it in. I loved to be alone with the cat. At first, my cousin and I would take the meat down, but the cat didn't like my cousin. As a matter of fact, I too hated him. One of the reasons for my pathological obsessions about defecation is due to him. We never had a toilet in the house until I was eleven years old, and when we worked on the railroads there wasn't even an outhouse; we used to have to go out on the plains.

"There was an old tree trunk — like a hitching post — where everybody, the women and the men, sat and did their duties out in the open. Everybody seemed to accept it as quite normal, and men and women used to sit there smoking cigarettes, carrying on conversations while they did it. But I found it offensive.

"One day, my cousin was sitting on this fence relieving himself. I was only about three or four and I had to squat on the ground. He reached behind and took his excrement in his hand and rubbed it all over my face. I never forgave that sonofabitch.

67

"Anyway, the cats also didn't like him, and this particular black cat hated him. Whenever my cousin was around, she would growl and wouldn't eat. I got him to go away. I loved having the big black cat to myself. The moment I'd come by she would purr in that rich organ way of hers. I used to dream about her. The fact that she was female also had a great deal to do with it. I thought she was the one woman in the world that loved me unconditionally.

"One day, while no one was around, I reached into the cage and touched her rich velvet coat. She was so tense, watching me. To this day I can still recall that soft, wonderful, shiny fur — and the danger. As I started stroking her very slowly, I could feel every muscle and fiber of that cat responding.

"Shortly after that I had to go to the county hospital for a tonsillectomy. In a huge room about fifteen children were lined up for an assembly-line operation. I saw one boy lying on the bloody table. I witnessed the whole gory procedure. I started screaming and straining to get away, but my hands and feet were all bound. After they wheeled the boy off, they shoved a mask on me; I felt the suffocating smell of ether. Things started to go round like Fourth of July fireworks, then it became black.

"I woke up in a small dormitory with about eight other boys. My father was sitting beside me. He sat there all afternoon.

"That night he wouldn't leave when the nurse said the visiting hours were over. He picked me up in his arms and covered me with a blanket. He carried me down the fire escape and all the way home. My mother has said he was rather undemonstrative but he kissed me that day and he took me home.

"My mother and my grandmother were terribly upset that he hadn't left me at the hospital. They were afraid that I would have complications, but he said, 'No, I'll take care of my son myself.' He sat there and he didn't go to work the next day until he was sure that I was all right.

"He had to go back and feed the animals; the panther had refused to eat. Later, he told me the cat looked around, as if to say, 'Where's the little boy? Where's my friend?' And my father started talking to the panther, saying, 'He's sick now, but he'll be back in a few days.' But she wouldn't eat, just kept pacing and pacing. Finally, he tried to force her to eat; he put his hand inside

he cage to hand her the food, and she jumped and practically
ore his arm off. He was in the hospital for two weeks hovering
etween life and death.

"I went to see the panther several times while my father was in
he hospital. I felt that she was sorry for what she had done. Her
eep growl was more like a cry asking me to forgive her. I petted
er.

"I went to see my father in the hospital and said that I had been
o see the cat. I confessed that I had been disloyal to him. He said,
Don't be silly, the cat loves you. And she's right, I had no business
ooling around with somebody else's girl friend. That's what a real
woman should be. You should only be lucky enough to find a
woman like that in your life, one who will kill anybody else who
omes near her. If you ever look for a woman, look for a woman
ike that cat.'

"He made me go back and feed her.

"Some time later we moved away and my great love affair with
hat sleek black beauty was over. I often wondered what hap-
ened to her — who fed her after I left. Did she fall in love with
im?"

# 4

TURNED OFF the highway and drove into a shopping center. I
ound a phone booth and called my wife in Santa Monica.

"Hello, Katie?"

"Yes, honey. How did it go?"

"Fine, fine. Listen, dear. I'm going to have dinner with the
octor and his wife."

There was a pause at the other end. "He's going to work with
ou at his home?"

"Well, he invited me to dinner, but I guess I will be under
bservation."

She laughed that intimate laugh I knew so well. "Don't be late, dear. The studio called to say your call has been changed and you have to be in makeup at 7 A.M."

Damn it, I thought. Right now I'm on the trail of some important truths, and I have to worry about make-believe. Then I realized I was being unfair because the world of make-believe had been my salvation. Make-believe was the only truth I *could* rely on.

"Okay, honey," I said. "How are the kids?"

"Fine. I took Duncan to the doctor to have his eyes checked. Kathy had her skin allergy tests; we'll know how they turned out in a few days. Chrissy has taken the television set apart and is putting it together again. And Vally is staying overnight with a girl friend."

"Any other calls?"

"Your agent. He said he has an offer for you in Europe."

I thought I detected a twinge of annoyance in the last bit of news.

"Okay, honey. I'd better get to the doctor's."

"Don't be home too late, dear. And Tony, trust in God. Everything is going to be all right."

"Yes, dear. See you."

I hung up.

I thought of her surrounded by the children I loved. I envied her. Here I was on a lonely, painful quest, when I should be at home "enjoying the fruits of all my labor."

I drove up the winding hill to the doctor's house. He had given me a map so I had little difficulty in finding it. Down below I could see the lights glittering in the clear cool night.

To me it was only right that the doctor should live in such neutral surroundings. I guess the man had to constantly "neutralize" himself.

He welcomed me at the door. He was smiling that opening "happy to see you" smile. At first, it had reminded me of all the red-necks I'd hated in my life — the railroad dicks, the vice principal at Senior High, the motorcycle cops and the U.S. Marines who liked to beat up zoot-suiters on Saturday night. Only lately had I begun to think there might be a modicum of sincerity about that smile.

He introduced me to his wife, who seemed gracious, warm.

70

As I looked about the room I could see that the same decorator had done his office — more Japanese silk prints hung on the wall, the same flower box for the rubber plant stood in the living room.

At dinner I earned my keep by regaling them with stories of my Uncle Cleofus.

When we were living on Daly Street on the East Side of Los Angeles, we lived in a perpetual earthquake. Trains roared by a few yards from our house, and we all seemed afflicted with Saint Vitus's dance. Everything in the house rattled, including our teeth.

And it wasn't only trains shaking us to pieces, but also the red streetcars that passed over the bridge in front of our house.

The "house" consisted of one medium-sized room and a small kitchen. At first, we all slept on the floor — Grandmother, Mother, my father, my sister and myself. Later, Father built a small lean-to that became his and Mother's bedroom. The room was only big enough to hold a bed and a side table with the kerosene lamp.

A piano crate in the middle of the "living room" served as our dining table, around which we all sat at breakfast, lunch and dinner.

My father hated the sight of the railroad yards on our left. He painted all the windows with different scenes. On the kitchen window he drew mountains with a stream meandering through a verdant valley. He even painted in the cows and the horses grazing forever on the grass. In the living room he let his imagination go rampant. One window was the Pacific Ocean with huge steamers going to an everlasting nowhere. The other was overlooking a small village with castles dotting the horizon.

Into our midst one day roared a stranger. I was told he was my Uncle Cleofus. Actually, he was my grandmother's brother. I can't remember what he said but two minutes after his entrance everybody was on the floor roaring with laughter.

At dinner he told us stories of his adventures during the revolution — like the day he had challenged Villa to a duel and Villa had backed down.

"Villa begged me, however, that on one terrain I must never challenge him. He had taken a long time to build up his reputation as a Lothario with women. He knew that if I ever wanted to

go on record his reputation would be destroyed. I kept my promise."

Uncle Cleofus turned to me: "Well, Antonio, being your father's son and my nephew you must have at least three women
stashed away somewhere."

I was then six and had had abortive attempts at sex while playing house with the little girl next door. My mother had caught me
and given me a whipping. I now looked to her for help. She told
Uncle Cleofus that she'd caught me "fooling around" one day.

"Only once? This boy is retarded," said my uncle. "And you
mean you stopped him? You might have ruined his health forever
Nellie. When the urge comes it's injurious for boys to restrain it."

Grandmother told him to hush up and said that he was still a
dirty reprobate.

"Sabina, you always had a misguided sense of sex. If God hadn't
meant us to use our appendages, he would have made them sea-
sonal. But, thank God, they are functional all the year round
Tony, tomorrow you and I will have a talk when these puritan
aren't around."

That night I could hear my uncle snore. It was the loudest
healthiest, happiest snoring I'd ever heard. He seemed to enjoy
himself even in his sleep.

Next day he took me out in the backyard and gave me my firs
lesson on the art of love.

"My dear boy, one's relation to women colors all one's life
Learn to handle them and you can handle anything from wildcat
to higher mathematics."

He looked around to make sure we were alone. "Just between
us men, you do have a girl, no?"

"Well, there is this girl at school . . ."

He roared his approval. "I knew it, I knew it. When I saw you
yesterday I said, here is the only man in the world who is going to
break my record! Tell me about her."

"There is nothing to tell. I like her but I think she likes another
boy. He buys her candy."

"Aha, one of those, huh? They are difficult, but they can be
broken down by ingenuity. She is probably not worth your attention if her affections can be bought with candy. A man who has
to hold a woman by gifts is not a man. He is a broker. Although

72

have already made up my mind she is beneath you, I can't have you grow up with a sense of failure. It could color all your life. What is your favorite approach?"

"What do you mean?"

"How do you get her to notice you?"

"I just look at her."

"Aha, your first mistake. Always ignore them, Tony. Never let them know you are interested."

"What should I do?" I asked. I realized I was getting a valuable lesson in life.

"Suppose I'm the girl and you want to get my attention. How would you walk by me?"

He made me cross the yard and walk past him. I was self-conscious and looked down at my feet as I passed him.

"Oh, son, you are going to need a lot of training. First you take your hands out of your pocket — and don't meander. Walk like you're in a hurry and you have no time to spare. If you want, you can cast one fast glance at her, but make it seem like you are looking through her, not at her. Now, if after a while that doesn't work, then you'll have to use another approach. A different walk. For instance, once in Guadalajara there was this beautiful arrogant rich señorita who wouldn't see me for spit, but I soon had her eating out of my hand. I developed a walk that stunned her and made her mine forever. I would take one step and tap with the foot behind, another step and another tap."

He got up and illustrated.

"Use it only in extreme cases, son, otherwise you will be swamped with women. They are suckers for that step."

For days I practiced it. The only thing was that when I did it for Lucy at school she thought I was crazy. I reported my failure to my uncle. He said, "Forget her. She is beyond redemption. She deserves guys who only feed her candy."

After a week or so my uncle had turned the house upside down. He had talked my father into financing an invention. That night the whole table had been held spellbound by his great discovery.

There was a lean-to in the garden that was part barn and part garage. Since we had no automobile, the only things it housed were some rabbits, three or four hens and one belligerent bantam rooster.

73

"Francisco," he announced at dinner, "I am going to turn that garage into a small factory."

"What kind of factory?" my father asked suspiciously.

"Sh-sh," my uncle hushed him in a loud whisper. "What I am about to tell you is only for your ears. No one in the neighborhood must know what is going on. Everyone here must be sworn to secrecy. One word and it will ruin all our plans. My dear boy, I needn't tell you how I esteem my favorite sister here on my left."

My grandmother scoffed.

"Sabina," he continued, "you hurt me when you take my affection lightly. You were always the dearest of all the family to me. After the death of your husband I was like a father to your son. Was I not, Francisco?"

"Whenever you came around," agreed my father.

"Son, we were at war. And no matter where I roamed the Quinns were always in my every thought."

"Never mind," said my grandmother. "Tell us about the factory."

The family had caught fire with the possibility of the riches he implied.

"Oh, yes, the factory. Francisco, do you realize how much a banana costs in New York?"

"No. How much?"

My uncle took his full dramatic pause. "Twenty cents for one banana."

The family as one were stunned. Twenty cents for just one banana! You could buy a dozen bananas in Los Angeles at that time for ten cents.

"Exactly. Imagine the profit if I can deliver fresh bananas to New York."

"Don't they grow bananas in New York?" asked Grandmother.

My uncle dismissed her ignorance of higher agriculture. "Bananas only grow in tropical climates. They transport them into New York from the island of Cuba or the tropics of Mexico. Only here in Los Angeles do they have crops to equal Cuba and the South. Now the problem is how to get them to New York before they rot. They are now transported east in refrigerated freight cars, which is why each banana costs twenty cents."

He quickly explained that on one dozen bananas the profit would be two dollars and thirty cents.

"Multiply that by a thousand dozen and you are a millionaire overnight."

He let that sink in. Every mouth at the table was agape at the simplicity of it all.

"What has the factory got to do with it?" asked my pragmatic grandmother.

He had saved the *pièce de résistance*. "Aha. I have invented a means of freezing which will make the refrigerated cars and the tons of ice necessary for transporting bananas obsolete."

After the dramatic announcement, my grandmother broke the silence. "When did you become an inventor?"

"Sabina, what do you think I've been doing all these years? I've been looking for the one thing that will make us all rich. I came to California expressly at the call of certain individuals who have heard of my secret. But after the few days I've spent here in the warmth of my dear family, I've decided I will not share my secret with strangers. I don't need them. All I want is a place to work and some simple tools — which Frank will provide. And he will be half-owner of the patent which I am registering in a few days."

He got up and left the room discreetly, saying he was going to the corner to buy some cigarettes. He knew that the family would want to discuss the possible investment in my uncle's invention.

Oh, the pros and cons that went on. My father had been won over by the promise of imminent wealth. He would back Uncle Cleofus to the hilt.

Two weeks later, the garage was boarded up tight and all the knotholes covered lest anyone peek in and see what my uncle was building. The hammering on metal went on all day long. Whenever he had to go off to town to buy important tubes and gauges for his "invention," he locked the "factory" up tight. The backyard looked like we had gone into the junk business.

After a while, his progress became "top secret." Only my father and he discussed how the invention was coming along. I remember that at dinner the talk was very gay and Father seemed to think the millions were just around the corner.

Occasionally, my grandmother complained that we would all

be driven to the poor house by my uncle's invention. She calculated that Father had already advanced ninety-seven dollars and the end was nowhere in sight.

"Ordinarily," my uncle defended himself, "this titanic undertaking would cost thousands of dollars, and the means which only a large factory can provide. Due to the limited capital, I am working day and night. I am completely aware of my responsibility to my nephew's faith. I will not soil that trust. However, if you all feel that I am in any way taking advantage of my own family, there are certain individuals who are dying to . . ."

My father grew impatient with such negative discussions. "Look, Cleofus, I said I'd go ahead, so you just continue. I think it's a great idea."

The hammering and the clatter went on for weeks in the backyard. Finally, the great day arrived. The unveiling was to take place. It was a Sunday morning, when all the family could be present to rejoice at my uncle's accomplishment, and dream about how to spend the millions. My grandmother was willing to settle for the hundred and forty-seven dollars my father had advanced, but we had all come to recognize her as the voice of doom.

My uncle opened the factory door with a flourish. We all rushed inside. There in the center of the garage was the "Invention." It was a huge oil drum with all manner of tubes wound around it, like a huge animal with all its guts on the outside. There were numerous gauges and faucets.

Uncle Cleofus went into a lengthy, detailed description of pressures and intakes and outlets, which only my father seemed to follow. Then he opened a door that creaked loudly. Inside we could see something that looked like a discarded oven. In the center of the ovenlike container was one banana.

My uncle took it out with great delicacy and we watched him peel it. He was like a magician peeling away the seven veils. Then he made all of us take a bite — my father first, who had priority as the big investor — then Mother, then Grandmother, then I took a bite, and Stella, my sister, got the last piece. God knows what we all expected but it tasted just like an ordinary banana.

"So?" asked my grandmother.

"'So' — is that all I hear, 'so'? My dear sister, that banana has

76

been in there for a fortnight and it is as fresh as if I'd picked it from the frond of a tree this morning!"

We were all impressed.

"How many bananas will that thing hold?" asked my grandmother.

"At present, twelve," my uncle smiled.

My grandmother calculated roughly that each banana would be worth ten dollars by the time it got to New York. He smiled sadly at her ignorance.

"Of course, this is only a model, my dear. As we increase in size so will the volume and the quantity of our cargo."

"In order for you to carry a thousand bananas you'd have to build a tank as huge as a skyscraper," my grandmother argued.

The family was beginning to realize she had a point. Uncle Cleofus tried desperately to revive the enthusiasm.

"Francisco, if one listened to women, electricity would never have been discovered; Columbus would not have crossed the ocean. Don't be affected."

But even Father's enthusiasm was beginning to wane.

Not to close the ceremony on a negative note, my uncle placed six bananas inside the contraption and locked it by turning several screws and faucets. He also regulated the valves and refilled a bottle with water which dripped one drop at a time into a receptacle that he explained was the cooling system. Then he lit the fire under the drum. He said vaporization would take place and that the vacuum created by the oxidization would create its own cooling system.

He promised that in three or four days we'd all be there when he opened the door and that the six bananas would be as fresh as when they were put in.

On the morning when the new unveiling was to take place I heard screams coming from the garage. It was my grandmother's angry voice. She had caught my uncle changing the bananas. She was in the process of throwing them into his face.

"I'm going to tell Frank and he'll kill you," she threatened.

My uncle tried to explain that something had gone wrong, but I noticed he had lost his note of assurance.

That evening he made a big announcement at dinner — the unveiling would not take place, but he was satisfied that his in-

77

vention worked. He was now going to meet certain important individuals in the East who would put up the necessary funds for the building of the Quinn-Espinoza Cooling Machine. He told Father he need have no worries since his name was included in all the patent papers as half-owner. There was no chance that he could be cheated.

It took several days for my uncle to clear up certain important matters, and his departure was scheduled for the following Sunday.

We all sat cross-legged at the piano crate. Though it was early in the morning, the women had prepared a feast. The piano crate was full of festive food. Four or five neighbors had been invited to see my uncle off.

These were many toasts, and finally my uncle got up to make a speech. Time was running short. We could hear the train whistle in the distance.

"My dear friends and dear, dear family. I have been here only a short time but long enough to feel the pangs of nostalgia at the thought that I won't share your warmth and affection for a long time to come. I feel we are on the verge of a great fortune. I feel that the revelation of my great invention was not given to me by God for my own selfish use. It was destined that I should share it with the beloved offspring of my dearest sister. I will leave you within a few minutes, but the benefits that the Quinn family will derive from my visit will be everlasting."

He gulped down a last glass of dago red. The train whistle was now much closer. He grabbed his knapsack and we all rushed out behind him.

The train was still going slowly as it came out of the yards.

He made a dash for an open boxcar. The knapsack got in his way and his first attempt was awkward. He almost fell under the wheels. However, he managed to wave back to us as if to assure us that all was well, and on the second attempt he caught the ladder and swung aboard the car.

He blew us all kisses and we all wept as he disappeared in the distance.

A week later my grandmother sold the invention to a junk man for eight dollars and no one ever spoke of it again.

After dinner, the doctor's wife served coffee in the study. She said she had some work to do and hoped to see me again soon.

After she left, the doctor asked me how my session with my mother had gone.

"Fine — nothing new. A slightly different treatment of some elements but nothing really new."

"So you didn't find any answers?"

"Doc, you told me to ask questions. I'm hoping you will find the answers."

"We will, Tony, we will. By the way, that's a lovely car you drove up in. What make is it?"

"A Continental."

"It's beautiful. A block long. You like powerful cars, Tony?"

"Look, I've read a lot of books. I know what the symbol of a car stands for. No, Doc, I have no penis envy, and I don't smoke big cigars."

He laughed. "I wasn't implying . . ."

"Doc, your racket is like mine; we're always working. So I will tell you something that should give you some homework to do. I drove the car to my mother's house in the complete knowledge of what I was doing. I wanted to show off to the old neighborhood, and even more important, to show my stepfather I'd become a bigger man than he was. I wanted to show him he'd never be as big or important as my father."

"That's sad, isn't it, Tony? I am sure the old man has lived in your father's shadow all these years. You're too nice a guy to want to keep rubbing it in."

"As a matter of fact, it didn't work anyway. He wasn't there. But 'the kid' was."

"You saw him again?"

"The sonofabitch won't get off my back. I can never please him. No matter what I do, what I accomplish, he sneers at it."

"How old was he today?"

"Ten or eleven."

It was late and I didn't want to open that can of peas. I had to work next day and I had to deal with fantasy — reality would have to wait. I said good-night to the doctor and he walked me to the car.

It was a long drive home, and all the ghosts sat in the back seat.

I was afraid to turn around. I played the radio real loud to drown out their voices.

# 5

"TELL ME MORE about 'the boy.' "

The doctor spoke very casually, as if asking about the weather. To me, the kid spelled storm clouds. Lately he had really been bothering me. Maybe he felt that the ring was closing in on him. He was fighting back.

I had seen him a few times on the set of the movie I was making. Then I'd seen him again at the studio commissary, where I was having lunch with a woman columnist who was interviewing me.

"Your childhood sounds fascinating, Mr. Quinn," she said. "I mean, your Irish father and your mother fighting in the revolution with Pancho Villa, and all that. I mean, now that you have won two Oscars, what are your goals?"

The kid pretended to go on eating at the next table but I knew he was listening to every word. I didn't understand why they didn't throw him out. He was dressed in corduroy trousers, white shirt, and that glee club green sweater. They probably thought he was some kid doing a TV series.

"Mr. Quinn, what are your goals?" The woman sat there with her pencil poised.

"My goals? To stay healthy and earn enough money so my children can get a good education."

"That sounds nice and healthy, but I was talking about your other career goals."

I looked toward the kid. I caught his eye and he just stared at me. The waitress was passing by so I asked for the check. I turned back to the interviewer and I kidded, "I let my agent make all those decisions — I just report for work."

At least I hadn't committed myself in front of the boy. Nothing for him to sneer at.

I told the doctor.

"What does he want?" asked the doctor.

What *does* he want? I thought.

"He wants the world," I said. "He wants the sky. He wants eternity. He demands things from me I can't give him. He wants purity and truth."

"Can't you give him purity and truth, Tony?"

"I give him the truth that's around today. It's the only kind available on the market. But he wants a different brand, one they no longer make. As for purity, where do you go to find it nowadays? To some monastery in the Himalayas? Do I become an Albert Schweitzer in the jungle?"

"Is it only religious purity he is asking for?"

"No, he wants purity of thought, purity of action. He wants complete honesty."

"You try to be honest. Your sessions with me have been pretty direct. You seem to me a man who is desperately trying to be honest."

"He doesn't think so. I keep saying I'm as honest as one can be in this 'naughty world' but he just scoffs."

"Well, using the kind of language you like, Tony, tell him to go fuck himself."

"I have, Doctor. He won't do it."

"When did he first appear?"

"He started coming around when I began acquiring things I thought would please him. The first time I saw him was when I bought the jazzy house on Sunset Boulevard. He was standing on the lawn one day wondering what the hell I was doing with such a mansion. It was during the war and big houses were going abegging so I thought what the hell, I'll buy it. The boy began to make me feel guilty about it so I used to let people use it to raise money for good causes. The only time I ever saw the sonofabitch smile approvingly was the night I gave a party to raise funds for the 'Sleepy Lagoon' case. That night the kid and I walked around the garden like real pals."

"What was the 'Sleepy Lagoon' case?"

"Around 1944 or 1945, twenty-two Mexican boys were being

tried for murder. It seems there had been a party in East L.A
and it had ended in a rumble, which wasn't unusual at those
parties. Some kids from another gang had tried to crash, there
had been this fight, and one boy had been killed. Twenty-two
Mexican boys were rounded up and now they were being tried
for murder. Certain groups in Los Angeles were up in arms; they
felt the kids were being railroaded. They called it another Scotts
boro case, where a group of Negroes had been found guilty of
rape in the South. The case was becoming a political football.
Some Los Angeles papers were saying that Mexicans had bad In
dian blood in them which made them violent. They were ferment
ing a great deal of anti-Mexican feeling.

"I was making a war picture at Camp Pendleton at the time and
one Saturday, after I'd finished work, some marines who were
working with us came and asked if I wanted to join them. They
were going up to Los Angeles to 'beat up some Mexicans.' Those
poor misguided bastards. They were trying to tell me they con
sidered me one of them. I guess my name being Quinn, they never
thought I was Mexican. I got into a fight with the asshole who
had invited me. He was a big bruiser. I guess luckily someone
pulled us apart.

"One day I got a call at the studio from my mother. She asked
if I had read about the 'Sleepy Lagoon' case. Christ! Even m
mother was caught up in it. I said of course, the papers talked
of nothing else.

" 'One of the boys' names is Levas.'

" 'So?'

" 'You wouldn't remember her but when we first arrived in
Juárez from Chihuahua she was the first person to help us. W
were starving and she made us some scrambled eggs.'

"I had to laugh thinking how Mother remembered the menu

"She went on. 'Anyway, she called this morning and was cry
ing. It seems that everything points to the fact that her son will
go to the electric chair.'

" 'Yes, I know,' I said. 'It looks like he was the ringleader.'

" 'I promised her that you would get him off,' my mother an
nounced.

" 'You what?'

" 'They have no money, Tony. They can't afford a good lawyer

All she wants is for her son to get a fair trial. All these years she's never asked for a favor in return.'

" 'Mama, I can't become involved in a murder case. Jeez, you've read the papers. Everybody who has come to the defense of the kids is being called a Communist. That's all I would need. Mama, we could be run out of the country!'

" 'Maybe we wouldn't be in the country if it wasn't for Trini Levas.'

" 'Why, because she fed us some scrambled eggs?'

" 'Perhaps she saved our lives.'

" 'Christ, Mama, how much do we have to pay for those god-damned scrambled eggs? All right, I'll give you a thousand dollars. You can give it to her. That should be more than enough payment for those eggs.'

" 'No, Tony. She doesn't want the money. She wants her son.'

"I argued. I pleaded for her to let me off the hook. She wouldn't.

"That night I called a friend of mine. He and his wife, Goldie, were good people. They were always fighting for causes. Whether it was the lettuce strikers, the dock workers, or the 'Sleepy Lagoon' case.

"I told them I would like to help the boys. What could I do? He said there was a committee being formed for their defense. I could help them raise money.

"I had had no experience with such things so I took the direct approach. I went to actors and directors that I knew and asked for cash. Most of them responded generously. Some were afraid they would be implicated politically. One famous star who had made his reputation playing gangster parts turned me down flat. He said the whole movement for the defense of the kids was being run by 'Reds.'

"I began making speeches at ladies' club luncheons. The papers picked up the news and one day I was called in by Darryl Zanuck, at whose studio I was then under contract. He told me that my involvement was endangering the investment they had in my pictures.

" 'Darryl, you have been one of the most courageous men I've ever seen in this business,' I told him. 'You've made pictures like *The Ox-Bow Incident, Grapes of Wrath, Gentleman's Agreement.*

You've never been afraid. Why do you want me to run scared now?'

"I explained the circumstances that had caused me to become involved. Now that I was in it, I said, I had begun to realize there were some ugly forces working against the boys.

"He nodded and said, 'A hell of an expensive plate of scrambled eggs!'

"When I walked away I didn't know whether I would be dropped by the studio. I wasn't. I have always been proud to know that some people in my business stand for more than mere self-interest. Darryl Zanuck certainly proved it that day.

"Soon after, there was a big benefit party at my house in Beverly Hills. We charged a huge entrance fee and some of the most famous people in Hollywood came to entertain, all for the cause.

"That night as I went about the garden welcoming the guests, 'the boy' walked beside me. I had never seen him so happy. It was the first time in years he seemed to approve of me. I thought he'd leave me alone after that. He didn't."

The doctor had listened patiently. Once or twice I'd seen him scribble on the papers he kept on me.

"Tony, would you mind discussing your political views with me someday?"

I must have given him a strange look because he threw back his head and laughed.

"I am not a representative of the Un-American Activities Committee."

The pains they had caused friends of mine kept me from joining in his laughter.

"No, Doc, I have nothing to hide. Let me say at the outset that I wouldn't give a damn if you were from the Un-American outfit. Sometimes I almost wished they had called me. To tell you the truth, I think 'the boy' hoped they would. He always prods me to stand up and be counted. I have never been a Communist. have never attended a cell meeting and, believe it or not, I was never proselytized or asked to join any so-called subversive movement. I was pro-labor for humanitarian reasons. I was anti-Fascist and anti-Nazi because they preached racial and nationalistic superiority which was diametrically opposed to my philosophy. To me

84

America was an experiment in humanitarianism which I did not want to see fail."

I began to sound like I was waving a flag. I knew the doctor was my friend when he didn't cringe.

"You've never seen 'the boy' happy since then?"

"Once, in Paris."

"Tell me about it."


"On the ship crossing the Atlantic to do a picture I had eaten some bad fish, and had developed a terrible allergy. My face had swollen up beyond recognition. At first, everyone thought it was temporary, but by the time I reached Le Havre it had gotten worse.

"I warned the producers that I might not be able to start the picture on schedule.

"They came to meet me on the boat to make sure it wasn't an excuse to get out of the commitment. They were appalled by my appearance and had to smuggle me past the authorities. I looked like I had a contagious disease.

"When we reached Paris I was installed in a garret apartment of one of the fancy hotels.

"The next day they began calling every skin specialist in Europe to diagnose my condition. I went from office to office. They performed all sorts of tests and cures, X-ray treatments to sandpapering my skin, all to no avail.

"I lived in the garret with a silk mask over my face. I refused to see a soul. I was completely isolated, except for the telephone calls from the producers, who had imported another specialist. At night I'd ride down in the service elevator and sneak out the back entrance.

"The picture was with Gina Lollobrigida, who refused to allow the producers to recast the part. She firmly believed that I would get well. But the pressure was on and the time was fast coming when they'd have to take someone else.

"I sat in that garret for weeks with that mask over my face. At first I too had thought it was a temporary condition. I enjoyed the time off to read and listen to music. Later, I stopped reading and rarely listened to music. I just sat and stared at the Parisian sky, convinced that I had a strange malady which was incurable.

"That's when 'the boy' showed up. He sat in that room for days. He was very quiet and had lost that sneer. We didn't really speak to each other. There wasn't much to say. I almost welcomed his company. One day we had been sitting there for hours in silence when I said, 'Well, kid, the ride is over.'

" 'It looks like it,' he said.

" 'You're happy, aren't you?' I said.

" 'No, not exactly. Not like this. I didn't want it to be forced on you.'

" 'What do you want, kid? What the hell do you want? What more can I give you?'

" 'I don't want more things. There is already too much. I just want it different,' he said quietly.

"Oh God! I knew what he meant, but I didn't want to think about it.

" 'What will you do if the crud doesn't disappear?' he asked.

" 'I don't know. I've been thinking of sitting on an island. Maybe going to live in India with the rest of the untouchables. After all, no one says that a writer or painter or even a builder has to have a Palmolive skin.'

"The kid laughed. He actually laughed. It was nice seeing him happy. We kidded back and forth about what I would do. He enjoyed dreaming of all the possibilities."

The doctor's voice brought me back. "So he was glad at the thought of having you to himself, wasn't that it? I mean, he didn't discuss taking your wife or your children to India, did he?

"No, you're right. He kept saying it would just be the two of us."

"A few days later I found the psychological reason why I had been sick, and I got well."

"Just like that?"

"The producers decided to take one last crack at it. They found a man who was a homeopath. He had a dingy office out in the Montmartre district. The place contained more books than medical equipment. The specialist sat behind his desk and pushed some books and magazines aside.

" 'Now, Mr. Quinn, what is your trouble?'

"What the hell did he think I was doing there in his office. I pointed to the blotches on my face.

"He shrugged as if that was unimportant.

" 'What are you doing in Paris, I mean?'

" 'I came to do a picture.'

" 'What's the title?'

" '*The Hunchback of Notre Dame*,' I answered. I hate doctors who act like movie fans.

" 'Well,' he laughed, 'now you know how it feels to be a monster, don't you? Now that you know, go home, wash your face with Evian water, and rub some camphorated alcohol over your face. In three days you'll be well.'

"He was right. In three days I was well.

"But that was the last time I saw 'the boy' smile."

The doctor was at the window. He was in his shirtsleeves, with his back to me.

"My God," he said, "I've never met anyone who is such a contradiction. You love life and you hate it, Tony. You believe in life and yet you go about surrounded by the dead. Your great companions, your great challengers, all belong to the past. De Mille, John Barrymore, Carole Lombard, all dead. Your father dead, your grandmother, and Sylvia, too. It's easy to fight them; they can't answer back. They stand behind you just picking at you to try to force you to move ahead, but you run hither and yon. The only one you haven't really tackled is 'the boy' because you know he can destroy you any time he wants. Yet you've kept him around because he is the only one who has a sense of direction. He wants to go someplace. He can't tell you where. He's never been there. Perhaps the place doesn't exist. Perhaps it is merely something his ten-year-old mind has invented. But let me ask you, Tony, would you let a child drive your car? Would you trust your life to a pilot ten years old?"

After that barrage from the doctor, I was ready with a monologue of my own, but I wasn't fast enough. He looked at that damn clock.

"We'll talk about 'the boy' again," he said.

As if I didn't know!

87

# 6

"How DID YOU START being an actor?" he began the next ses sion.

"Doc, you sound like all those silly journalists who come t interview me and are thoroughly unprepared. They hope I wil do their homework for them. I have told that story over and ove again. I'm bored with it."

"Yes, I've read several versions. I just wondered which was con rect."

"By now, I don't know myself. If you repeat a lie often enough you get to believe it yourself."

I could see the doctor leafing through some clippings he'd col lected. I had to give him credit, he was doing his homework. Ou sessions lately had become easier. He had told me a week or s before that he looked forward to our "visits." As a matter of fac he had scheduled me at six o'clock so that I could be his las "visitor."

He picked up a clipping. "It says here your father was a cam eraman at a studio and that you began acting when you wer eight years old. Is that true?"

My father a cameraman!

It's like the old joke about the producer who had just bough his first yacht. He arrived home in his white duck pants, double breasted jacket with brass buttons, and a captain's hat. He wa met by his mother at the door:

"Gregorovich — what's that on your head?"

"It's a cap. I'm a captain."

"So to you you are a captain, but to a captain are you a cap tain?"

Was my father a cameraman? Yes, we have a tattered photo graph of my father cranking a camera, but I doubt that he wa cameraman. He did work at Selig Studios, where they filmed sequences that had to do with animals. That's where he fed the black panthers. After a year or so he was promoted to cranking the camera while they were filming.

One day they were to do a sequence in a picture that involved two grizzly bears and a cub. They had two trained grizzlies but no cub. Someone had the brilliant idea of dressing a child in a bearskin. When everyone said it could be dangerous for a child to work with two grizzlies, whether trained or not, my father said he had a son who wouldn't be afraid. They said, "Okay, bring him tomorrow."

That night he brought the skin home and announced that I was about to make my film debut. After dinner all the family sat around while I had my first dress rehearsal. I walked around in that bearskin for hours. I even did a somersault as I had seen the cubs do, putting my shoulder to the ground and rolling over slowly. Before we went to bed, my father announced we would be leaving for work at seven in the morning.

I couldn't sleep for the excitement. No actor has ever worried over a part as much as I did that night lying near the stove. I must have played the role in my head a hundred times. In the morning I woke up in a sea of urine.

My mother saw that something was wrong. She felt my forehead and found I had a high fever. My father was furious. He said it was stage fright, and that probably I was afraid to get in with the big grizzlies.

I swore it wasn't true. I cried that I was all right, but both my mother and grandmother refused to let me go.

Finally, it was decided that my father would pick up my cousin, who was my size and whom I hated, to take my place. I wept all day.

I saw the doctor make his now familiar chicken scratches in my dossier.

"Most of all," I continued, "I was hurt because my father thought I was scared of the bears. How could I have been scared? I thought of them as Mama and Papa. That's why a few weeks later we had the incident with the car."

"Tell me about it."

I was dying to tell it because it was the first time I had equaled my father.

My father had just acquired an old jalopy, the first car he had ever owned. He had driven it home and all the neighbors had stood around looking at our wonderful acquisition. We were the only family in the area who owned a car. He had just gotten a small raise and he had bought it from one of the workers at Selig's. My grandmother always referred to it as the "tarantella." She was terrified of my father driving it.

She said, "Do you know how to drive?"

My father was annoyed at the question. "Aw, come on, Mother, of course I know how to drive."

We were constantly amazed by the things that my father knew how to do.

He turned to me. "Come on, Elephant, get in the car."

I felt sorry for my mother and my sister, who were obviously dying to ride in the car, but he said to them, "The Elephant is going to be the first one to ride with me. Later, I'll come back for you."

We went off and headed for the Lincoln Park hills. The whooshing air almost took my breath away.

"Well, Elephant, what do you think?" he shouted over the motor.

I yelled back, "It's a wonderful car, Papa."

"Isn't it a beauty? Some day, when you get a little older, I'll teach you to drive it!"

"Oh, you don't have to teach me. I can drive this car if I want to," I called back.

He looked at me quizzically. "What do you mean, you can drive this car? You've never driven a car before."

"I've been watching you. It's not so difficult. I can drive this car, too."

We were going down a long winding hill.

"You really think you can drive this car?"

"Sure," I shrugged. "There's nothing to it. You just turn the wheel, wherever you want to go."

So with that, he picked me up and he put me behind the wheel.

nd he moved over to the side. And suddenly, I had the wheel in
ny hand, and I couldn't hold it on the bumpy road.

I said, "Papa, Papa, please — I can't!"

He said, "No, you go on. You said you can drive — you drive."

I said, "But Papa, I can't — I can't." And I started crying.

He yelled, "Look, you sonofabitch, you said you could drive
his car, so goddamn it, you drive it!"

I said, "We'll get killed!"

"So we'll get killed. From now on, don't say you can do some-
hing if you can't do it. You drive this goddamned thing."

What had started out as a nice, charming adventure turned
nto a hysterical nightmare. I was weaving from one side of the
oad to the other, terrified that we might meet another car.

My father lit a cigarette and was looking out at the country-
ide. The gas-line lever was on the right-hand side of the wheel.
shoved it up and the motor started chugging along, but the car
till had a great deal of momentum going downhill.

I couldn't reach the brakes. Father went on smoking noncha-
ntly. We reached the bottom of the hill by some miracle. We
adn't gone over the cliff! We hadn't crashed! The car coasted
or a hundred yards or so, then coughed and stopped.

My father puffed on his cigarette.

"You drove very well, Tony. I didn't think you could drive.
)o you want to drive some more?"

I said, "No, Papa, you'd better take the wheel."

He got out and cranked the car. It started up again and he got
ehind the wheel. We went on with our drive as if nothing had
appened.

Outside it was growing dark. Most of the offices in the building
cross the way were closing. I could see the dentist putting away
is white starched coat and changing into a loud checkered sports
cket.

The doctor seemed to be lost in reverie.

I waited for him to come back. He turned around in his swivel
air.

"I was thinking how much our fathers were alike. In my case
was a tractor. We lived on a farm and almost the identical

scene happened. Only I chopped up half of our crop for that year and the tractor crashed into a barn wall."

I was pleased that this man who was helping me find the answers, and whom I often considered square, had similar experiences to mine.

"I guess our fathers were tougher than our generation," he sighed. "Well, Tony, let's get back to your motives for becoming an actor. That time back there with the bearskin, do you suppose it was there that it started?"

"Maybe even earlier.

"When I was three, my grandmother used to take me to 'cine.' Her favorites were Antonio Moreno and Ramon Navarro. I can remember how she gripped my hand as she watched the screen. She would relive the movie all over again on the way home. As a matter of fact, I'm sure she planted the seed in me. All the time I was growing up and talking of becoming a great preacher, or a boxing champion, or an architect, she was unimpressed. But the day I started to study acting, she perked up. I suppose to her it meant easy fame and wealth. The poor soul at that time was very sick with cancer, and she kept saying that she would refuse to die until she knew I was on my way."

"Your grandmother had an enormous influence on you, didn't she? Her death left a great void in your life?"

"You ask me a question and I would love to tell you everything, but in a few minutes you're going to look at that clock. Like a train about to enter the station, I'll have to start putting on the brakes."

The doctor smiled. "That's why I told my wife I wouldn't be home for dinner tonight. I know you don't have to work tomorrow, so there is no clock to pressure us. Just don't cheat and dodge with me, that's all I ask. You were talking about the motivation behind becoming an actor."

"It's complicated, Doctor. I remember one of the most difficult things I ever had to say in a picture was, 'We have all been traitors for one simple reason. We have all failed to *love*.'

"The night before I had to do that scene, I couldn't sleep. The statement haunted me. I think an actor would give his soul to re create one crystal moment of truth on the stage or screen. Oh they often say, 'How I long for a part that I can get my teeth nto.' It's a cliché, of course. What they really mean, and I'm talking of the good ones, the serious ones, is that they are looking for the part that will allow them to hold up a mirror to all their muttered dreams, all their longings and loneliness, a part that will give them a permanent place on the wall of absolute truth. The actor wants to give that ultimate moment to the world — what the actor wants is to give. That is why I love the profession. But today, Doc, I was on that set for ten hours and I couldn't give a goddamn thing."

"What? Why didn't you tell me that at the beginning of the session?"

"I didn't want to talk about it. I still don't want to go into it."

"Tony, I sympathize with you, but it is precisely the difficult things that we *have* to go into. What happened today?"

"I don't know. I've never had such an experience. For years I've taken pride in the fact that I was a one-take actor. Today I had to do twenty-seven takes! It was such a simple scene — and yet the moment the director said 'Camera,' my mind would become a blank.

"All the actors became aware that I was having trouble. The director knew that I was going through an emotional problem, but rather than understanding or trying to help, he became annoyed. Around the twentieth take he became furious.

" 'What the hell's the matter with you?' he yelled.

"The other actors and the crew cringed. I have a reputation for being difficult, not a man that people yell at. They expected fireworks. Instead I stood there and took it.

" 'Goddamn it,' the director continued angrily, 'if you can't do the scene we'll change it.'

"I bowed my head. They were paying me a small fortune to do the part and I couldn't deliver the goods. He was right to be angry. Inside, my guts were knotted. I tried to hold back the panic.

"What the hell was the matter with me, Doctor?"

"Go on with what happened."

"The female star of the picture — a sex goddess — came over to me and held my arm.

" 'Easy, Tonito, easy. Can I do anything to help you?'

93

"I looked into those well-known bedroom eyes and the coiffured blond hair. I knew that she too had known panic, indecision and loneliness. I knew that she would have understood. But I couldn't bring myself to confess my pain.

"Even 'the kid' was concerned. He stood on the sidelines waiting.

"The director called us all back to try the scene once more. I blew it six times in a row. It was getting late. I knew that if the company went on overtime, the cost would be enormous. I called the producer, who came running. He tried desperately to smile and make a joke of the whole incident, but his usually cherubic face had a slight twitch.

"'Look,' I begged, 'I don't care if I have to stay here all night, I'll pay all expenses, but I *have* to do this scene. Please ask the crew if they're willing to go on overtime.'

"'Tony, Jeez, we'll rewrite the scene. It's not *Hamlet.* You're just tired. Go home and get a good night's rest. We'll take a new crack at it tomorrow.'

"'No. If I don't get this scene, I'm through. I beg you. . . .'

"'Okay.'

"The crew agreed to go on. Somehow the pressure was off and I got the scene on the next take.

"Normally, I would have been pleased when the crew broke out in applause, but I felt humiliated. I felt like the guy who comes in last at a marathon and the crowd breaks out in derisive cheers.

"I know actors have been known to fluff scenes. The stories are legion of Barrymore, Gable, Tracy, and others blowing twenty or thirty takes. But, goddamnit, not me. They could laugh at their fallibility. I'm too insecure to laugh at myself.

"What the hell is all this analysis doing to me, Doctor? I seem more mixed up than ever."

"What was the line you kept stumbling over?" he asked.

"A stupid line."

I tried to say it but again I found my tongue could not form the words. He waited patiently. Finally, I stammered it out: 'I'm sorry I'm late. I was held up by some unforeseen complications.'

"'Unforeseen complications'?"

"That's right."

"Now, Tony, the way you work you often find strong identification with the character, don't you?"

"Christ, you wouldn't have thought so today."

"Having these sessions with you, I understand something about the way an actor works. I mean the way your conscious and subconscious are in constant oscillation. We've often talked of how sometimes a character takes over and then you yourself become involved emotionally."

"Goddamnit, Doctor, I'm not here to discuss the Stanislavski method. Today I couldn't do my job. It's the only fucking thing I've been able to count on lately. If I fail at that I might as well put a bullet through my head."

"But the fact that you had difficulty with a line of dialogue is not the end of the world, Tony."

"It's the end of the only world I know."

"But don't you see why? You couldn't say those words because you have come up against a wall of 'unforeseen complications' yourself. You see, to be an actor you have to be in full control of your emotions. Today the subconscious was stronger. Turbulence inside does not respect contracts or obligations to anybody. I don't give a damn about your career, Tony. I am trying to help the man, not the actor. I know how important acting is to you, but you are functioning on five cylinders. I want you to function on all eight, maybe ten. I'm happy about today. We've made a big breakthrough."

"I wish I could believe that."

"We have. Recognizing the problem is one step in solving it. Now let's go back. The last time we met you were telling me about your father. You repeat constantly how much you love him. Do you really? In all our lives we have to make choices. We can't follow God and Mammon. We can't have two masters. Whose voice do we listen to, our father's or our mother's? Have you talked yourself into this great love for your father because in loving him you wouldn't have to compete with him? Or is he really unworthy of your love, and you're afraid to admit it to yourself because then you would have to supplant him with another figure — yourself — and you don't know if *you're* worthy?"

Then I thought about that time with the grapes.

"Extra, extra, mister — read all about it."

The passengers were getting off the streetcar. My father was not among them.

I looked over at the clock above the lumberyard. It was a few minutes to six o'clock. He would surely be on the next one, due in about ten minutes.

I went back to pitching pennies with the other newsboys. For some reason I can't remember, I got into a fight with one of them. We scuffled on the ground and tore into each other. After a while I heard the streetcar clanging. The fight broke up about then. I ran back to my pile of papers.

Every afternoon I looked forward to the ritual of selling a news paper to my father. I loved the easy way he jumped down from the streetcar. I admired the hugeness of him. He towered over everyone. He'd walk over to me, look at the headlines. He'd put his hand in his pocket and pull out a five-cent piece. The paper was only three cents, but he'd say, "Keep the change, boy." He'd smile that secret smile I loved. I would watch him as he walked away in that princely way of his.

Later, when I'd sell all my papers, I'd rush across the street to the bakery and buy some dessert for the family, but really it was only for my father. He never let me down. He'd take a spoonful of the cake or pie and roll his eyes toward heaven. He'd pretend he was in ecstasy.

"Nellie," he'd say to my mother, "this is the *greatest* pie I've *ever* tasted in my life."

He'd offer me a piece. I'd refuse, saying I wasn't hungry. Watching him eat *my gift* was greater than any sweet in the world. But on that particular day, I saw him get off the streetcar. I waited for him to approach me as he'd always done. I held the paper out for him to read the headlines.

"Paper, mister."

He looked over my head as if he was searching for someone. Then he walked away without once looking at me. He stood on the corner for a second, then disappeared down the street. Hadn't he seen me? Was he sick?

I couldn't wait to finish selling my last batch of newspapers to get home and find out. I called Carlos Ramirez and asked him to ake over my corner. I ran to the grocery store to buy the dessert. A beautiful bunch of grapes caught my eye. They were the first of the season — twenty-seven cents a pound. I blew my whole day's earnings and bought two pounds.

When I got home my father was already seated at the table. My mother and grandmother hovered over him, setting plates of meat, beans and tortillas in front of him. My sister was sitting beside him. When I entered, he barely glanced at me.

I went over to the kitchen sink, washed the grapes, and put them on a plate. I set them in the center of the table. He ignored the whole action and began making a fuss over my sister, whom he called Princess. My grandmother and my mother were aware that something was wrong between my father and me. My grandmother took me aside.

"Go wash up and then change your clothes," she said.

I went to wash and comb my hair. She handed me a clean shirt. When I went to the table, my father looked up. He smiled.

"Hey, Elephant, where have you been? I looked all over for you when I got off the streetcar. I didn't see you."

"But, Papa, you walked right by me. I went up to you and you acted like you didn't know me."

"I didn't see you. I saw some dirty little Mexican kid who asked me if I wanted a paper. He looked a little like you, but he wasn't my son. My son might be poor but he is never dirty. No matter what he does he stands proud and always looks like a prince."

He looked at the grapes as if for the first time.

"What's this? Grapes!"

He took one and savored it.

"These are the finest grapes I've ever tasted, Nellie."

Now, as I told the doctor about it, I wept. I couldn't hold back the choked feeling I'd felt long ago.

How I'd hated my father when he called me a dirty little Mexican. How I hated him when he said that that boy was not his son.

"Papa, you stupid sonofabitch, does your loving me depend on the way I look, on how I behave? Don't you love me for me, for myself? My mother makes no demands on me. She doesn't care if I am filthy dirty. She doesn't mind if I stink of shit. But you will only accept me if I behave like a prince. I am no prince. I am me

97

with all the fears, the shame, the cowardice, the frailties and stenches of a growing kid. Can't you love me as I am? Must I always bring my offerings to you, the great Jehovah? What lamb must I sacrifice at your altar? I am from your loins. You made me in your own image. Who in the fuck are you to expect more from me than you yourself can deliver?"

I was weeping. I was back there as a child waiting to beat the shit out of my father for hurting me, for having denied me.

I would surpass the sonofabitch one day. Who in the fuck was he, giving himself airs, when he was just a lousy wetback like the rest of us? I had seen him sweat in the sun driving rail spikes. I had seen him work as a common, ordinary fruit-picker. Who the hell was he? What the hell was his own mother but a Mexican? Did his two spoonfuls of Irish blood make him so superior to the rest of us?

"I got news for you, Papa. You're no better than the rest of us."

The doctor watched me in silence as I tried to destroy my father. He let me cry myself out.

"Strange, Tony, most of the stories about your father are painful stories and yet I feel that you loved him a great deal."

"Yes, you're right. I guess they do make him sound peculiar. In retrospect, I feel maybe he knew he would die soon and he was in a hurry to get it all in before he left. I think he was in a hurry for me to become a man. I felt he just stayed with my mother because of me. There was some mystery about his stay in Pennsylvania. Mother always claimed he had found another woman there. I don't know, but when he came back to El Paso, Mother feels it was because of me. Yes, his lessons were harsh, but I understood somehow. I knew they were done with love. I felt he didn't belong in that atmosphere. I felt he was atrophying, being with us. I sincerely felt aware of the sacrifice he'd made because of me. For instance, just after we'd come back from the fields up north in San Jose and Santa Paula, where we'd followed the different crops – walnuts, apricots, peaches, tomatoes, lettuce, stringbeans — even though I was four or five years old, I felt sorry for my father picking fruit like the rest of us."

"You felt he was too good to do ordinary labor?"

"Doc, picking fruit is not ordinary labor. Not only is it back breaking work but it's considered less than menial. It's humiliat ing. White men have always used minorities — Filipinos, Chinese, Negroes and Mexicans — to do it for them. The pay is poor and the living conditions subnormal. To spend all day on your knees is demeaning, and damnit, I hated to see my father do it."

"You felt it was all right for your mother and grandmother, but not right for your father?"

"Don't try to catch me, Doc. Nobody should have to earn a living on his knees."

I told him another story.

When we were living on Daly Street, one of the family rituals was that my father would take me out on Saturday nights. We would go down to Main Street, by the Plaza, and he would wander around looking for friends whom he had known in Mexico during the revolution.

The Plaza was surrounded by little green stands where they used to have small stoves, and inside each stand a woman or man would stand cooking "carne asada." For ten cents you could get a huge plate of meat with fried beans and rice. My father and I would go over and sit on the benches and get a shoeshine. I used to watch the boy who was shining our shoes to make sure he was doing it right, because I was a very good shoeshine boy myself. Sometimes I would give the boy some advice on how to do it.

One Saturday we were walking around the park and he stopped and talked to a couple of fellows. Then he said, "All right, Elephant, now we will go and eat."

On the way over to the stand he reached for the money in his pocket. As he pulled his hand out, a coin dropped and clinked down the sidewalk into a gutter. I ran to get it. My father took me by the arm.

"Don't bend."

"But Papa, the fifty cents — you've got to pick it up."

"Come on."

I was starving. I could smell the frying steaks and the beans and rice. My father started walking away as if he had just had a great meal. I followed him, looking back to see if anyone was picking up the 50 cents. A couple of men were watching my father as if he were crazy, and I knew that the minute we turned the corner they would pick up the money.

99

"But Papa, why?"

"Son, no money is worth bending for."

The doctor sat up straighter in his chair, but I launched swiftly into another story.

One time when my sister Stella was six years old and I was nine, I saw a man taking her into a small tunnel near our house where the creek passed by under the street. As I crept up to see what was happening, I saw him playing with my sister; he was touching her between her legs.

I ran into the house and got an ax. I sneaked behind the man and hit him on the head with the flat side of the ax, and kept on hitting him and hitting him.

My sister started screaming when she saw the blood. Some people came and stopped me and took the man off to the hospital. He was half dead.

That night, when my father came home, my mother told him what had happened. The police had been there, and my mother and I had explained to them that the man had been molesting my sister and nobody bothered me. My father came up to me and said, "Let's you and me go outside." He put his arms around me and said, "I'm very proud of you; you were very courageous. It was wonderful that you saved your sister, but I'm going to whip you." He took off his belt. "The first time you hit the man was for what he was doing to your sister. That was right. The second time you hit him was in anger, and that might have been all right, too, but the third and the fourth time was because you're a potential murderer, and I'm going to whip you so that you'll never lose your temper to where you can kill someone."

I took my whipping like a man.

"You know, Tony, your father was a patriarch. But as you've taught me yourself, the Mexican is in constant struggle between a matriarchal and a patriarchal society. Even in his religion he is much closer to the Virgin Mary than to Christ. Here in America we all tend to romanticize our mothers. I mean, a boy can say he hates his 'old man' and be forgiven — but God help him if he calls

*100*

his mother a cunt. And let's face it, I'm sure many men have mothers who deserve being called that.

"Historically the world's societies have had this struggle. The Jewish religion — the Old Testament is devoted to a patriarchal concept. But momism has been making inroads for centuries.

"A matriarchal society is romantic and sentimental. It makes little demands on us. As with our mothers, we have unconditional love by just being. We have to do very little to deserve mother love.

"The patriarch demands more from us. We have to deserve God's love. The God of the Old Testament is a demanding one. He wants obedience — He demands perfection on all levels.

" 'Gird up thy loins like a man, for I will demand of thee and answer thou me.'

"Then God goes on to list all that he can do. He asks Job if he himself is prepared to challenge God.

" 'Hast thou given the horse strength? Hast thou clothed his neck with thunder?' "

The doctor put down the Bible from which he'd been quoting.

"He's a pretty tough guy, this God. He says, 'Okay, son, if you want to challenge me you're going to have a hell of a fight on your hands. But, boy, you'd better gird up your loins like a man.'

"Well, I think the moment has come. The 'unforeseen complication' is that you're looking for the unconditional love of the mother. Of course, she loves you even if you are full of shit. But your father doesn't accept that. He says, 'Boy, if you want my love, you're going to have to deserve it. You're going to have to fight for it. Gird up your loins like a man.' "

I knew what the doctor was talking about. When I'd started working with the "Holy Rollers" I'd read Job. That God of vengeance had scared the hell out of me. He made you feel so insignificant. Sure He could shake mountains and shut up the sea with doors, when it breaks forth. He could bind the sweet influence of the Pleiades, and loose the bands of Orion. But He was God. He had a hell of a head start. And who was *His* father? Whom did *He* have to beat?

"As you know, Tony, it isn't my practice to prescribe, but tonight, if you'll forgive me, I'm not your doctor. I'm your friend and I'm treading on dangerous ground. You have made your father your God. He demands perfection from you. Now what do we do? Do we take him on?"

# 7

THE TENTH OF JANUARY, 1926, was a lovely crisp Sunday morning. I'd already been to church. I had started going by myself when I was six years old. I can't remember ever having gone with either my mother or my grandmother. Certainly I never went with my father. I never heard of his going to church.

Sometime around the age of six I discovered that I could make a small fortune on Sunday mornings shining shoes in front of the Catholic church. Men liked to walk with nice shiny shoes. I could usually count on picking up forty or fifty cents. My enthusiasm occasionally extended itself to shining a man's socks. I remember once a man looking down and seeing that I had stained his white socks.

"Thanks, boy. Here's a quarter — I'll pay you to stop."

From then on I used to put a piece of cardboard between the shoes and the socks. But one day, after I had run out of customers, I stood in the doorway of the church and watched Mass. I loved the candlelight, the smell of incense, and the ritual of the priest. How I envied the altar boy in his long red robe with the long white lace surplice. I felt he had an inside track to God.

A young priest standing by the door invited me in. I parked my shoeshine box by the door and he led me inside. He seemed like the kindest, most understanding man I'd ever met.

People that I knew in the neighborhood knelt all around me. They had changed from their everyday selves to something different. They behaved like little children full of hope and wonder. As they crossed themselves I saw their yearning to be good. I wanted to be part of that world of hope, faith and love.

After Mass I asked the young priest if I could come back the

ollowing Sunday. He said of course. For years we were close
riends — later I was to hurt him, but that is another story.

Now it was four years later and I had just come back from
church. My father was out in the yard with two of his friends. One
was José Arias, a big hawk-nosed man who had fought beside my
father in the revolution. The other was a man named Bob Wilson,
who worked with my father at Selig's.

My father was showing them the rose garden my grandmother
had planted.

As I walked up, he introduced me to his friends. He seemed
proud of me. He bragged about how I already knew how to drive
a car and how he could die easy because I was already a good
provider.

The two men laughed, but the mention of death disturbed me.

We all had lunch out in the yard under an arbor covered with
a grapevine. The men drank some wine and "aguadiente," burning water made from pure alcohol. While the women did the
dishes and brought out the homemade ice cream, my father and
José entertained Bob with stories of the revolution. To them it
had been a time of action, adventure and hope. At first, they had
dreamed of destroying poverty and ignorance and substituting a
Utopian state. Then they had seen their friends, brothers, uncles
and fathers die for nothing. Nothing had really changed. Hunger
and ignorance still reigned, although politicians glorified the revolution and exploited it, keeping alive the hopes of peoples who
were still waiting for the fruit of all their spilled blood. Yes,
thought the people, they would get their land one day. Their
children would never again know hunger in their bellies. They
would learn to read and write and become lawyers and doctors.
Peonage would disappear from the face of that beautiful sun-
baked land. The longed-for Utopia was near at hand — mañana,
mañana, mañana.

Bob asked if it was true that Mexican men considered their life
cheap and therefore were always willing to lay it on the line in
front of a bull or a gun. He'd heard about how Pancho Villa
would often play Russian roulette with his lieutenants to prove
they had "cojones." Was it true about the Mexican's great pre-
occupation with "machismo"?

My father didn't answer. Instead he picked up the guitar. José

and he started to sing some of the songs of the revolution. I loved
to hear the men sing. It reminded me of the happiest moments of
my life when after work in the fields the men would gather and
sing around the campfire.

> *Borrachita, me voy*
> *Y para olvidarte.*
> *Te quiero mucho*
> *tú también me quieres.*
>
> *Borrachita, me voy*
> *Hasta la Capital*
> *Pa' servir al patrón*
> *Que me manda llamar*
>    *anteayer.*
>
> *My dear little drunk, I'm leaving*
> *To forget you.*
> *I love you very much*
> *And you love me.*
>
> *My dear little drunk, I'm going*
> *To the Capital*
> *To serve the boss*
> *Who sent for me*
>    *day before yesterday.*

My father suddenly put down the guitar and said to Bob, "Are
you afraid of death?"

Bob thought a second and said, "You're damn right I am."

"Would you be afraid to know when you're going to die?"

"Yeah, I don't want to think about it."

"I think about it all the time," my father laughed. "And it
doesn't scare me. My kids don't really need me. Maybe they'd fight
harder if I wasn't around."

"Aw, come on," said Bob, "let's have some more songs."

My father turned to me and asked me to go into the house and
bring him the big pair of scissors in my grandmother's sewing
basket. When I came back he cleared a place in the middle of the
table and put down the scissors.

"Bob, I'm going to spin these scissors. Whoever the sharp end points to is going to die first."

José laughed. "Good, let's see who will be the first in hell."

Bob said, "Oh, Frank, it's a stupid game. You don't believe that shit, do you?"

"Yeah, I'm willing to take the scissors' word. It's as good as anybody else's."

Bob agreed reluctantly. I asked my father if I could play.

"No, Elephant. I want you to live a long time. I've made my deal with the Devil — he can take me if he'll leave you alone."

He spun the scissors. They pointed at him.

José laughed. "That's what you get for tempting the Devil."

Bob looked relieved.

My father smiled that secret smile of his.

"Come on," laughed José, "let's see who is going second."

My father spun the scissors again. Again they pointed at him. Nobody laughed. My father picked up the guitar and began to sing.

> *Yo ya me voy*
> *Al puerto donde se halla*
> *La Barca de Oro.*
> *Sólo vengo a despedirme.*
> *Adios, mujer,*
> *Adios*
> *Para siempre — adios.*
>
> *I am now leaving*
> *For the port where I will find*
> *The Golden Barge*
> *I've just come to say good-bye.*
> *Good-bye, woman,*
> *Good-bye*
> *Forever — good-bye.*

There was nothing tearful or sentimental in his voice. It was just a quiet statement. My mother and grandmother, who had entered during the last spin of the scissors, were furious. My grandmother scolded her son.

"I don't like these stupid games."

She grabbed the scissors and ran into the house. She was crying.

The men continued to sit under the arbor, exchanging stories while my father strummed his guitar. Some boys came by and invited me to go to the Unique Theatre to see *The Green Hornet*, but there was something about my father that forbade me to leave him alone that afternoon.

The sun was going down and the evening was turning chilly when Bob and José Arias decided it was time to call it a day. They got into the old Ford coupe that my father had sold José a few weeks before for fifty-five dollars. José kept teasing my father that he'd been robbed. My father cranked the car up for them while José pulled down the spark. Finally the car spluttered and they drove away.

Father and I walked into the house, where Mama and Grandmother were already cooking dinner over a kerosene stove. In the center of the table Mother had already lit the kerosene lamp. Soon we heard José's voice calling from across the street.

"Frank — hey, Frank."

Father and I went out to the stoop and could see José beside the stalled car. There was a steep incline as you turned in from our street into Brooklyn Avenue. The car had refused to make the hill. José had just learned to drive a few weeks before and didn't know how to coax the car.

My father turned to me.

"All right, son — you go in the house. I'm going to give them a hand."

Did I imagine his smile? Is it because it comforts me to think he was letting me in on the secret? Is it because he knew what was coming and was trying to tell me that it was okay?

The next thing I heard was the loud crash. Then José's voice calling my mother and grandmother, and I knew.

I ran into my father's bedroom and jumped onto his bed. I huddled against the corner and stared at his coat hanging on the wall. Under the creases of the coat I could feel the muscles of his strong arms. I knew that those arms would never hold me again.

A few seconds later I heard my mother's agonized scream, "Francisco! Francisco!"

My sister ran into the room and stared at me. I resented her

ntrusion. I wanted to be alone with my father. I felt him in the
oom. I felt he wanted to say good-bye to me alone.

Soon the house was full of people consoling my mother and
grandmother.

I could hear people asking how I was "taking it." I didn't leave
he room.

Next day I took a shovel and covered my father's blood which
till stained the pavement where another car had crushed him
while he was pushing José's car up the hill.

A few days later at the funeral I refused to look at the man they
had in the box. I knew it was not my father. My father was off
omewhere on a Golden Barge.

# 8

"YOU KNOW WHAT that sonofabitch kid accuses me of? That I was
ecretly glad when my father died."

The doctor nodded and scratched away on his pad. "You keep
alking about this kid, Tony, and I don't really see him. Can you
describe him for me?"

"He's eleven years old. Big for his age, maybe five foot six or
even. He's a dark, lonely kid with a twisted smile."

"Your father's smile that you keep talking about?"

"I guess so, only he never quite makes it. It's just a smirk."

"You don't like the kid?"

"I hate his 'holier than thou' attitude. I mean, all that church
usiness, first as a Catholic wanting to be a priest, and then with
he 'Holy Rollers.' It was an escape. He was afraid of life and
wanted to retreat into some kind of sainthood so that no one
would challenge him. He was terrified of losing, so he avoided
ighting. He never put himself out on a limb. He felt if he got
lose to God maybe he could hide under His robe."

"In other words, if you could go back you'd change him?"

"I owe the boy a lot. But goddamnit, I've paid him back ten-fold. Yes, there are a lot of things I'd change about him."

"What?"

"Like the fighting, like all that crap he took from the other kids and turning the other cheek. I think he took Jesus' advice too literally."

"But the boy believed it at the time, didn't he?"

"He believed it for the wrong reasons."

"You think he was yellow?"

I couldn't help but feel hurt at the doctor's blurting it out like that. How I hated all those words as a kid — "chicken," "lily," "sissy," "yellow," "mama's boy," "chicken-shit," "teacher's pet," "spic." I came to the kid's defense.

"He took on Walter Mears, who towered almost a foot over him, that time in the school playground. He'd also beat Valentín that night under the walnut trees. Then there was the time he took on that football player in high school and only stopped because the other kids were screaming for him to kick the shit out of the dirty kike."

"Was there someone back there that you would have liked to have been like?"

"I would have liked to have been as good with my hands as Carlos Ramirez. He was a small, chunky, five-foot-four kid that took on all comers and kicked the shit out of them."

"That's your childhood hero?"

"No. There was Mario Nardini, who couldn't fight his way out of a paper bag, whom I really admired more. He was a handsome Italian kid — always neat and well combed — who could paint like a young Michelangelo. But I guess I would have liked to have been a combination of both."

"In other words, the boy wasn't a total loss. He did win a few fights and he did show some kind of guts, but there is something about him that bothers you."

"I've already told you about that religious stuff."

"But besides that. . . ."

"Besides that I want him to leave me alone. He keeps wanting things from me."

"Like what?"

"Like wanting me to go back to religion, being some kind of saint. He wants me to — oh, Christ — the sonofabitch wants to be Napoleon, Michelangelo, Shakespeare, Picasso, Martin Luther and Jack Dempsey all rolled up into one. He wants me to read every book that was ever printed and be able to sing every song ever sung. He wants the whole fucking world in a neat package. Nothing I ever do satisfies him. He wants perfect love — from me, from my friends, my enemies and my women. He won't let me make concessions. He wants the sky. I want him to let me be, just let me be!"

The doctor rocked back and forth in his chair. I could feel the wheels turning.

"You know, Tony, we might have to kill the kid."

I looked up. He was serious as hell.

"What do you mean, kill the kid?"

*"You may have to kill the boy!* If he is merely another ghost who keeps you from self-realization, you may have to destroy him. You have a responsibility to a much higher being than the ghost of an eleven-year-old boy. But does he deserve to die? Just one word of warning. Hear him out before you pass judgment."

"That scares me, Doc," I said.

"Okay, let's not rush it. Tell me about the boy after your father died."

"I didn't go to my father's funeral, but I heard my mother and grandmother say there was no money for a headstone. His grave was unmarked except for a cheap brass plate. I went and asked the teacher who ran the workshop if I could make a headstone for my father's grave. He let me make a cross with a big heart-shaped wooden plaque. Then he helped me with the lettering:

FRANK QUINN

Born – 1897
Died – 1926

*In Love*
*His son, Tony*

"I went out to the cemetery one Saturday and planted it in the grass in place of the brass plate."

"Have you ever gone back to visit his grave?"

"No. I don't like to think of him down there."

"You never accepted the fact that he had died, did you?"

"No. I hate to talk about it."

"Have you ever had anyone else close to you die?"

"Christ! Please, please, Doctor — don't, don't ask me to remem
ber. *He* isn't dead. He'll *never* die — that was worse than m
father dying. Don't take *him* away from me. I loved him mor
than my father, more than myself, more than Christ or anybody
Don't ask me to even acknowledge he's not here. Please, Docto
leave him alone."

The doctor respected my silence and tried another tack.

"Well, what was life like after your father's death? How did yo
and the family manage to live?"

"My mother started on the night shift at the Goodyear Rubbe
plant. She used to go to work at three o'clock in the afternoon an
come home about three in the morning. I used to set the alarm fo
two-thirty in the morning and go and meet her."

"Weren't you afraid?"

"Sometimes. Anyway, I carried a pocketknife, just in case."

"You never had to use it?"

"Once. I arrived late and I saw my mother leaning against th
wall of an office building on the corner. He had his hand on he
shoulder. I took out my knife and rushed at him. My mothe
screamed as she saw me about to stab him. She quickly explaine
that he had only been keeping her company until I arrived.
didn't believe her. I yelled at the frightened man: 'If you don
get away from my mother, you sonofabitch, I'll cut your balls off
My mother started crying and the man ran off without saying
word. On the way home my mother pleaded with me to forget th
whole incident.

" 'You whore, my father is dead six months and you're fuckin
around with other men,' I shouted. 'If I see you talking to an
man I'll kill you, I'll kill both of you.'

"My father would have done the same, and *I* was now the ma
of the house."

"Did you ever forgive your mother?"

"No, never. That's where it gets mixed up, Doc. The kid in m won't let me forgive her. He's never let me forgive her. It was shortly after that that he shifted all his affection to my grandmother. Grandmother had only known one man in her life. She was the only woman who lived by the concept of 'One man and a wall three feet wide for the rest of the world.'

"You know, Doctor, the first time I came into your office you asked me if I believed in love. I felt the subject was too complex to answer at the first session. I merely answered yes.

"Knowing the workings of the mind, you can imagine all the images and questions that raced through my brain, all the pros and cons. After all our 'investigations' you no doubt have become aware of the areas where I fail in the arenas of love. To give love and to accept love unconditionally — that to me is the highest goal. To be unable to love unconditionally — that to me is the original sin, the one that engenders all the others. However, I answered yes because if I give up the hope of finding love I would find life intolerable. Everything I stand for, everything I preach, would be a lie.

"My first love was obviously my mother, but when my father came back to stay in El Paso I became number two. I became a number. Later I dreaded knowing what my number was with the various women I fell in love with.

" 'Sylvia, what number am I?'

" 'Susan, swear to God I'm number one.'

" 'Joannie, thank you for making me number one.'

" 'Lorie, you bitch, why didn't you tell me? What the hell did you lie to me for? You know how I feel. Christ! I feel lost. Where the hell do I run to? What the hell do I do now? How do I go back to loneliness?'

"That night when my father returned, I was full of confusion. He was a giant. A giant who could destroy me. He had taken my place. Once again I found myself on the floor. Even though I had an infant sister to keep me company, I couldn't help but feel that we were both out in the cold.

"Then came my grandmother. She had lost a son, I had lost a mother. We were both rejects, in a sense. Suddenly we found ourselves together. Finally, I had someone all to myself. We would go to movies, for walks — everything together. Oh, I knew she had once rejected me, but I was getting even. I was rubbing her rejection back in her face. I would make her fall so much in love with me that I would become her number one — then we'd see.

"I don't have to tell you how children are the greatest wooers when they want to be. I used every trick — and had her eating out of the palm of my hand.

"I remember once, when I was six or seven years old, I neglected a duty my father had assigned me. He was raising rabbits and I forgot to feed them for two days. I had gone off to play under the bridge instead. The mother rabbit died.

"When Father found out it was through my neglect, he gave me a whipping and locked me up in the cellar. I was afraid of the darkness. I screamed in terror. He forbade anyone in the family to pay attention to me. I could hear them upstairs having dinner. The cellar was full of ghosts and wild beasts who wanted to eat me alive. I clung to a small air hole where I could see the stars. I sobbed my heart out.

"When everyone had gone to bed I heard footsteps in the garden. I was sure it was some monster coming to chew me to pieces. Instead, it was my grandmother bringing me food. My father had taken the key to the cellar and so she sat there in the garden and talked softly to me until I fell asleep on the floor.

"She sat there until dawn, then she went into the house lest my father should find out. But I had won a major victory. I could make her take my side against my father."

"In other words, you had replaced your father — something you'd never been able to do with your mother. I mean, not after your father had come back to stay."

"I've read Freud. I know all about that shit. No, I never had a mother complex. I never found my mother sexually attractive."

"And your grandmother?"

"I thought she was one of the most beautiful women in the world. I'm paying you too much to be dishonest. I *never* had a twinge of sexuality about her. About my sister, yes, but about my mother and grandmother, definitely no."

"You're pretty definite."

"I used to get into bed with my grandmother when I was frightened or couldn't sleep. I felt protection and warmth from her. I felt love. When I became sexually awakened — and not through her — I stopped sleeping with her because I was terrified I might

ave a sex dream and she'd become aware of it. I knew she'd scold
the hell out of me. As a matter of fact, once she found my under-
pants stained from a childish orgasm I'd had on the streetcar and
she made a big scene about it. I told her she was crazy, that the
stain had come from some cream I'd had to put on because my
skin was chafed."

It was the first laugh the doctor and I had had in days. Then I
told him about the time she'd dug up the street.

Grandmother had been watching the men digging out on the
street for five days. At first there had been an army of engineers
surveying with their transits and levels. The neighborhood had
been excited by the rumor that we would finally get a sewer pipe,
which would spell the end of the backyard two-holers.

The men had marked the street with red and yellow chalk
marks, put pegs down, and then had disappeared. After two or
three months the only memory of their having been there was that
Widow Alonzo's daughter was left pregnant by the head engineer.

Then one day three trucks arrived, unloaded men and equipment, and the digging began. Grandmother kept close check on
their progress. They dug about a cubic foot and a half per man
in one week. According to my grandmother, she dug more than
that an hour in the vegetable garden surrounding our privy.

Every night as she prepared our frijoles and mustard greens,
she cursed the injustice that we should be starving while those
men out in the street were getting the enormous wage of three
dollars a day, enough money to feed our family for a month.

One morning she couldn't stand it any longer and went out and
accosted the fat foreman.

"I want a job!"

"Doing what, lady?"

"Digging like these men."

"Are you kidding, lady? That's man's work."

"Look, mister, I can lean on a shovel as good as they can. I've
been watching them all week. A dog can dig faster."

"Look, you got any complaints, go to City Hall."

"I just want a job. I've got two hungry kids to feed."

"Go and do some sewing or washing."

Feeling challenged, my grandmother pulled a pick from th[e] hands of a stunned workman and began to tear up the street.

The foreman tried to wrest the pick out of her hand, but sh[e] threatened him with it.

"I'm going to dig here all day. If you don't think I've earne[d] my money at the end of the day you won't have to pay me."

The foreman shrugged and walked away. All the men, who ha[d] gathered around to watch the spectacle, laughed uproariously [at] her. An hour later, when she was still furiously swinging the pic[k] the men started to gather off to one side and mutter about goi[ng] on strike. Meanwhile, various spectators had gathered on the sid[e] cheering.

The men finally went back to their work, at the insistence of th[e] foreman, who seemed to hope the old lady would disappear an[d] that it was all just a bad dream — a nightmare. After a while, th[e] superintendent showed up and was amazed at the sight th[at] greeted him. The foreman rushed up to him and explained. Th[e] superintendent looked at the other workers and said, "From wh[at] I can see, this is the first time these bums have done any wor[k] Maybe she's right. Maybe we should let her work."

He walked over to Grandmother and said, "Lady, stop a mi[n]ute. I want to talk to you."

She went on digging.

"Lady, listen to me. You can't work like a common laborer."

"Why not?"

"I don't know," he said, "but it don't look right. Besides," [he] smiled, "you're making them all look bad. You're right, they a[re] bums, but this would start a revolution, lady. My business is [to] get this street done. I don't want to be involved in any cra[zy] revolution by women picking and shoveling like ordinary labo[r]ers."

The old lady stopped for a second and considered.

"All you want is this street done, right? I promise you, with m[e] among them, you will get it done in half the time."

"I don't doubt it, lady, but there'd be an awful lot of explai[n]ing to do. I beg you to leave the men alone. Look, tell you wh[at] I'll do. I understand you've worked three hours already. I'll p[ay] you for the whole day. We'll be around for some time and you ca[n] bring the men water. I'll pay you for a full day's work."

For the rest of the month, the men had the best water carrier f their lives. My grandmother took her job very seriously. In the 1orning she would make ice-cold lemonade for the men working ut on the street. Sometimes she would vary it and put in strawerry. No group of pick-and-shovel workers ever drank such nectar s she made. I think they were a little sad when they finished the ob and had to move to another neighborhood. But that month 1y grandmother made a grand total of sixty dollars, which kept s in three square meals a day for a long time.

The doctor smiled. "How long would sixty dollars last you now, ony?"

"An hour with you, you thief," I kidded him.

"I'm just a drop in the bucket. I hear you spend money like it's oing out of fashion."

"I suppose I do, but as someone once said, once you've known overty you can never feel rich. I have no respect for money, eally. The worst thing about poverty is the embarrassment. Not 1e need, because one can go without food for days. It's the inignity of poverty that one can't escape. There's a bad smell to overty, a stink. I remember my first day at junior high school. Ve were supposed to go to gym and the teacher said that I had o take off my trousers and put on gym clothes. I didn't have any ym clothes, and besides I was embarrassed because I was wearing ome patched-up shorts. The shorts. The shorts had the mark of flour bag and I was embarrassed that the other kids would see it. he gym teacher reported to the principal that I had refused to ike my clothes off. The man gave me a whipping without even sking why."

"But certainly you were one of many at that school who knew overty, Tony. You've explained how the East Side of Los Aneles is a ghetto. You certainly were not alone."

"Christ, Doctor, you sound like a Pollyanna. Just because everyody is up to his ass in shit does not mean one has to accept it. hated poverty. How the hell can you feel like a man if you go round apologizing for yourself? If you are made to feel dirty and nwanted because you are poor, you even begin to think that God ates you when you are poor."

"But if you hadn't known that poverty you might not have bee driven by ambition."

"I don't remember having any particular ambitions, except t escape that cesspool. My one great fear was anonymity. Once on very hot day, I was looking for a job, walking down First Stree Today I can still recall the steamy asphalt, the smell of grease, an suddenly feeling that I was nobody. If I died nobody would kno that I had lived. Strange thoughts occurred to me. I would d anything, but I would not die unknown. I could not die withou the world hearing from me or knowing I had lived. I think would have murdered, but I could not have faced —"

Suddenly I couldn't go on. "The boy" was standing by the doo

The doctor saw the look of fear on my face. "What's the matte Tony?"

"He's standing at the door."

"Who's standing at the door?"

"The boy."

"Good," the doctor said, "I've been anxious to meet him."

For a moment I thought he was merely humoring me. Did h think I was mad or could he, too, see the boy there with a smir on his face?

"What do you want, young man?" asked the doctor.

"He won't talk to you, Doctor."

"Then you talk to him. I want to hear it all."

I hesitated. Then I thought, what the hell.

"Okay, Doc," I said. "Here's the way the boy talks to the ol man. I'll even include a few stage directions."

MAN. Okay, kid. Spit it out. What the hell do you want?
BOY. I want it different.
MAN. Like what?
BOY. I want the truth.

I got up from the couch and yelled:

MAN. What fucking truth? It's tough just staying on your feet.
BOY (scoffing). You're doing a fine job, aren't you? That's wh you're here looking for crutches.
MAN (pleading). Can't I ever do anything right?

OY. Rarely, but I have to admit a couple of times I was proud of you.

AN. When?

OY. Not the times you think. Not for the awards or the applause, or the limousines and big houses and famous paintings — and all that shit.

AN. When then?

"Say, Doc, are you sure you want me to go on? It's not too crazy?"

"Sanity," the doctor said, "is being able to relate the fantasy world to the world around you. Sanity is bringing the two into focus."

I continued.

OY. You're paying this guy fifty dollars an hour for that sort of advice? What is he saying? Accept things as they are? Don't fight City Hall? Niggers and Mexicans and kikes should stay in their place. Poverty and war are necessities of nature. Fuck the quack, it's too easy. Change the world, old man. Don't ask me to change myself.

AN. Who are you to change the world? You couldn't even read until you were nine. I remember that time when you memorized the sign in the streetcar: "Expectorating on floor of vehicle strictly forbidden by law." What a great quote to live with.

OY (surprised). You remember it?

AN. Word for word. Imagine if we had stopped there? Imagine if I hadn't gone beyond and read Rolland, Thoreau, Wolfe, Schopenhauer, Nietzsche, Plato —

OY (interrupting). Spare me the long list. I know them all. What original thought have *you* come up with?

AN. I try. I'm looking.

OY. Horseshit. You used them all to help you collect things.

AN. You'd like me to be living in that hut we called home? You'd still be squatting in that two-holer you hated.

OY (starting for the door). I didn't shine all those shoes, pick all that fruit, choke on all that dust so that you could wear hand-made Italian shoes.

117

MAN. Where the hell are you going? Let's have it out right her
and now.

BOY. You listen to him (*pointing to the doctor*) — he's got all th
answers.

MAN. At least he doesn't have a pitchfork up my ass every fiv
minutes.

BOY. He's a fifty-dollar-an-hour yes-man. You two have a nice mu
tual admiration society going on. I wouldn't want to break i
up.

The doctor was saying, "To put it in movie terms, reality an
fantasy are like the negative and the positive."

"Who is the positive and who is the negative, Doctor?" I aske
looking toward the door. The boy was gone.

It was late when I pulled into the driveway. The light was o
in our bedroom. I knew that Katie was waiting up for me. I stoo
there in the dark, listening to the roar of the ocean down belo
The smell of the magnolia blossoms permeated the soft night ai

I walked down the path to the front door. Katie opened it as
was reaching to put the key in the lock.

"Hello, dear," she said. "Did you have dinner?"

"The doctor and I sent out for some pastrami sandwiches."

"I'll make you something to eat."

We went into the kitchen. It was immaculate. The frame
prints I had inherited from the Barrymore estate hung on th
wall. The clock on the stove read one-thirty in the morning.
could feel Katie's eyes on me.

"You were with the doctor until now?"

"Sure, where the hell do you think I've been?"

"I knew you had an appointment at six o'clock."

I didn't bother to explain.

"Where were you, in his office?"

I was too tired to go through analysis twice in one day.

"Damn it, Katie, we had a tough night and a lot of ground t
cover."

She set a steak before me. "Is he helping you?"

"Not yet."

"You're awfully tense lately. Is it good for you to go through all this while you're making a picture?"

"Probably not. But I think my life is more important than any picture. Anyway, I'm probably trying to do more than the lousy film merits."

"Why did you accept it if you didn't like it?"

"Because we have to eat, and the agent says it will make me a romantic movie star."

"Is that what you want?"

"No, but I'd like to know that I could be if I wanted to. I don't want to feel I'm not as acceptable as other guys who have made it."

"Why do you envy them? What do they have that you can possibly want?"

I put down the knife and fork hard on the table. "You know fucking well what I want. They have it and I don't."

"Please don't curse."

"I'm sorry. I got swinging pretty good with the doctor and I guess it's hard to stop."

"Isn't it possible, dear, that some of them envy you? A lot of these men depend on their looks for their success. You don't have to."

"You mean my homeliness might someday become an economical advantage?"

"You're too hard on yourself."

"I just want to know how it feels to be number one — once."

"To me you're number one."

"Don't give me that shit. Remember the game of anagrams?"

"Sweetheart, can't you forget it? God, it was just a game."

"None of it is a game to me, baby. I play everything for keeps. Maybe I won't amount to a pile of shit, but if it's only manure I can come up with I want my woman to think it's gold. I fell in love with you that day when you said, 'Tony, I have a feeling that if you were a newsboy you'd try to be the best newsboy in the world. If you lived on an island you'd build a castle out of sand.' I want to build you a castle. I'm trying like hell to be a king, and I haven't been able to deliver."

"I don't want to be married to a king."

"But now *I* want to be one. Only as a king can I beat those fucking ghosts. Only as a king can I command them to go away.

Who the hell is going to listen to a Mexican peon? Baby, you must never, *never* again root for anyone else but me. Don't ever laugh when someone beats me at anagrams, tennis, or even pitching pennies. Even if I come in last, stand up and cheer me as the winner. Because, you stupid bitch, I'm trying to win the crown for *you*. don't want to wear the fucking thing!"

"Tony, I grew up differently from you. We played card games at home and we all tried to beat each other. They were just games."

"I didn't grow up playing games, honey. I grew up with kids throwing shit at me, not tennis balls. And there was no applause or laughter, only dull shame when you didn't make it. I'm tired of losing. I want to win a round or two. And I don't want you to be in my corner rooting for the other guy to knock me out — even at a lousy game of anagrams!"

Later that night, long after we'd turned out the lights, I knew she was still awake.

"Tony?"

"Yeah?"

"I'm sorry."

"I know, honey. I know. And that's why I'm trying to work it out so that maybe I'll stop eating out my guts, so I can be a nice man and a good father. I swear to you I'm doing my best."

"Good-night, dear. I'll pray for you."

"Good-night."

"Dear?"

"Yeah?"

"Do you think that maybe I should go and see a psychiatrist too?"

"No, honey. One nut in the family is enough."

She laughed softly. "Good-night."

The sleeping pill had begun to work. I felt the kindliness sleep overtake me. Then a familiar scene.

I was a little boy awakened by my parents, who were yelling each other! They seemed to be angry one second and laughing crazily the next.

I got up and went to their bed. My mother sat up. Though her eyes were wide open I knew she couldn't see me. Yet she w

creaming for me to go back to sleep. I went to my father, who
eached up, still lying on the pillow, and smacked me across the
ace. The blow hurt tremendously but I refused to cry. I choked
ack the tears. Soon my parents quieted down.

I tiptoed out of the house into the pitch-black dark. Though
here wasn't a cloud in the sky, there wasn't a single star in
eaven! It seemed as if God had drawn a black tarpaulin across
he sky. I became terrified and started to run back into the house.
ut when I turned I saw that the house was gone! I was alone in
hat immense darkness.

Was I in hell? Had I died and was my spirit now condemned to
verlasting night? Had I gone blind?

I began to run. I felt the asphalt pavement under me. I ran
ster. Even in the dark I knew I was climbing up a steep grade.
hen the incline leveled out and I knew I'd climbed so high I
uld touch the tarpaulin.

I stretched my hand above my head. The tarpaulin was made
f tissue paper! It tore at my touch. Wind started to rip the tissue
iolently.

The whole sky was coming apart. I saw three stars, but the sky,
I knew it, was not there — just three huge shining objects
thought were stars. Where the sky should have been there was
lorless space, a flat dead mossy green.

The wind blew harder. I couldn't stay on my feet. I was thrown
the ground and I rolled about like a tumbleweed. Suddenly
e wind died as abruptly as it had begun. I got up slowly.

Huge gray moss was hanging down in long endless streams from
eaven. In the center of the moss a huge wide carpet was being
lled down by seven deadly white angels. The carpet was a bril-
ant purple. It hit the ground and the angels kept on rolling it
ward me.

Then I saw, as far as the eye could see, multitudes of people.
hey were looking at the top of the carpet, as if over a huge
ountain. It was just hanging there in space!

There was no sound from the masses of people. Not one cried,
one knelt in prayer. Yet they all knew that the end of the world
d come! They waited silently.

Then I heard the piercing sound of the trumpet! I knew that
od was coming!

I saw the people start over the high crest of the velvet highway. First the band of trumpeters, followed by hundreds of chariot. Behind them a light — a Blinding Light!!! I turned my head I couldn't look.

Then I became aware I was holding something in my hand. It was the rolled-up tissue paper. I had the sky in my hand! And God was coming down to claim it back!

# 9

THE DOCTOR looked up after entering his notes in our growing folder.

"That's straight out of the Book of Revelations, isn't it?"

"There's a similarity."

"Do you often have such vivid dreams?"

"Practically every night."

"Do you have a recurring dream?"

"Several. One is about a house I am constantly building on top of a hill. It overlooks a magnificent emerald bay. Another is about a huge house divided into two parts, like a duplex. I live on the side which is musty and dark. I can't find the door to the other more cheerful side."

The doctor was having a field day with his pen. "What about the dream you had last night? Have you had anything like before?"

"Yes. In fact, it recurs more often than any of my night vision. Part of it, I mean. I very often dream of the world coming an end."

"Is it always the same?"

"More or less. I always hear the trumpet, and the host of angel coming down the never-ending purple carpet from Heaven."

"When did it start?"

"When I was about eleven years old. After my father died, my grandmother became very sick. I started going to the Catho.

hurch more frequently. I seriously thought of becoming a priest.
went to study with Father Anselmo, who was quite young him-
elf. He talked to me a good deal about fate and God's will, and
accepted what he said. He told me that my father was not dead,
hat he had gone to Heaven. I was relieved to hear someone say
his, since I had never accepted the death of my father. I was glad
e was in Heaven because he was certainly deserving of a much
etter life than we had had in that terrible neighborhood.

"Whenever I wasn't working or at school I would go to see
ather Anselmo. We would talk about what it meant to be a
riest. 'It's not an easy life, Tony,' he would say. 'Don't have any
lusions about it. It's very hard work.' I wasn't frightened by hard
ork. I also liked the thought of the robes, the incense, the music
– detachment from the hard ugly material world.

"One day, I came home to find several strangers in the house.
1y grandmother had terrible stomach pains. She could hardly
reathe. The people were from a Protestant group we called the
Ioly Rollers,' the popular name for the Foursquare Gospel
hurch of Aimee Semple McPherson. They were praying for my
randmother.

"To me, it was like seeing the Devil; anybody who wasn't
atholic was anathema to me. I became furious, pushing them
nd shouting, 'Get out of my house. You're evil, you're disciples
f the Devil. . . .' One man held me and said, 'Tony, we're not
oing anything wrong. We're praying to the same God, maybe in
different way. We know you're a Catholic, that you have aspira-
ons of being a priest, but your grandmother is going through
reat pain. She believes that we can help her. Please let us stay
ere and pray for her.'

"My grandmother lifted her head from the pillow and said,
Tony, they're not doing anything wrong. They want to help me.
have terrible pains.'

" 'Grandma, I'll go to the church and have a Mass said for you.
he priest will come and pray for you.'

" 'Tony, I've heard that these people can do miraculous things.
want them to stay.'

"I ran out of the house. I went straight to Father Anselmo and
•ld him what had happened.

" 'Tony, I don't worship like the Protestants, but we mustn't

be so narrow as to think they are devils. There are many way
to reach God. If your grandmother believes these people are th
way, fine. Let them come.'

"I relented and got used to seeing them at the house. The
would arrive in little groups of three or four. They called eac
other 'brother' and 'sister.' I began to see they were nice peopl
They weren't allowed to smoke or drink. They never went t
movies, and generally didn't believe in worldly things. There wa
a kind of communal feeling about them. Slowly I began to accep
these Protestants. My grandmother gradually felt better.

"One day, a young man from the group said they were formin
a band at the church and would like me to play the saxophon
with them. I said, 'Look, I don't mind your coming to my hous
but I'm not going to your church, let alone play my saxophon
for you.'

" 'Tony,' my grandmother intervened, 'I don't have the pair
anymore. These people have helped me. I want to go to thei
church, and I'd like you to come with me.'

" 'Grandma, I'm not going.'

" 'We owe them something,' she persisted. 'I think we shoul
both go and give thanks. I promised that if I got well I'd giv
testimony.'

"My grandmother and I went to our first revival meeting. T
my amazement I found it tremendously moving. The crowd wa
different from what I was used to at Mass. There, it was all qui
and cautious. Everybody tiptoed around as if apologizing fo
being human, as if God would not forgive them if they mad
noises.

"Here, everybody was laughing and seemed to be at a picni
People were patting each other on the back — 'Hello, brother' -
'Hello, sister' — 'Glory, Hallelujah!' — and smiling. I recognize
several Negro boys from Belvedere Junior High. I'd always see
them with a chip on their shoulders around the playground. He
I saw them smiling and grinning. They felt at home, accepted.

"Then the singing and shouting started. I had never seen fi
hundred people happy at the same time. The preacher was tal
ing about the usual things — sin, redemption, angels, hell and tl
Devil — but he also threw in a lot of 'Glories' and 'Hallelujal

d every time he spoke, five hundred people would roar back,
lory, Hallelujah!'

"'One moment he'd be scaring the life out of them with images
brimstone and hellfire; in the next breath he was shouting,
's all right because the King of Heaven, who loves us so, is
ing to let us sit at His right hand. Behold, He cometh through
e clouds and every eye shall see Him.'

"'Amen!'

"'And they also which pierced Him.'

"'Amen!'

"'His head and His hairs are as white as the first snow and His
es a flame of fire!'

"'Glory, Hallelujah!'

'Brothers and sisters, in His left hand He holds seven stars!
d in His right hand a two-edged sword, and His countenance
s the sun.'

"'Amen! Glory be! Glory, Hallelujah!'

'And he that cometh and keepeth my works, unto the end,
him I give power over the nations! And I shall give him the
rning star!"

'The Negro families had their arms over their heads, as if
ey wanted to catch the stars when they started falling.

'And the stars of Heaven fell unto the earth, even as a fig
e casteth her untimely figs, when she is shaken of a mighty
nd!'

"'Yes, brother!'

'The band began to play. The trumpets blew loud.

'And white robes were given *unto every one of them* and it
s said unto them: "They shall hunger no more, neither thirst
y more, for the Lamb which is in the midst of the throne shall
d them, and shall lead them unto living fountains of waters.
d God shall wipe away all tears from their eyes!!"'

'The music rose to a crescendo. Five hundred people were rais-
; their arms to Heaven. Every soul was waiting for the skies to
en. Unafraid of seeing the wonder of Heaven, they were ready
that voice of thunder!

'I caught sight of my grandmother. She wore a beatific smile
he looked up toward Heaven.

'The preacher yelled over the wailing of the congregation,

'And He said unto me, it is done. I am Alpha and Omega, t
beginning and the end. And He carried me away in the spi
to a great and high mountain!!!'

" 'AND I, TOO, SAW THE GLORY OF GOD!!!'

"My grandmother jumped to her feet. 'Brothers and sisters
was sick,' she began. She talked about my father, about me a
about the great miracle that had been performed and how s
had believed. She seemed illuminated from inside; the congre
tion hung on her every word.

"When we went home that night, I knew there had beer
transformation in me. I had witnessed something enormous.
had brought me to a point of decision in my life, but I s
couldn't accept having Protestants in my house. The next da
came home and a group of them were sitting around eating a
laughing. A madness came over me. I started yelling terrible
scenities at them. I picked up a knife, threw it at one of the m
but hit my mother in the back instead. She fell. I thought I I
killed her. I rushed up, took her in my arms, and burst out c
ing. The group surrounding me started praying. A man put
hand on my head and said, 'Brothers and sisters, let us pray
this boy. He has the spirit of a leader. He believes, but in
wrong thing, and we're going to pray that God shows him
way. We're going to pray, brothers and sisters, here and n
Everybody kneel, please, and pray for this boy.'

"Suddenly I was the center of attention.

" 'Brothers and sisters, you have just seen the evidence o
beautiful soul, one who believes in the blood of Christ. We w
this boy as leader — "And a Child shall lead us," says the Go
Book!'

"The following Sunday I went to the Catholic church; I v
an altar boy at that time, helping the priest during Mass. I s
denly knew it was the last time I would go there. After the serv
in the vestry I helped the priest take off his robes.

" 'Father, I have to talk to you.'

" 'I think I know what you are going to say.'

" 'You do?'

" 'I've watched you wrestle with this problem for a long ti
I know your mother and grandmother are going to the ot
church. I can only tell you that you must follow your heart. '

126

for a while if you wish. I know that you will return a better atholic than ever.'

"I went back into the deserted church and prayed for hours. felt a tap on my shoulder. A cleaning woman asked me to get ut. She had to sweep the floor before the evening Mass. I was urious. I said this was my church and that I would stay as long s I pleased. She called the sexton and he asked me to leave.

"The following day I told the people from the Foursquare ospel that I would be happy to play my saxophone in their and.

"While I worked at a variety of odd jobs and attended school poradically, I became deeply involved with the Foursquare Gos- el Church. I started going out into the street, playing my saxo- hone with three or four of the younger people. We'd stand on orners and play hymns. Crowds would invariably gather round nd we would take turns preaching, mostly in Spanish.

"I was fourteen when I met the most magnetic personality I as ever to encounter. Years later, when I saw the great actresses work I would compare them to her. As magnificent as I could nd Anna Magnani, Ingrid Bergman, Laurette Taylor, Katherine epburn, Greta Garbo and Ethel Barrymore, they all fell short that first electric shock Aimee Semple McPherson produced in e.

"I sat in the orchestra pit of the huge auditorium at the An- :lus Temple. Every seat was filled, with the crowd spilling into ie aisles. Many were on crutches or in wheelchairs. Eventually ie congregation settled down, the lights dimmed, and a hush me over the assembly. Even the whimpering of children stopped.

"A spotlight illuminated a lectern with an open Bible. We aited for what seemed an eternity. One could hear a feather op in that huge auditorium, which seated about twenty-five indred to three thousand people. I could actually feel people lding their breath. Suddenly a figure with bright red hair and flowing white gown walked out to the center of the stage.

"She lifted her arms in that immense silence. Then that rich elodious voice began slowly, 'Glory! Glory! Glory!' I could feel e audience exhale. We shouted, 'Glory!' She smiled and the ngregation felt truly blessed. She closed her eyes, leafed through e Bible, and let her finger fall. She read the passage, caressing each word. She began to interweave sudden bursts of emotion 'Hallelujah! Hallelujah, brothers and sisters!' All the congrega tion replied, 'Hallelujah!'

"The orchestra got its cue and we started playing. In a very few minutes the audience was rocking. People were screaming fainting. Finally, with the audience at the height of frenzy, Aime raised her hand and stillness descended. In a soft voice, almos a whisper, she said, 'Brothers and sisters, is there anyone here wh wants to be cured tonight? Let him come up and if he has fait he will be cured. Those who are blind will be able to see; thos who are deaf will be able to hear; those who are crippled will b able to walk. I beg you to come up now if you have faith. If yo have faith, brothers and sisters, come up, come up. . . .'

"They started getting up all over the audience, shouting, 'Ha lelujah, hallelujah, sister. Hallelujah!' Long lines formed to reac her. She stood center stage and greeted each one. 'What is you name, brother? What is your name? What is your name, brothe What is your name? What is your ailment, brother?' One ma said, 'I can't see out of one eye.' 'Do you believe, brother?' sh asked. 'Do you believe that I can make you see? Do you believ in the Lord, my brother? Do you want to see?' Transformed, th man started shaking with emotion. 'You can see, brother!' Ca you not see, brother?' And suddenly, the man cried, 'Yes, siste I can see, I can see!' And the audience went crazy.

"To a woman dragging herself across the stage on crutches sh said, 'You don't need a crutch, sister. You can walk. The Lor wants you to walk. The reason you needed a crutch was that yo weren't walking in the way of the Lord, sister. But if you wan to walk in the way of the Lord, if you want to follow his footstep you can throw away the crutch. Throw away that crutch! An follow me!' Suddenly, the woman threw away her crutch and ra into Aimee's open arms. I left that service exhilarated, renewe

"This was all during the height of the Depression, when hung and poverty permeated America. Many Mexicans were terrifi of appealing for county help because most of them were in th country illegally. When in distress, they were comforted by th fact that they could call one of Aimee's branches at any time the night. There, they would never be asked any of the embarra ing questions posed by the authorities. The fact that they we

ungry or in need of warm clothing was enough. No one even
asked if they belonged to Aimee's church or not."

The doctor nodded. "Back in the Middlewest we'd heard about
Mrs. McPherson, but of course we only read criticisms of her, and
gossip."

"I remember all that horseshit. I couldn't have cared less about
her private life. To me she was a good woman and gave people
faith."

My voice started to rise in anger. The doctor held up his hand.
"Whoa — whoa — I didn't say they were right. When did you
meet her personally?"

"She had been at several of the band rehearsals. She always had
a warm smile for everyone, but I could never look into her eyes.
I knew she'd be able to see through me. One day, I was tooting
away on my saxophone when I felt someone's eyes on my neck.
I knew it was Aimee. I tried not to turn around but the pull was
so great. During a pause I turned and there she sat behind me.
Our eyes met for the first time. I felt no fear, no embarrassment,
no awe — just complete acceptance. She smiled as if to say, 'I
know you. I like you.' It was so simple.

"When she walked over to me I was amazed that she knew my
name. 'Tony, I understand you've played with the band the way
I did when I was a young girl. My mother used to make me play
on streetcorners standing on an apple box. I'd gather people
around so that she could preach to them. Tony, I have the feeling
that the Lord has singled you out to become a great preacher. It's
a wonderful calling, and people need help. I want to work with
you. Next Saturday, we're going into the Mexican district; we
want to build a temple down there. Will you go with me?'

"I said I would be honored and delighted.

"Saturday afternoon I arrived at the temple. There was a long
line of cars. She asked me to ride in hers. She had a way of making you feel so wanted, so needed, so accepted. It was as if I'd
been waiting an eternity for such acceptance.

"When we got down to the East Side of Los Angeles, an enormous crowd lined the streets and surrounded the tent. We got
out of the car. There was no applause, only respectful silence and
obvious awe. She very sweetly held me at her side as we walked
through the crowd.

"On this particular night, after the congregation had quiet down, she thanked them and said she was very happy to be among her Mexican brothers and sisters. She apologized for not being able to come down more often, but noted that she didn't speak Spanish. She said she felt that the preachers who were handling the congregation were doing an excellent job. And then she said 'I've asked a young boy, who I think is going to be one of our great preachers, to translate for me for the benefit of those who don't speak English.' She called me to her side and I found myself translating for my goddess, Miss Aimee Semple McPherson. At first, I was terribly frightened, but she put her hand on my shoulder and an electrical charge went through me, dispelling fear or embarrassment. I spoke out loud and clear. I was her voice that night, the extension of that great power."

I looked at the doctor to see how he was taking it. He had the impassive look. I had learned that it was not a lack of interest on his part but a way of digesting information. Trying to fit the jigsaw puzzle together. I waited. He picked up the pen and put it in his mouth. He had given up smoking recently and was going through the withdrawal pangs.

"What's bothering you?" I asked.

"I was thinking about the kid. I wondered why you pinpointed him as being eleven. It seemed that the period with McPherson had a tremendous effect on him — I mean you."

"No," I insisted, "the boy is definitely eleven."

The doctor started putting away my folder and tidying up the desk so I knew the session was over.

We both put on our jackets and started down the deserted hallway. The doctor seemed lost in thought. We were talked out. When we got to the sidewalk in front of the building he surprised me by putting his arm around me.

"Good-night, Tony. Sleep well. We're doing fine."

He headed for his car and I walked across the parking lot. It was late and my car was the only one left.

I was shocked to see "the boy" sitting in the front seat, waiting for me. I looked back to see if the doctor was still in sight. He wasn't. There was nothing to do but climb in beside the boy.

I drove out of the lot and headed for Sunset Boulevard. Crossing it I almost collided with another car.

The kid laughed. "Hey, take it easy. You want to kill us both?"

"What the hell do you want?"

"I came to see how you and your pal are getting along. Has he straightened out your head yet?"

"Watch out," I said. "We're getting closer."

"Exit the ghost, huh?"

We were driving west toward Pacific Palisades now. The boy looked out at the big luxurious homes lining the Boulevard.

"Christ, back there you never thought we'd get this far," I said. "Why can't you be satisfied? Why don't you stop bugging me?"

The boy didn't answer. I had turned on the radio and Peggy Lee's haunting voice filled the car.

"What did you tell him tonight?" the boy asked.

"We talked about Aimee."

"Oh." He nodded noncommittally.

MAN. Did you really ever think of why you changed religions?

BOY (*quickly*). For my grandmother.

MAN. No, I've thought about it for a long time. You had already been to Aimee's and you liked the uniforms the orchestra wore. You liked the idea of sitting in front of that huge crowd blowing your horn.

BOY (*starting to protest*). That's not . . .

MAN. Sure, sure, I know you were religious, kid. I'm not saying you were a complete fake. It might surprise you to know that I've done a lot of soul-searching myself. I often wondered where the acting bug hit us. I know now.

BOY. Go on.

MAN. Aimee Semple McPherson influenced your life. She really rocked you. I don't mean the way she rocked everybody, but you knew you were seeing the greatest actress of all time.

BOY (*smiling*). Remember how she'd walk down that long ramp and stand there in the middle of the stage and hold that crowd?

MAN. What did you call it?

BOY. What?

MAN. You called it a stage. That's what it was to you. Not a pulpit, but a stage. That's why you changed religions. There was a chance for you to get on that stage. As a would-be priest it was doubtful you'd get to say Mass for years. But with Aimee all you needed was the guts and you could get up on the stage with her.

BOY. She was a good person.

MAN. Nobody is saying anything about her. She was fine. We're talking about you not seeing it for what it was. She was the biggest star you'd ever met!

BOY. And probably the biggest you'll ever meet.

MAN. I think you're right. God, how I'd love to be on the same stage with her now.

BOY. Well?

MAN. I know you'd rather have me be an evangelist than an actor.

BOY (*sarcastically*). How humble you sometimes are.

MAN (*angrily*). Oh, I've been eating humble pie for so long I've decided to try the other. Maybe it's sweeter!

As I pulled into the driveway of the house the boy jumped out. I saw him start down the street and disappear into the dark night.

# 10

IT WAS the twenty-third of December, 1929. My sister and I were standing on the porch, watching the rain come down in sheets and singing: SINGING IN THE RAIN.

The sky had just fallen in on America. The Depression had begun. To us, it was merely an abstraction; we had been living in the backwash of poverty all our lives, and had learned to laugh at hunger. In a few days it would be Christmas and Stella and I knew that for us, once again, there would be nothing.

We saw Mother coming down the slushy road, carrying two huge shopping bags. We rushed through the rain to help her. When we reached the cover of the porch she told us they contained our gifts. My sister and I were beside ourselves. We were going to have a Christmas after all.

In the morning, we all gathered around and Mother started to open the shopping bags. Out came suits and dresses, shirts and ties. They were used. They certainly weren't a perfect fit, but to Stella and me they were the most elegant clothes we'd ever seen.

It was the best Christmas we had known. My mother explained to us that everything came from some people she had met, very nice people; their name was Bowles.

A couple of days later, a man rode up in the latest Model-T Ford coupe. He was a very well-groomed, well-dressed man.

My mother went out to meet him at the car and they spoke for a few minutes. Then she brought him into the house, and there was something about him I didn't like. Not him personally, but I didn't like the way my mother talked to him. She just introduced him as Frank Bowles. Later, we all got into the car and went for a drive. I didn't enjoy it very much because my mother was sitting in the front seat with him, and my grandmother, my sister and I sat in the rear. I didn't like the back of the man's head. I couldn't wait for the ride to be over.

Finally, he drove us back home. He stayed for dinner and then left early. My mother called me into her room and said, "I might as well tell you that Mr. Bowles has proposed to me and I've accepted." I was surprised when my grandmother took the news rather calmly. She seemed to be in complete agreement with what my mother was doing.

As I was fourteen years old at the time, I felt that I could take care of the family. I didn't see any need for a new man to come in, and as far as I was concerned my mother had no right to look at another man after my father's death, anyway. I told her so.

"Well, Tony, I know how you feel. I've always known that you would feel this way. Mr. Bowles and I have talked about it and we're going to get you and Stella and Doña Sabina a little house by yourselves. I will go and live with Frank."

I looked to my sister for help but she was already trying on the hand-me-downs and seemed happy as hell with her new-found treasures.

I realized now that her dresses, along with my suits, silk shirts and ties, had all come from the man who wanted to take my father's place. I picked up the clothes and threw them across the

room. I would never accept a thing from him. I would neve
accept him, period. I ran out of the house in tears.

"She did marry him, didn't she?" said the doctor.

"Yes, but I didn't go to the ceremony. I could never understan
how Grandmother could condone my mother's sleeping with an
other man, why she didn't fight for her son's interest."

"Did Mr. Bowles keep his promise about the separate hous
for you and your grandmother?"

"Yeah. One day a pickup truck arrived and we piled in all ou
belongings and drove across Main Street to our new house, whic
was just a few blocks away from Angelus Temple. It was part c
a duplex. It consisted of three rooms. In front, a living roor
dominated by a big bay window looking out into the street; th
center room, which was the bedroom; and the back room, whic
had a kitchen and a newfangled miracle — an inside toilet!

"All I knew was that I was being relegated to the number-tw
spot, so I demoted my mother to number three!"

"Divorces and remarriages are tough on kids," the doctor sai
"Where was your mother living now that she was Mrs. Fran
Bowles?"

"She lived in a house overlooking Echo Park Lake. She sti
lives there."

"Have you ever forgiven your mother?"

"No. I understand why she did it. She was only twenty-si
when my father died. Frank offered her security, and maybe sh
deluded herself that eventually he and I would work things out.

"You couldn't adjust to him?"

"I could never swallow the fact that he bore the same name a
my father. I swear that if his name had been George or Harr
I might have been able to accept him. But what fucking righ
did he have to be called Frank!"

"Perhaps your mother was drawn to him because she had real
loved your father and couldn't bear to love a man with anoth
name."

"Yeah, I thought of that. It was no consolation. I rememb
one Saturday afternoon I was in the front room playing my sax
phone when I saw Frank's coupe pull up to the curb. My moth

and he got out. They were loaded down with shopping bags. They'd only been married about six months at the time.

"My sister and grandmother ran to the front door to let them in. My sister Stella was always a sucker for packages.

"My mother handed my grandmother two big bags full of food. I could see a lemon meringue pie on top. Stella was handed a big box that she immediately put on the floor and started opening. She pulled out two starched-looking dresses. She was delirious with happiness.

"My mother looked pleadingly at Frank. He seemed uncomfortable as he handed me a big box.

" 'This is for you, boy.'

"I always hated that 'boy' shit of his. It reminded me of El Paso, Texas. As a matter of fact, Frank was born in Uvalde, Texas, and had all the attitudes and prejudices of that region.

"I took the package from him and put it on the table in the middle of the room.

" 'Aren't you going to open it, son?' asked my mother, with false gaiety.

"She put it in my hands again and motioned for me to open it.

"I hated the way everybody stood around while I unwrapped it. When I opened the box I saw a pair of two-toned black and white shoes!

"I knew I couldn't look up because they would see that I had tears in my eyes.

" 'Thank Frank, hijito,' my mother was saying.

"I looked at Frank. He was peeling an orange. 'Thank you, Frank,' I squeezed out of me.

" 'That's all right, boy. You can work them off in four or five weeks.'

" 'What do you mean?'

" 'You don't think your mother and I are going to give you those expensive shoes for nothing, do you? You will help me wash windows every Saturday afternoon until you pay us back!'

"I picked up the shoes and threw them in his face. He, in turn, threw the orange at me and hit me right in the mush. The women were screaming as Frank and I made for each other. I was pleading with my grandmother to let me kick the shit out of him.

Oh, how I longed to get my hands on him, as my father would have done."

The doctor couldn't help but laugh at the nice family scene with shoes and oranges flying about.

Yes, in retrospect I could laugh too. But not then. I remembered how Frank had stomped out of the house saying I was an ungrateful bastard, and that I would freeze in hell before he'd talk to me again.

" 'Are you coming?' he yelled at my mother.

"I begged her to leave him, to stay with us. I promised to earn a living for us. I had started boxing and swore to her that within two years I'd be a champion earning thousands!

"My sister was crying in fear and grabbed at my mother. She disentangled herself and headed for the door.

" 'He is my husband, son. A woman has to obey her husband.'

"I saw her get into the car and drive away with him. That night as I walked around the lake, I looked up at their house. All the lights were on. I could hear the player piano going full blast."

"At this same time, you say you wanted to be boxing champion?" said the doctor.

"That is right."

"You were certainly juggling a lot of balls all at the same time."

"I guess so. When Katie and I were first married, we'd go out to dinner and I'd be telling stories and I'd say, 'Now when I was an electrician' or 'When I was working as a butcher' or 'When I was a cement worker. . . .' One night, coming home from a party, she said, 'Honey, do you mind if I tell you something?'

" 'What?'

" 'You're always talking about all the jobs you've done. I'm afraid people must laugh at you because nobody could possibly have done them all. People will think you're making it up.'

"I was furious. 'You think I'm lying?'

" 'Well, dear, I do think you're exaggerating.'

" 'That's the trouble with you goddamn rich people. You have no idea how the poor live. You only worry about when the lazy Mexican maid is going to bring you your fucking tea and crumpets. I sweated as a kid, I didn't perspire like your friends. And I *did* work as an electrician's helper, sold papers, shined shoes I *was* a clean-up man at a meat-packing plant, emptying out the slop. I *did* work on the Los Angeles sewer system carrying water to the men who were building it so that the shit of your rich friends would be unimpeded on its way to the Pacific Ocean.

" 'Yes, I did pick fruit, drive a cab, deliver telegrams. I washed windows and polished floors. I sold cheap perfumes. I cleaned dirty toilet bowls. I *did* work in a mattress factory. I *did* box for five dollars a night. I'm sure there are a dozen other jobs I've forgotten to mention, that I took because I had to live. So if your friends are sneering at me, they can kiss my Mexican ass.' "

The doctor laughed at my passionate speech. "You hate rich people, Tony?"

"No, Doc — I just hate the people who are unaware of the inhumanity of poverty. Like the time when I was a waiter in a short-order restaurant and I served this red-necked sonofabitch ham and eggs. After he'd paid the bill he stood in the doorway. 'Here, boy,' he said, and flipped a dime through the air. It clinked on the counter, then rolled around onto the floor. I picked it up and threw it back in his face. He called me an 'ungrateful Mexican.' The boss agreed with him and fired me."

"You keep talking about red-necks. You've told me that when you first came to see me you thought of me as a red-neck. Why do you hate them so?"

"I guess it started in Texas. They had a way of acting like they owned the fucking world. I could see in their beady eyes that they felt superior. To them everyone else was 'boy.' It didn't take much intelligence to know that they considered themselves the only 'men.'

"Then I guess I got to hate those bastards up in San Jose. We arrived in cattle-cars to pick the grapes, and they started to play the Mexicans against the poor Filipinos and the poor whites.

"They have a fat-assed walk. Their masculinity is in the width of their shoulders and the lard of their asses, rather than in their cocks."

The doctor threw back his head and laughed that wonderful full laugh of his. "By the way, just to change the subject for the moment, did you ever envy *your* father's penis?"

He had a way of suddenly throwing me a curve, hoping to catch me unawares.

"No, Doctor. I only saw it once, to the best of my memory It was soft and not very impressive. If you really want to know I thought: Jeez, it doesn't look too different from mine. Y'know Doc, I've never *really* felt a man's masculinity was in his penis As Barrymore said to me years later, 'How can I be proud of tha in which every chimpanzee is my equal and every jackass m superior.' "

We both laughed.

"Tell me about the years after your father's death," said the doctor.

"I picked up odd jobs, like the ones I've mentioned, but some where along the line I got a brilliant idea. I was very good a drawing. I began to copy photographs of famous actors. I did them in Crayola colors. I started to mail the drawings to every impor tant star in Hollywood. I waited for the money to start pourin, in. I would run to meet the mailman every day. Finally, one letter arrived. The only one. It was from Douglas Fairbanks. The not merely said 'Thanks,' but he had enclosed a ten-dollar bill. No on else wrote me.

"Since my art project had failed I took a new tack. I'd become a famous orchestra leader. Rudy Vallee was the idol of the mo ment. His example led me to the saxophone, the instrument later played in Aimee's church. When I went shopping for one, found out they cost anywhere from fifty to a thousand dollars.

"I inveigled my mother into buying me one from the Wurlitze music shop in downtown Los Angeles. She had to pay five dollar down and a dollar a week. What with interest, it seemed we wen on paying for that damned horn for years. Then there was th money for music lessons and sheet music. It was a drain on m poor mother, so when I heard that the Martinez family down th street was going up north for the summer to pick apricots — the had sons my age, Luis and Valentín — we made a deal that would pay my way if I could go with them.

"We drove over the Conejo Pass. The old car kept overheatin, every five miles and we'd have to park by the side of the road t let it cool. It took us five days to reach Camarillo. Today one ca make the trip in an hour and a half.

"When we got to the Camarillo Ranch there were hundreds o families waiting to be hired, but Mr. Martinez had applied week

before so he was taken on. Since I wasn't on the list, it looked like
I'd have to bum my way home. I was heartbroken.

"I went up and spoke to a big blond man named Mr. Green —
the owner of the ranch — and told him my problem.

" 'What's your name, son?'

" 'Antonio Quinn,' I said.

" 'Quinn, eh?' He thought for a second. 'Think you can handle
people?'

" 'What do you mean, sir?'

" 'Think you can give people orders and have them obey you?'

" 'I think so, sir.'

" 'Okay. I'll make you foreman of the sulphur sheds.'

"He walked me over to the sheds and showed me how the half-
cut apricots had to be shoved into the sulphur sheds on long
wooden trays, then laid out to dry in the sun.

"The Martinez family changed toward me after that. I guess
they thought I'd joined the enemy camp of the 'Bosses.'

"Valentín called me a gringo and we fought it out in the
orchard. He was tough, but I had the reach on him and was able
to keep him away with my left hand. After a while, his nose
started to bleed and I knew I could beat him.

"Mrs. Martinez told me next day I'd have to move away. I
found a tree out on the edge of the field and set up camp. I made
a deal with another family to feed me for twenty cents a day.

"The woman was not the most generous with her servings and
I had to replenish my diet with apricots. To this day I can't look
an apricot in the face.

"The thing that kept me going was the knowledge that I
would arrive home at the end of the summer with a small fortune.
I had a mental picture of walking into the house and dumping all
that money in the middle of the room, and saying, 'Here it is. I
have earned it all for you, Grandma, Stella and Mother. I am now
the *man* of the house.'

"The scene became an obsession to me. I kept dreaming of a
bigger and bigger pile of money.

"It got so that I resented having to spend anything. I scrounged
and scrimped all summer. I was afraid to keep money on me, because there were always robberies going on, so I asked Mr. Green
to hold it for me. I liked him a great deal and trusted him, espe-

cially after the day he came and said to me, 'You're doing a good job, son. Your father would be proud of you.'

"Finally, the summer came to an end and the camp began breaking up. Many of the families were going off to work in the bean fields, but I couldn't stand the suffocating dust and dirt. Besides, I wanted to go back to school.

"I went to Mr. Green to get my money. He handed me an enormous wad of money — eighty dollars!

" 'Here you are, son, you've earned it. I've watched you these last two months. You did very good. By now maybe you've learned that being a boss is a lonely job. Everybody thinks you're his enemy. I watch people come here and work these fields every year. Not one ever comes to thank me for putting him to work. Believe it or not, sometimes I lose money on the season, but I like having all these people around with their campfires and their guitar music. It makes a nice summer for me.'

"I had never known my grandfather but this man was what I always thought a grandfather should be.

" 'Mr. Green, I came to thank you. And maybe I'll see you again someday.'

" 'I hope not, son. I mean I'd like to see you but not working the piscas, not fruit-picking. There are better jobs for a man. What are you going to do with all that money?'

" 'I'm going to give it to my grandmother and mother, sir.'

" 'Where are they?'

" 'In Los Angeles.'

" 'How are you going to get home?'

" 'I guess I'll bum a ride.'

" 'No, you're not, son. Someone is likely to roll you.' He reached into his pocket and took out a ten-dollar bill! 'Here, you go down to the bus station and take the bus home tonight.'

" 'But, sir, the fare is only a dollar seventy-five.'

" 'You can use the rest of it for a a good dinner.'

"I wanted to hug him — that lovely red-neck.

" 'Thank you, sir.'

" 'What are you going to do with your life, Tony?'

"It was the first time he'd called me by my first name.

" 'I don't know, sir. I want to draw and build houses and — oh I don't know. Right now I want to learn to play my saxophone ıd maybe someday have an orchestra so I can afford to study rchitecture, or something.'

" 'Architecture, huh? Why architecture?'

" 'I think it's nice to build things, build nice houses for people ꜧ live in — nice buildings. I don't know.'

" 'But right now you're going to learn to play the saxophone, ı?'

" 'Yes, sir.'

" 'Okay, Tony. Someday when you're playing a tune, maybe ᴏu'll think of me.'

"I took his hand and could find nothing else to say.

"On the bus back to Los Angeles I sat in the back seat. Every ᴏw and then I'd feel the wad in my back pocket.

"I relived the scene of my arrival home endless times. It was ke seeing a movie you like over and over. I never tired of the ᴏse-up on my grandmother's face as she saw the pile of money d saved.

"The bus let me off at Sixth and Main and I took the streetcar ᴏ Belvedere. By the time I got to the corner of Rowan and ᴏooklyn it was night. I ran all the way home. They were all sit-ng at dinner. I walked in and threw the pile of money on the ᴏle with great casualness, as if I was sprinkling the table with ᴏse petals. The look on those women's faces was worth all the ᴏeals I'd missed and all the sulphur my lungs had inhaled. It was ᴏst as I had seen it on the screen of my mind."

The doctor smiled. "The kid was really happy that day, wasn't ᴏ?"

"Yes."

"It all worked out just as he had imagined. Even to the close-up ᴏ your grandmother."

While he pulled down the blinds to block out the glare of the ᴏtting sun, I asked, "Doctor, how long is all this going to last?"

"What?"

"All this digging. When can I expect a clean bill of health?"

"Why, do you still feel sick?"

"Knock it off, Doctor. I'm not exactly a Charles Atlas emotion-ly."

"Thank God," he laughed. "He was just a load of physic muscles. *We* hope to build up emotional muscles."

"So how long is it going to take?"

"I don't know, Tony. Maybe we'll find out you're not sick at a and that I'll have to make you sick enough to be able to exist a sick world. It's not easy to unlock the subconscious. It can tough as hell. In your case, and *because* you are an actor, yo conscious and subconscious are constantly oscillating. In your j as an actor you are always bringing it to the surface. The stror identification with the characters you play often makes you reca painful or joyful experiences.

"As you quoted one day from your friend Oscar Wilde: 'He wl lives more lives than one, more deaths than one must die.'

"You've told me of the pains you went through to play chara ters like Gauguin, Quasimodo, Zapata's brother, Mountain River and the character in *Tchin-Tchin*. It seems to me that there great danger of the actor's using his craft for psychotherapy. The is a danger that he will become self-indulgent, but there is also tl chance that that wonderful magic can happen when the charact and the actor meet. And when it *happens* it must be the mo satisfying moment in the world. It must be like sexual gratific tion."

I had to agree. "I know that if I'm not working well, I *don* enjoy sex. It's only after I've really earned my bread that I fe liberated enough to give myself over to sex."

"Do you often give yourself completely to sex?"

I wanted to be honest with this man. I knew he was trying help me. At times, I had tried to win his approbation and goo will by regaling him with anecdotes. It was like going to a denti or having an operation; you try to make small talk to stave off tl pulling of the tooth. I struggled with his pointed question.

"No," I said finally.

"Why not?"

"I've never found my ideal woman."

"Is it you that hasn't found her, or is it the kid who hasi found her?"

"I don't want to blame the kid for everything. I'm trying learn not to cop out. But I guess it's a combination of both of us

"Do you have an ideal woman in mind?"

"Yes. I know it sounds naïve and it almost embarrasses me to talk about it . . ."

"Tony, we've talked about so many intimate things. What's to embarrass you now?"

"Well, when I was a kid, before I knew about anything, I thought men and women made love by coming together. I mean, some kind of fusion, like there would be this cloud that would envelop them and they'd waft into space, and there would be heavenly music, then this clash of thunder and lightning, not as we know it, but the huge crashing of a thousand cymbals and drums, and the lightning would be multicolored like the Aurora Borealis over the North Pole. To be able to achieve this, I thought the ideal woman had to be a kind of a virginal goddess."

"But after the affair she would no longer be a virgin, would she? Does that mean you'd have to find another virginal goddess?"

"No, as long as she was only mine and no one else existed for her, each time would be like the first time."

"So you never found her?"

"No."

"Why, do you suppose?"

"Because there aren't many goddesses around, and there's certainly a shortage of virgins."

"So you've never really enjoyed sex?"

I burst out laughing. "Let me say that though I haven't found perfection, I've had a hell of a good time looking for it, Doc. Of course I've enjoyed sex. Many is the time I've heard the bells ring and seen a flash or two of lightning. But you asked about perfection. God knows, I've been willing to settle for a good healthy sexual experience, but the kid wants it all — the way he saw it back there."

"And what do you think keeps him from being satisfied?"

"The aftermath. That's when he stands over in the corner and shakes his head. I'd hear him saying, 'No, this is not it. It was good, but not really it.' "

"What was missing?"

"I'd start to see the ghosts."

"What ghosts?"

"The other men in the woman's life, the other men she'd been with, even the imaginary men she might find in the future. He brought them all to me and they stood around gloating that they'd been there before, or would come after. The kid wanted to be number one from time immemorial and beyond eternity. He reminded me of the question that Solomon had asked himself when he was hung up on the kid, Shulamite: 'I shall leave all this unto a man that shall come after me, and who knoweth whether he shall be a wise man or a fool? Yet shall he have rule over all my labor. . . .'

"The kid is always reminding me, even at the times when it's good — and at times it has been very good — that the young shepherd is standing in the wings."

The doctor and I sat quietly for a long time. He no longer looked at the clock. He had his secretary run out for some pastrami sandwiches and pickles, and we began to eat them. He gave me two packets of sugar because he knew I liked my coffee very sweet.

"The kid back there, Tony, what was his sex awakening like? I mean, why is he so demanding? Is it because he experienced that moment in the clouds and wants to recapture it?"

The pastrami tasted good. I liked the spicy taste and the hot mustard.

"I think it's all tied up with religion and that time when he started going to church. I know you've asked me not to analyze myself, but no doubt the organ music and the multi-colored lights of the stained-glass windows are what he is dying to recapture in sex. And I don't have to tell you where he got the 'clouds and virgins' image. Then, his few early brushes with sex were far less satisfying, if not downright disgusting. I mean, like that degenerate cousin of mine showing me his indelicate anus, and the boy jerking off."

"How early was that? How old were you?"

"I was about eight at that time. I was asked to join a gang in somebody's cellar. It was dark and smelled of musty rot. This one big kid — he was about fourteen — took out his huge, black thing that looked like a piece of garden hose and started to play with it. The other kids looked around self-consciously and started to unbutton their pants. I was terrified of not being considered manly so I took out my sad little peter.

"The big kid really had it down to a science. He spit on the

alm of his hand and said, 'All right, the last one to come is a
mother-fucker.'

"I didn't have a very clear idea of what my objective was, but
then the big kid said, 'Go!' and everybody started to pull their
rods. Their hands were going up and down like pistons.

"Suddenly the big kid started to laugh insanely. It scared the
hell out of me. Then I saw this huge stream pour out of the end
of his wang. It looked like a big angry cobra spitting venom. The
whole thing kind of scared me. For a long time I associated sex
with that dank-musk smell.

"Then there was a young tubercular-looking kid, named Alonzo,
that all the bigger kids kind of used as a mascot. I learned later
that they were buggering him. Those young kids they buggered
were known as 'slaves.' But somehow they didn't associate it with
homosexuality. The kids made fun of the only fairy in the neighborhood, because he powdered his face and used rouge. They
didn't associate their physical ambidextrousness with homosexuality. A fuck was a fuck."

"Did you ever try buggering another boy?"

"Jeez, you sound like Kinsey, Doc. I was interviewed by him
once and he asked questions like he took it for granted that everyone had fucked everything — from goats to lizards. But to answer
your question: When we were living on Daly Street we had some
rabbits and I used to have to go out in the fields to gather grass
for them to eat. One afternoon, my cousin went with me — he was
about four years older. While we were gathering the grass he
pulled down his pants. At first I thought he was going to squat
and take a crap; instead he bent over and asked me to shove my
little thing into his behind. But as he bent over I got a good look
at his anus and it disgusted me. It looked all puckered up like a
baboon's ass. I ran away. For days he had me thinking I was some
kind of degenerate because I couldn't corn-hole him."

I wondered what the doctor was writing on his pad. Jeez, maybe
he thought there was something wrong with me too.

"What about when you got older?" he asked.

"Oh, I don't think my experiences were different from anyone
else's. Sure there were a lot of guys that tried to make me when I
started working in the theater. But that's to be expected. There
was one famous director that showed me some dirty postcards,

then made a grab for me. Then there was a movie star I was visiting. He brought out a pair of pajamas and suggested we go to bed together. I wasn't interested, but it never bothered me."

The doctor scratched away. "Your early sex life surprises me," he said.

"Why?"

"Well, you do have a reputation as a Don Juan. That obviously came later. Your early experiences were really rather insignificant, weren't they? And slightly pathetic."

"The one beautiful memory was at the age of twelve when we were living on Fisher Street. There was a beautiful, red-haired lady who lived down the block. It was a shingled cottage, always well kept, and by far the richest-looking house in the district. Her husband was a railroad man and he was always busy.

"She often used to call out to me, 'Hi there, good-looking.'

"I think of her now as looking like a Renoir painting. Soft pink hues. Lush and full. I don't suppose she could have been more than twenty-four or twenty-five.

"One night, when I went outside, I saw the light come on in her bedroom. It was a hot night and the window was open. I saw her come into the bedroom, rubbing herself with a towel. Her body was still glistening from the bath.

"She sat on the side of the bed and wiped her toes very carefully. I saw her naked breasts and her lovely navel. She leaned back and stretched out on the bed.

"Her body was facing away from me but I could see her hand rub her thigh. Her eyes were closed. She spread her legs slowly and her hand disappeared between her thighs.

"Soon I hear her moaning. It was such a lovely, tentative sound, like the sound of a cello in the distance. Then the music of her sighs started to come faster. Her lips were parted with such yearning. They moved as if whispering to someone.

"Then I saw her body arch, and she let out a slight scream. I was too young to know what was going on, but I felt the wetness start to run down my legs.

"For weeks afterwards I relived that vision. I think it was around that time that I became afraid my grandmother would see the stains on the bed, so I became an expert at taking a handke chief to bed with me. It was a hell of a substitute for that Renoir redhead!

"Actually, I had become aware of women at the age of six."

"Six!"

"Yeah," I laughed. "I was precocious. Some friend of my mother's was visiting one afternoon and she was sitting on the edge of the bed. I was playing catch with a red ball and it rolled under the bed.

"I went down after it. As I looked up I saw the woman's milky thighs. I longed to touch them. My little peter got hard and I stayed under the bed until it went back to normal."

"At six?"

"Oh, come on, Doctor. I've seen my sons have erections at three. We're Latins, don't forget.

"But outside of showing a girl-cousin my penis through a knot-hole in the fence at the age of twelve or thirteen, I had no real sex experience until I was fourteen.

"We had had a picnic out at Seal Beach. One of the few times I went out with Frank Bowles, who was then courting my mother. A lot of other people were there.

"I hadn't really wanted to go, but my grandmother had had a long talk with me and said that if anyone was to resent another man in my mother's life it was she, since it was *her* son who had been my mother's husband. She said that my mother had every right to have another husband. After all, she was young and Frank could help her support us. I'd finally agreed to go along to the beach since my sister had counted on it for weeks. So off we went.

"My sister and I spent most of the day playing in the ocean. There were a lot of other kids that belonged to Frank's friends. Among them was this big girl. She was seventeen or eighteen years old. Earlier in the day she had asked me how old I was and I had lied. I was five feet ten at the time so I could get away with saying that I was eighteen too. A couple of times, while riding the waves, I came into contact with her wet body. I pretended to be swimming and touched her breasts and thighs. After the sun went down, a big bonfire was built and people started eating from the huge picnic baskets they'd brought. This was still Prohibition time but everybody was making homemade beer in their homes, so soon those great big tubs came out filled with bottles of homemade beer. It was then that someone proposed a toast to Frank and my mother and their wedding, and I started to get drunk. After a few bottles, my head started to reel. It scared me to feel the earth spinning and not being able to control it. Suddenly, the girl was standing beside me.

" 'You feel sick, Tony?'

" 'Man, I just feel drunk. I want to sober up.'

" 'Why don't you lie down for a while?'

"I said I couldn't because the earth kept going around and it made me sick. She took me by the hand and led me down the shoreline. We walked for about a quarter of a mile. I started to feel better. In the distance I could see the bonfire going and the silhouettes of the people. I could hear the laughter and the singing.

" 'Do you feel better, Tony?'

" 'Yeah.'

" 'Come on, lie down.'

"I fell down on the warm sand. I looked up at the sky and it was no longer reeling. The girl sat beside me quietly. Neither of us said a word. The beer and the warmth of the sand lulled me to sleep. When I awoke, I had the strangest sensation. I felt someone licking my penis. It was the girl. She took me into her warm mouth with great tenderness. I was afraid that if I moved, it would break the spell and embarrass her. I pretended to be asleep. Soon my penis was hard and she went at it with more relish. I erupted in her mouth. I tried to do it as quietly and unobtrusively as possible, still feigning sleep. She wiped me clean and put me back into my pants. She sat there beside me. After a while I pretended to wake up.

" 'Did you sleep well?' she asked.

" 'Fine. How long have I been asleep?'

" 'Oh, about a half an hour.' "

"Neither of us acknowledged what had happened. After a while we walked back and joined the group. I never saw that girl again. But I dreamt of her often. She had made love to *me*. She had found me desirable and asked for nothing in return. She had found *me* an object of *love*."

# 11

"I HAVE A NOTE HERE to remind you to tell me about the mattress factory." The doctor laughed as he began the next session. "I suppose your stories about your early sex life brought to mind mattresses." I joined in the laughter.

"That was my senior year at Belvedere Junior High. I was fifteen years old and a lot of my friends had dropped out of school, going to the Piscas, etcetera, to help support the family. Though I had started to earn a few bucks playing the saxophone with a small orchestra away from the temple, my knocking Rudy Vallee out of the box was a hell of a long time away. Someone said that a new factory was opening up at Downey and they were looking for help. I went and applied. They asked me how old I was and I said eighteen. Nobody questioned it. The foreman, an American kid about twenty years old, took me down to my cubbyhole and showed me what I was suppose to do. There was a machine at the end of the assembly line that made the goddamndest racket as it spit out the steel springs. They fell onto a big rubber conveyor belt. As the springs came down the fan belt, they were still hot. The small ends were sharp as needles. You had to insert your forefinger into the spring, squeeze it into a sideboard against your body, then insert it into these long steel rods. When the rod was full, you inserted it into sewn sections of burlap. You would pull the pin and release the springs, which would then be sewn in place by the woman opposite you. If you didn't work fast the springs would pile up at the end and they'd become all tangled up, and the machine would have to be turned off. There were about ten assembly lines working, besides the women who followed behind tying up the springs in place. It wasn't complicated once you got the swing of it, except that after an hour or so your hands began to cramp up from squeezing the springs, and your fingers were bleeding from the sharp ends. We were all paid by piecework, so you had to move like hell to make fifteen or sixteen dollars a week. I became pretty good at it. It was a matter of rhythm, and by the end of the second week I was making seventeen and eighteen dollars.

"My mother, at first, had been furious at my quitting school, but I threatened to leave home if she insisted I go back. The truant officer had started coming around the house wanting to know why I wasn't at school. My grandmother told him I was out of town visiting a sick relative. Before I left for work each morning I'd send her out to see if the truant officer was hanging around. I managed to avoid him for two months. Most of the workers at the factory were Mexican, and the American kid who was foreman had a tough time telling them what to do. He invariably asked me to translate. The boss came in one day and saw this. He walked over to us and said, 'All right, Tony, from now on you become the floor foreman and you, Jim, go and work in the office.'

"The workers were glad about my promotion because they knew that I was one of them: I knew how tough the work was and would be more lenient. Sometimes when the springs started to bunch up I'd grab a rod and help the boys on the assembly line. I really enjoyed the job, the smell of the burlap, the sound of that machine, the lunch break when the workers would gab with me. Also my paycheck had been raised to twenty dollars a week. I was making only three dollars less than my mother. I knew now that I could support my grandmother and sister, if necessary, and we wouldn't have to take any shit from Frank Bowles.

"One Friday afternoon, as I was walking down the alleyway between the assembly lines, I felt a heavy hand on my shoulder. When I turned around I knew who it was. That sneaky face could belong to none other than the truant officer. My employees must have been surprised to see their foreman being dragged off to school by the scruff of his neck. I wish I could have made a more dignified exit.

"Having lost my job at the factory I desperately looked around for something to take its place. I refused to accept help from Frank or Mama.

"On Saturday morning I'd go with Sidney and Willy to the market down on Central Avenue and help unload the trucks

e'd make a dollar a day. A far cry from the twenty dollars a
eek I'd been making at the factory.

"One day I ran into a kid named Buddy, whom I hadn't seen
r some time. He was wearing a flashy new suit and two-toned
oes. I asked him if he'd pulled a job. He told me he was making
enty-five dollars a night.

" 'Doing what?' I gasped, hoping to get a hot tip.

" 'Boxing,' he said, throwing a fast jab that missed me by a
isker.

"Of course, I thought to myself, what an idiot I'd been. Demp-
y and Gene Tunney had become millionaires from one fight. I
iftly saw myself as the champion of the world, with a deadly
ght cross. Buddy gave me an address of a man who booked
okers.

"Next day, I went to Spring Street and waited in a long line of
piring pugilists to be interviewed by a big heavy-set man sitting
hind a desk. The walls were covered with idols of mine — News-
y Brown, Mushy Callahan, Bert Colima, Dynamite Jackson,
entleman Gen del Monte, Tunney, Dempsey. I couldn't wait till
y picture would grace the wall. I knew exactly the kind of pose
1 assume: my chin tucked into my left shoulder and my dynamic
ght cocked for the knockout blow. I'd wear a sneering smile, but
y eyes would be cold and hard.

"The man asked me what weight I fought under. I said 'Welter-
eight.' He gave me a slip of paper. 'Give this to the man out
ont.' I was booked to fight in Gardena in a four rounder. The
inner was to get five dollars, the loser three. Buddy took me un-
r his wing. I did two miles of roadwork at the crack of dawn
ound Echo Park Lake. He taught me how to bob and weave. I
as tall for my age, but weighed only a hundred and forty-five
ounds. As the great night approached, I began to feel I could use
hell of a lot more time preparing. Buddy kept assuring me he'd
 in my corner when I made my debut, so I felt better. He and I
de the red streetcar to Gardena, where the businessmen were
ll at dinner. They were all having a hell of a time. As I crossed
e hall toward the dressing rooms I heard some man say, 'Kid,
m betting on you.' I nodded, reassuring him he could rest easy,
s money was riding on the future champion of the world. Buddy
d brought his fighting togs for me to use. Now that it was about

to happen I began to feel fear as I had never known it in my li
Not so much of being hurt as of being ridiculous in front of
those men. Several other guys came into the dressing room a
changed. Very little was said. I figured they were all going throu
the same qualms I was having.

"Buddy told me to warm up. He held his hands up for me
hit. My own were heavily bandaged. Then I put on the glov
They were much heavier than I had anticipated. I was to go on
the third bout.

"Someone came into the room and told me the first fight h
ended in a knockout, and the second wasn't going to last long. V
went to the door to see how the fight was coming along. A t
dark stringy kid was reeling under the punishment a husky blo
boy was dealing out. Some men were yelling: 'Kill the greezer.'
the belly, hit the Mexican in the belly.' The tall kid dropped st
as a board from a looping right. He didn't stir as the refer
counted him out. His handlers rushed into the ring and carri
him through the aisles to a dressing room.

"Buddy pushed me toward the ring. Suddenly, I was under t
glare of the overhead lights. Buddy was rubbing my back as t
referee called the other kid and me to the center of the ring f
instructions. I barely heard what was said. I kept looking at t
boy I was going to fight. He never looked at me. He kept stari
at the floor. It was only when the bell rang for the fight to beg
that I saw the fear in his eyes.

"Though I had run miles training for the fight, I never kn
how long twelve minutes of fighting can be. By the end of t
fourth round I could barely lift my hands. I can't say it was t
most exciting fight in the annals of fisticuffs, but we both earn
our money. Buddy had done a good job of teaching me how
bob and weave and throw a jab. I was awarded the decision.

"It was a happy ride back home that night on the streetcar. V
had been fed well by some men who had bet on me. So I was
my way to fame and fortune. I could see myself as a contender f
the title, with a big roadster full of blonds.

"After that first night I fought quite regularly. Along about t
eighth or ninth fight, I was booked to meet a red-headed kid w
was making a name for himself. He was chunky, with arms li
hams. When we met in the center of the ring I could see hate

My maternal grandmother. She is holding my sister Stella.

This is Frank Quinn 1—the husband of Sabina—my Irish grandfather
Cork, Ireland.

My paternal grandmother, Sabina.

My father Frank (or Francisco) at the age of 26.

My mother with Stella, 2 years old, and me, 4 years old.

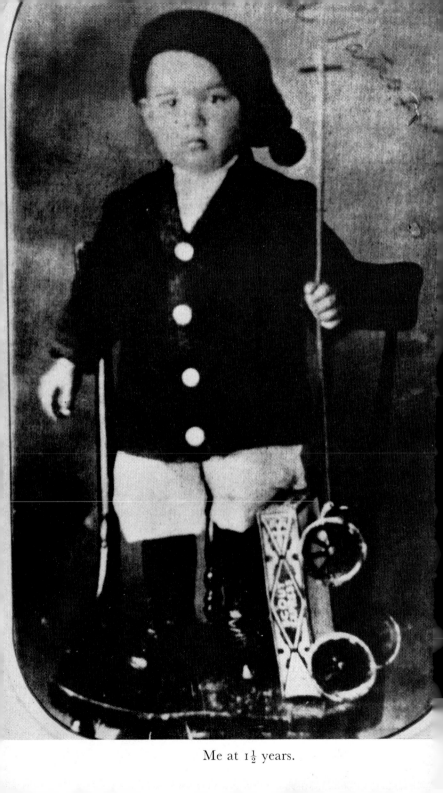

Me at 1½ years.

Me at $4\frac{1}{2}$ years with my sister, $2\frac{1}{2}$ years.

As a boy at the age of 11 or 12 years.

Wearing my glee club sweater at the age of 14.

left, at the age of 22.
top, At 20.
bottom, in my first film, a documentary

At the age of 22.

is eyes. All the other guys had tried to scare me by looking mean
nd tough, but I somehow knew it was all an act. This guy really
nade me feel he hated me, that he would have killed me with no
ompunction. When the bell rang I knew I was in for a bad night.
uddy had insisted I run backward a half a mile every morning,
n exercise I put to good use that night.

"During the first round, the red-headed kid threw a left hook
t my kidney and I blocked the punch with my right, hurting it.
or the rest of the round I wasn't able to lift it. I fought to sur-
ive. Buddy used to tell me I had style, that I looked good in the
ing. That particular night I fought very well, despite a bruised
ight, and beat the boy. After the fight a man came in to the little
ressing room and said that he'd been watching me. He thought I
uld be great. 'How old are you?' I was sixteen at the time, but I
ed and said I was eighteen, the minimum legal age for fighting
t smokers.

"He said, 'Well, if you let me train you, I promise to make you
champion.' I said that was fine. 'How many smokers have you
ught?' I lied. I told him a dozen. 'All right, kid, from now on
e don't fight any smokers; we don't do any of this. Do you need
oney?' I nodded.

" 'All right, I'm going to give you ten dollars a week. You don't
ave to fight yet, but you have to train. You fight when I tell you
fight.' I said, 'Fine, all right. But excuse me, who are you?'

" 'I'm Jim Foster.'

"Well, it was like saying to me, 'I'm the President of the United
tates' because he was well known at that time as a star manager.
Vhen he said he wanted to handle me, it was almost like a guaran-
e that I would become a champion.

"I went home and told all the kids. Buddy was impressed,
ough he was a much better fighter than I was. He said, 'All
ight, I'll train with you.' We used to get up in the morning, put
n heavy sweaters, sweat clothes, and go out and run two or three
iles around Echo Park. Then we would shadowbox. When I
ame home, I'd have a big breakfast and a nap. I was living like
real boxer. In the afternoon after school, which I attended peri-
dically, I would meet Buddy at a Main Street gym, where I saw
e big stars, Sandy Casanova, Newsboy Brown, Mushy Callahan
nd others.

"I seldom saw Mr. Foster. He had made arrangements for me to get into the gym, and was paying the fees. And people there were very impressed. I could hear them whisper, 'That's one of Foster's boys.'

"He appointed a trainer who supervised me, correcting my faults. Among others, I had developed a very strong left hand at the expense of my right.

"Eventually, Jim sent me out to fight. In those days they had boxing rings in every little town — Anaheim, Long Beach, Downey, Watts, all along the periphery of Los Angeles. Usually, managers kept thirty per cent of whatever you made, but I was making so little that Jim would give me all my money. I was getting anywhere from twenty to thirty dollars a fight.

"There are different categories on boxing cards: the semi-windup, the preliminaries, and the headliners. I was usually third or fourth on the list, already heading for some kind of stardom. I won all my fights.

"During this period, Primo Carnera became champion of the world, and he came to train around Echo Park. They hired a lot of us boys, including Buddy and myself, to box with him. He was a big, slow, lumbering man and they wanted to make him faster, but even then it was pretty well known that he wasn't a very good fighter, because he was so slow. But he was such a sweet man, the poor soul, one of the kindest men I have ever met in my life.

"They hired us to go out and train with him and paid us five dollars for about five minutes. I kiddingly say that I fought with Primo Carnera; actually, it was no more than shadowboxing. We were very young and I don't think he really tried to hit us; he weighed about 230 or 240 pounds, one hundred more than any of us. It was like getting into the ring with a big bull who didn't have any horns. It was an experience.

"Jim selected the fighters I was to meet, boys he thought wouldn't be too tough on me, and when I'd had about thirteen or fourteen fights he said he was going to get me a semi-windup. That's like saying to an actor, 'I'm going to give you the second lead in a picture.' The only drawback was that the fight was in Watts, and there were certain neighborhoods that we hated to go to because the kids were very tough. Watts had the toughest.

"I went out there and I fought, and I was very lucky; I beat the

oy and had no trouble. I had made good on my first semi-
windup, and the trainer congratulated me. I made a lot of money
that day, fifty dollars. So I became a big guy in the neighborhood,
and, of course, all my friends were proud of me.

"Then I had another preliminary fight, this one in Downey,
and I won that. And finally the trainer said, 'Well, Tony. Kid, I
think you're ready. We're going to get you a good boy to fight,
then we'll talk about maybe going some place outside of Los
Angeles, San Francisco or maybe San Diego, and you can really
start making a reputation for yourself.'

"They got me a fight in Long Beach. It was a semi-windup
against a black boy. The stadium was full. As I was waiting in the
dressing room, Buddy was there rubbing my shoulders, and all my
pals showed up, Willy and Sidney and everybody, and it was like
I was making the big time, like I was suddenly appearing on
Broadway. Of course, I was nervous as hell, you were always
nervous before a fight.

"Finally, somebody called, 'All right, you're on, kid!' and I put
on the robe my grandmother had made for me — made specifi-
cally to Bud's specifications. My grandmother wasn't very much
for my boxing, but I was bringing money into the house and she
never saw me getting hurt, so I had been able to convince her that
it was all right. I had been very lucky up until then. I had never
been scratched or marked very much. Most of the boys of my age
had broken noses or teeth, or cauliflower ears. But I had been
lucky. Of course, at the smokers we'd fought with bigger gloves,
not with eight-ounce gloves as you did in the semi-windups.

"So I was walking down the aisle and suddenly people started
calling my name. Most kids at that time chose some kind of fighting name. I didn't. I always liked the name Tony Quinn. It
meant something to me and I never wanted to change it.

"As I climbed into the ring my friends started applauding and
yelling and the crowd decided it liked me. I must have learned
some kind of showmanship from Aimee Semple McPherson. When
the black boy I was to fight walked up the aisle, they started
booing. Sometimes audiences will do that in a fight and it is supposed to be good-natured fun, but I always thought there was
something sad about it. I felt sorry for the boy. As he climbed into
the ring, I heard somebody say, 'Hey, Smoky, this kid's going to

kill you.' Smoky meant Negro, and not in a complimentary way
I didn't like it. My friend Buddy was black, too, and there in the
ring with me as my second; he was the guy that would hand me
the water to gargle between rounds. He was rubbing a towel on
me and I was embarrassed that Buddy had heard it.

"The referee called us together to give us instructions. You hear
the same goddamned instructions every time you fight; it's a silly
ridiculous ritual: 'All right, boys, I want a good fight — keep it
clean. When I touch you on the elbow, that means break. Don'
hit in the clinches . . . et cetera.' Nobody is listening. Every
body is worrying about his own problems. You're sizing up the
other boy and you try to avoid his eyes. But I couldn't avoid this
boy's eyes; and as I looked up he was gazing at me, as if to say
'What's going to happen?' There was something in the boy's eye
that I liked.

"We went back to our corners and Buddy put in my mouth
piece. It was really a used mouthpiece of his. The way he put it in
my mouth, the way he looked at me, I felt like saying, 'Gee, how
can I fight one of your people, Buddy?' God only knows what he
was thinking.

"Suddenly the bell rang and the boy came right at me. By that
time, I had learned to be kind of a fancy dancer and I sidestepped
shot a left at him that connected, feinted a right cross, and hit him
a left in the stomach. The boy was rather surprised at my speed
He hit me a couple of times and got me over in a corner, but
had learned a lot of tricks from Buddy. I took the boy's elbow and
pushed him away and hit him with a right cross. I had good con
centration. The fight now was really fun. I had fought boys who
weren't that good, but this boy was classy, so I had to show my
best.

"The first round went well. In the second I could do almost
anything I wanted and I heard people saying, 'Knock him out
Knock him out!' I feinted with the right, the boy would drop his
hand, and I'd throw in the hook; but I could only fight well with
my left hand. I won the second round too. Buddy said to me
'Come on, step up the fight!' I said, 'What's the difference, Buddy
I can beat him. It's a six-round fight, why knock him out?' He
said, 'You're fighting, that's why.'

"In the fourth round, I felt so comfortable that I thought

ould really beat the boy any time I wanted. I got a little careless. Suddenly he caught me with a right, and I had never felt a punch as strong. The fact that I could be hit, that I could be stunned, shocked me. I found myself against the ropes. The stadium was going around and all I saw was this form come up. I crouched down and covered my head. He hit me with a left hook and miraculously everything cleared. He could probably have knocked me out but the fact that he hit me on the other side of the head kind of stabilized me. I was back in focus, able to finish the round. I was never so happy to hear the bell in my life, because I was really in trouble.

"When I went back to the corner, Buddy was furious because I hadn't followed up my advantage in the beginning of the round and had let the boy catch me. The fifth round was coming up. Buddy said, 'All right, go out and get him.' I must admit I felt that if I didn't get the boy now he was going to get me. Because I'd won the first four rounds, I still had a slight advantage. I was wary now, more careful of the boy's right hand. The crowd was urging me to come back, but I was still in a partial daze from his right.

"Almost a minute into the fifth round, I feinted with a right and caught the boy with a hard left. His guard went down and I kept hitting him with my left. I threw a right at his stomach, he went down, I hit him again with a left hook, and he began to reel. I heard these people near the apron of the ring chant, 'Come on, kill the nigger!'

"I remembered a year before when I had had a fight at school and I hadn't been able to hit the boy because they had been calling him a Jew. Here they were begging me to 'kill the nigger.' I didn't follow up my advantage. The boy straightened up and started moving away. I just kept jabbing him. I could hear Buddy calling to me, saying, 'Throw the right!' The boy's guard was down and I saw his jaw unprotected. I knew that if I threw the right I could nail him, but I felt blocked. I couldn't throw my right. I kept jabbing. The bell rang, we went back to our corners, and again Buddy bawled me out.

"I couldn't say to him that I couldn't hit the boy because of what the crowd was yelling. I told him not to worry, that I was winning by a big margin.

"The bell for the sixth round came up. The crowd had less interest in me because I hadn't thrown a right hand in the round before. They seemed to be with the black boy now. I heard somebody yell, "Come on, hit the Mexican, he's yellow!' I turned for a second to see who had been talking when a hammer blow hit me on the right side of my jaw. It felt like my jaw had cracked; everything started reeling. I had become a piece of wood. I couldn't move my jaw and I couldn't stand up and I couldn't fall down. I felt a hard blow on my stomach. I tried to get against the ropes but my legs were paralyzed. Next thing I knew, I was on the canvas, surprised as hell. I heard the referee count. At the count of seven I tried to get up. I got up on one knee . . . at nine, I started to get off my knee . . . and I collapsed. I just couldn't make it. That was the first time I was ever knocked out in the ring.

"Buddy came and picked me up. He sat me in the corner, washed my face with cold water, sprinkled some water over my head, and I came to. I had no more than a slight headache. I wasn't too hurt at having lost. I realized that I had paid for one moment of carelessness, but I didn't feel I had put on a bad fight.

"When I got back to the dressing room, which we shared with all the other fighters, Jim Foster walked in. I looked up sheepishly as if to say, 'Well, it's no disgrace, the best fighters in the world get knocked out.' But he was furious at me.

" 'Why didn't you throw that right in the fifth round?'

" 'Well, I didn't have a chance.'

" 'The boy was wide open. You had him reeling. Why didn't you throw a right?'

" 'I thought he was just faking and trying to suck me in. Look, get me another fight with him and I promise you I'll beat him.'

" 'Not only will I not get you another fight with him, but if I ever see you in the ring again, I, myself, will climb up and beat the hell out of you.'

"I was surprised by the tone in his voice. He sounded like an angry father reprimanding a son he loves very much.

" 'I never want to see you in the ring again. You're not a killer and you don't belong in this game unless you're a killer.'

"On the way home I said to Buddy, who had witnessed the scene with Foster, 'Gee, Bud, what do you think?'

"And Bud said, 'I think Jim's right. I don't think you should fight.'

"I knew he was right. I had no killer instinct, I would never make a great fighter.

"Although I liked the glamorous part of boxing, the performance part of it, I didn't like the competitiveness. I liked the drama, those bright lights, the kind of strangely festive atmosphere in the audience, and the comradeship with the guys. I hated the dressing room with its odors of rubbing alcohol, iodine, wet leather, cheap soap and dirty, stained towels. I hated the tawdriness behind the scenes, all those sweating bodies, the frantic efforts to achieve something with your fists.

"That night my grandmother said she was happy about what had happened. She thought it was for the best, and she had been praying for some months that I would stop. I think we both knew, deep down, that it was just a stopgap to get some money.

"A few days later, I ran into Baby Ariesmendi, one of the world's greatest fighters. He had started fighting just to strengthen his legs, because he'd been afflicted with polio, and ended up becoming the champion of the world in his class.

"The week before, I had seen him in a fight with one of the top boxers of his era, Lew Ambers. In the seventh round, Ambers had caught Baby against the ropes.

"I said to him, 'Baby, I saw that fight between you and Lew Ambers, and in the seventh round he hit you hard. Did he hurt you?'

"It was a long time before he answered. 'Tony, everybody hurts you.'"

# 12

So you gave up boxing?" said the doctor.

"Yes, and I was running out of fast moneymaking schemes. Besides, the last scheme had hurt. I don't mean emotionally, because

I agreed with Mr. Foster the next day when I found myself peeing blood from the blow to my kidney in the sixth round.

"Willy and Sidney had made a few fast bucks entering dance contests.

"The winner would usually get a cup, which you could always pawn or sell back to the management for five dollars. There was a dance hall down on Olive and Fifth that was very fancy — you had to wear a tie there. And then there was one down at Ocean Park, and another place called the Moonlight Dance Hall in East Los Angeles. We decided to tour the whole circuit, entering contests to try and make some money.

"We all went into training for the big event. Since I was the only one who had a radio, the gang would gather at my house every night. The living room became our rehearsal hall.

"We made a pact that we would be a team. Willy, of the swivel hips, would be our rumba representative; Sidney, with his short piston legs, would be the fox-trot expert; Dan, with his wavy hair was perfect for the Viennese waltz; and I, with my pomaded black hair, would be their representative in the tango. My sister stood in for all our future partners.

"At school I could hardly keep my mind on the goal of the moment, being a great architect. The thought of being under the spotlight dancing with some vision of loveliness, with thousands of eyes on my every move, was far more exciting than calculating the stress on a steel beam. I was willing to forego Doric and Corinthian columns in order to be another Rudolph Valentino. I read that to dance the tango well, you should move as if you had a knife in your teeth. My grandmother's butcher knife served the purpose as I stalked about the living room every night.

"We gave the team a month to prepare for the big onslaught of the dance circuit. At our dress rehearsal, Dan, Willy and Sidney arrived in their Sunday clothes. My sister put on her best dress and I was all talcumed and greased down. I had borrowed one of Frank Bowles' floor-polishing machines and our rough floor was like glass.

"Willy exhibited his rumba. He would have put Marilyn Monroe to shame with the subtle movement of his hips. When he and my sister finished, we knew we had a great contender. Next Sidney did his fox-trot. We couldn't vouch for the grace of his teps, but his feet moved with such velocity we were afraid he'd reak through the floor. Dan was a picture of grace and beauty as e pirouetted about the room, swinging my sister. The Archduke f Austria could have learned a point or two from him. Next came ly turn. I swept my sister into my arms as I had seen Valentino o with Vilma Banky. When we finished, my grandmother's ap-lause was vigorous. We were all excited. We were ready.

"Then came the big discussion of shoes. We all wore regular loes. They wouldn't do. A great team like ours could dance in othing less than patent leather. We were disconsolate, since one of us could afford patent-leather shoes. But Sidney had an lea. We would buy one pair and share them among us! Sidney sed an eight, Dan a nine and a half, Willy an eight and a half, nd I a ten. So we settled on a pair of tens that would serve us all, lore or less.

"Our first contest was at the Moonlight Dance Hall, an old omping ground of Belvedere. None of us had girl friends so we ad to hope that the wallflowers would be good dancers. We were ) learn that, invariably, the uglier a girl was the better she anced. Beautiful women seemed to think it was enough to let you old them in your arms. Ugly women really put themselves out to e accepted.

"Unfortunately, we hadn't taken into consideration that our utines would have to be adjusted to pickup partners. The only ne who was unperturbed was Sidney. He managed to jump, omp and hop to his own rhythm, using a partner only as a eographical reference point. I ended up with an old schoolmate ho had been in my home-room class. She had always had bad :in, and the years had not been kind to her acne.

"The fox-trot contest was announced; Sidney was to be the first ) wear the well-vaselined shoes. We wished him well as the music .arted.

"The judges walked around among the jumping dervishes, tap-ing on the shoulder the ones to be eliminated. Finally, it was idney and his girl and three other couples. We were cheering im on, but he got the finger and was eliminated. Still, one of our oys had come in fourth on our first time out!

"Sidney rushed off the floor and exchanged shoes with Willy, ho was to be next in the rumba. Willy came in third! In the

waltz, Dan came in second. His prize would be five dollars. W
were in the money!

"I was beginning to worry about my pimply partner. I won
dered if she could possibly compare with my sister. I had begge
my grandmother to let my sister come with me; I knew that wit
her I could sweep the field, but my grandmother was keeping m
sister for better things.

"I squeezed into the shoes, which pinched a bit, and led m
partner out for the big event. The music started. The pimply gir
got stage fright and started to pull away.

" 'I can't tango.'

" 'Why did you accept the invitation, then?'

" 'I wanted to dance with you.'

" 'But I came here to dance in the contest. I'm here on busines
Who the hell wants to dance for pleasure?'

"The poor girl ran away in tears.

"I turned in panic. The music was starting. I asked the first gir
I saw if she would dance with me. It wasn't until I stepped ou
under the twirling lights that I saw she was old enough to be m
grandmother.

"Once I put my arms around her sweaty back and went int
my adagio, I knew I was involved in a disaster. The woman ha
learned to dance with Montezuma. She did a war dance while
tried to imitate Valentino. Fate was with me, however, and w
were tapped early in the conflict. I thanked the lady for the wres
ling match and went back to meet my friends.

"They were kind and commiserated with me.

"We all waited around while Dan was given his prize — fiv
dollars — then we went to an all-night beanery and celebrated b
eating ourselves sick.

"One night a few weeks later, at the Santa Monica Pier bal
room, I saw a tall, willowy girl who I knew would be great fo
the tango. She walked like a queen — anyway, a princess — an
she was wearing a long dress, which helped. It would look goo
when we did our stuff.

"She was sitting with a couple of girls. I started to go up to he
but I'd never approached such a classy lady before. What if sh
said no? So I ran back to Danny. 'Hey, I don't know how to as
her.'

" 'Come on,' he said. 'I'll ask her for you.'

"His approach was very smooth. He went over and introduced himself. I thought he was a man of great worldliness — he had savoir faire. He bowed very courteously, a low bow. Everybody, no doubt, said, 'Who's this nut; who's this nut bowing?' In those days, bowing, mind you! He said, 'My friend has been observing you.' He used very big words. To overcome his complex about being Mexican and ignorant, he used to read books and he always used enormous words. Here he was, sixteen years old, talking to a girl, saying, 'My friend has been observing your terpsichorean ability. He finds that you dance, er . . . deliciously and would be very grateful if you would do him the high honor of entering the tango contest with him. May I present my friend, Anthony Quinn.'

"This girl was taken aback by this speech. She got up and shook hands, while the others at the table giggled.

" 'Well, I'm not a very good tango dancer,' she said softly.

"I said, 'I'm sure you are. I've watched you and I would like to enter the contest with you.'

" 'Fine, all right — nobody's asked me, yet.'

"As I started to walk away, I said as dashingly as I could, 'When the tango comes up, I will ask for you, if you don't mind.'

" 'Fine,' she said. 'But look, kid, don't you think we ought to rehearse or something?'

"I looked over the huge hall. There must have been at least a thousand people dancing, and not only kids. At that time, coming there was a kind of snobbish thing to do and many of the Hollywood people used to show up, famous directors and movie stars, to watch the dancing. For them it was like slumming.

"As we went out on the floor it occurred to me that I really had only danced with my sister and with the old bat who was my Waterloo. I had never danced with a girl before. When I got on the floor, feeling this girl, this tall, pretty girl, the smell of her, it was heady and romantic. The ceiling had lights that twinkled, and to me it was very romantic: this delightful thing in my arms; outside, the ocean lapping against the pier.

"We found out we danced quite well together. I learned that she was twenty-four years old. I was going around the floor with a really sophisticated lady!

"I fell in love.

"'Then came the contest. The tango was called. I excused my self and made a mad rush and put on *the* shoes. I led the young lady to the floor. The music started. I guess there must have been about a hundred couples dancing. And this man was moving around. When he would put his hand on someone's shoulder they stepped out, eliminated. I saw him approaching us and thought, I'm with this girl and they're going to throw me off the floor.

"He passed by us. He tapped another couple. Oh, the relief. Finally, there were about twelve couples left. The band started up once more. Now that I had survived the first three rounds I started doing fancy steps. The girl followed beautifully. I would lift and twirl her around and we would dip down to the floor and come up slowly.

"The man came around and I thought, this time we're going to get it. Again, the music stopped and we'd been left on the floor. Now there were three couples. We were under the spotlight. I loved it. I was someone; every move I made counted, everything that I did was important.

"The crowd applauded as the spotlight settled on each couple. My team whistled and stamped when it hit us. We were given the gold cup. As I accepted the cup, I reminded myself to smile like a winner.

"As I led the girl back to her table I asked her where she lived. Not far from where I lived, it turned out. I asked her if she had a way home. She said no.

"The guys were all very impressed with this beautiful, sophisticated twenty-four-year-old in her diaphanous dress. The young lady showed great class when she didn't complain about riding home with us in the pickup truck Sidney had borrowed from his father.

"I took her up to the door and said, 'Good-night — I'll see you next Saturday, maybe.'

" 'Aren't you coming in?' she asked.

"It was a long way home and already around twelve-thirty and I wasn't used to being this late. My grandmother always insisted I be back by eleven. But I couldn't say no. It didn't seem the sophisticated thing to do.

" 'Let's have a nightcap,' she said invitingly.

"I went down to the boys and said, 'Look, fellas, she's invited me to have a drink.'

"They all made obscene signs as they drove off.

"I went back into the apartment. I had never seen such luxury. I estimated quickly that she probably paid about twenty-five dollars a month for it. There were Kewpie dolls all over the place, soft red lights, and a phonograph that you wound up.

"She murmured, 'Do you mind if I get into something comfortable . . . ?' Wow! Those were exactly the words that Joan Crawford said in pictures. I was in the big leagues now.

"She came out of the bedroom in a robe you could see right through. She complimented me on my dancing and poured me a drink that started the rockets in my head. Before I knew it, I found myself in bed and she was undoing my trousers. Then there I was, lying naked, and I felt so embarrassed because I had an erection, and I thought, my gosh! She's going to see it and think I'm a dirty fella!

"Then she took off her clothes and got into bed with me. I thought, poor girl, she's probably tired and I should let her go to sleep. I tried not to disturb her. But I didn't know what to do with myself. She moaned a little and turned over; her hand fell across my chest, so I couldn't get up. Her hand just kept going on down. . . . Oh my God, I hope she doesn't touch it, because she's going to feel it's hard. What will she think of me? I'd told the girl I was twenty-two but I was only sixteen and didn't have much hair down there. She was feeling around. Oh God, now she's going to know everything about me. I drew in my breath, thinking she would probably pull her hand away. I was becoming more sober by the moment. To my amazement, she kept her hand there. I thought, she must be asleep — she doesn't know what she's doing.

"Pretty soon, she rolled over on top of me and started rubbing herself against me, and I thought, oh . . . oh, is that the way it's done? Poor girl, she's probably drunk too much and tomorrow she's going to hate me for it.

"But I was a gentleman, and I said hesitantly, 'May I?'

"She whispered, 'Please . . .' — and my first affair happened.

"The girl was wild. My conception of sex up to that moment was that there were pink clouds, soft music, that you touched somebody and got this feeling of floating in space. To me it had nothing to do with moaning and groaning like animals. I didn't know whether to be revolted by all the sounds she was making. I didn't know whether I liked it or not. I thought, am I hurting her?

"She rolled over on her back and pulled me on top of her. She was doing all the work, while I was busy trying to analyze the strange grunts and moans. It didn't occur to me that she was enjoying it.

"Finally, she let out a long frightening scream and we both burst. I looked down and thought, oh my God, what have I done? I've done a terrible thing! To me it wasn't related to love at all. I disentangled myself and pulled away. I got out of bed and dressed. All this time she was still moaning. I thought, my God, if she wakes up and finds me here, she may call the police, she may start yelling and accuse me of rape. I went out of the house and ran all the way home.

"Of course my grandmother was waiting for me. She was furious. It was now about one-thirty or two in the morning. She smelled the liquor on my breath and started slapping me. I had just been making love to this sophisticated girl, and here was my grandmother spanking me, sending me to bed like a teen-ager, which I was.

"While she was undressing me, she said, 'You're drunk. I knew that you and those boys would get into trouble.'

"I tried to tell her that we'd won the contest and been out celebrating, but it didn't impress her at all. And then she saw my shorts; they were still wet.

" 'What have you been doing?' she said, suspiciously.

" 'What?' I asked, pretending innocence.

" 'Why are your shorts wet?'

" 'Because I was perspiring, because I was dancing,' I said, heading for the bathroom.

" 'You take those shorts off. Let me see.'

" 'No!'

" 'Let me see.' And she pulled down my shorts. She took hold of my thing and saw that it was still wet.

" 'Who have you been with?'

" 'Nobody,' I said. 'Maybe I've got a cold or something.'

"Then she did a terrible thing — she smelled it.

" 'You've been with a woman.'

" 'No, Grandma,' I said. 'No, I haven't.'

"She picked up a shoe and beat me with it.

" 'Don't you know that you can get a disease from those dirty women?' she said. She was irate. She made me wash myself with soap and water. The next day she wanted to take me to a doctor to get some medicine before my thing fell off with some terrible disease. I felt awful. Every day for a week she made me take it out and show it to her to see whether it was rotting or not.

" 'It'll take nine days,' she told me. 'Nine days and then the pus is going to start coming out.'

"I lived in terror for nine days. I didn't go out of the house in all that time. I was expecting it to turn green and fall off any second.

"She explained to me that women get pregnant and that men get diseases. She made it all sound complicated and awful. Of course, the boys wanted a full report. I was the big hero for a week because maybe I had gonorrhea. Boy, if you had gonorrhea, you really were a man! The fact that I had gone 'all the way' made me a hero, and they wanted to know every detail about the evening. I kept dramatizing it more and more to them. Everybody followed the progress of my penis for quite a while.

"About ten days later, when I found out that my penis had not turned green, I went to the girl's house. She was alone, cooking something.

" 'Come on in,' she said.

" 'I want to apologize to you.'

" 'For what?'

" 'The last time. I think you were drunk, and I was drunk. I don't know if you know what happened.'

" 'What happened?'

" 'Oh, don't you know?'

" 'Well, did something happen?'

" 'Well, I don't know if I should tell you, but I think you should go and see a doctor right away,' I said.

" 'What do you mean? Do you have gonorrhea or something?' She was very matter of fact.

" 'No, no, but . . . I mean, you may be pregnant.'

"She giggled. 'How old are you, really, kid?'

" 'What do you mean?'

" 'Tell me something; was that the first time you'd done it?'

" 'Are you kidding? No, I've had a lot of women.'

" 'How old are you?'

" 'Aw, I'm . . .'

" 'You lied. You're not really twenty-two, are you?'

" 'Well, to tell the truth, I'm eighteen.'

" 'The truth!'

" 'Sixteen,' I confessed.

" 'That was the first time, wasn't it, kid?'

" 'Well . . . yeah, it was.'

" 'Don't worry, I'm not pregnant.'

" 'How do you know?'

" 'Well, girls know. And besides, I know how to take care of myself; don't worry.'

" 'You're sure you're not pregnant?'

" 'I'm not pregnant.'

" 'If you are, you will tell me?'

" 'What would you do about it?'

" 'Well, I'd marry you.'

"She took me in her arms and kissed me on the brow, when the knock came on the door. She left me standing there while she went and let in an older man of twenty-five, or so. She introduced us.

" 'Well, Tony, I have to dress now. I'm going out with George.'

"She went into her room. George turned to me and winked. I didn't know what the gentlemanly thing to do was. Should I smack him across the mouth or give him the big wink? Instead, I ran out of the house."

I heard "the boy" laughing.

BOY. What a lousy story. Tell your quack how you cried all the way home. Tell him how that cunt haunted you until you met Sylvia. You always had cheap taste in women. You thought love came wrapped in cheap tinsel.

MAN. Who the hell started it? You, you little hypocritical shit. You wouldn't open your eyes when that girl sucked you on the beach. You didn't have the guts to show Rita your cock when she asked to see it. You had to hide behind the fence and put it through a knothole for her to examine it.

BOY (*defensively*). That was a long time ago.

MAN. Come on, you dirty little bastard, deny that you wanted to make it with your own sister!

BOY. Is that some more of your sick crap? Yes, I loved her. I loved her a lot when she was a sick kid back in El Paso and I used to take care of her.

MAN. Okay, don't get mad, kid. I was just thinking that your sexual awakening wasn't the most normal in the world, was it?

BOY (*bristling*). What the hell are you saying?

MAN. Because you got a kick watching Rita's reaction when you showed her your penis through the knothole. You were a sneaky little shit. Why didn't you just take it out and show it to her?

BOY (*angrily*). Because, you dirty old bastard, she was my cousin!

MAN. It didn't stop you from fucking her later, did it?

BOY (*almost in tears*). I confessed it all to the priest. Besides, I didn't really do what you said. We just rubbed each other. Anyway, the priest forgave me.

MAN. Sure, you had him forgiving you everything in those days. But you won't forgive me anything . . .

BOY (*interrupting*). I was only ten years old.

MAN (*softly*). I'm not condemning you, but I think it would have been healthier if you'd been more honest and direct. (*man starts laughing*) And Jesus, kid — weren't you a jerk that night on the auditorium steps with Connie?

BOY (*smiling*). Yeah, I never understood that. I was so in love with her, but when she said, "I love you" right out like that I didn't know what to do.

MAN. After all these years, it's still a tough moment, kid. In my case I don't believe it anyway, so I just play along.

BOY. You're screwed up.

MAN. Come on, let's get back to Connie.

BOY. She had green eyes . . .

MAN. Like the panther.

BOY. Yeah.

MAN. Her hair was the same color as that cat, wasn't it?

BOY. You mean I wanted to fuck that big cat?

MAN. Didn't you?

BOY. Jeez, you *are* sick.

MAN. Okay, come on, what happened that night with Connie?

BOY. Her breath smelled like apples when I got close to her there at the bottom of the steps. We were all alone in the dark. We stood there looking at each other. I could have stood there for years just looking at her — breathing her in. And then she said it so simply, "Tony, I love you . . ." (*the boy can't continue*).

MAN. You started crying, you jerk. Instead of taking her in your arms and kissing those beautiful lips, you smacked her in the stomach. (*the boy nods in pain*) She stood there, not understanding. But she wanted to understand and you ran away into the night.

BOY (*crying*). Maybe she was the one.

MAN. Yeah, but you screwed it up.

BOY (*sobbing*). Why didn't she run after me then?

MAN. After you hit her? She was wise, kid, but not that wise. Besides, she was only thirteen.

BOY (*trying to escape the man's strong grip*). It was the only way I could tell her I loved her. I was hoping she'd understand.

MAN (*laughing*). No female understands a shot in the solar plexus after she's told you she loves you. Okay, what others did you really like?

BOY. I liked Evie. She would have understood the slap.

MAN (*uncomfortable — it's a subject he wants to avoid. He takes out a cigarette and lights it nervously*).

BOY. I know you don't like facing it, but of all of them Sylvia was the champ. She understood the slap better than anyone in the world.

# 13

IT HAD BEEN a lovely Sunday.

I had finished the picture. It was not one of my best performances, but at least I'd survived. There had been times when I thought I'd go under.

"The boy" had stuck pretty close to me all through the rough period. He hadn't approved of the picture from the beginning. He knew that I'd done very few things in my life that were consciously dishonest. This time I had been a whore. I had rationalized why I was being dishonest and I'd been able to talk myself into believing that I was doing it for a bigger purpose, like my children's security and advancement of my career, but the boy knew it was all a lot of crap. He would point to all the "goodies" that I would acquire to compensate for my guilts as a constant reminder that I had been a whore.

The boy had haunted me with my favorite quotation from *Cyrano de Bergerac:* "Shall I labor night and day to build a reputation on one song? Palpitate over little paragraphs and struggle to insinuate my name into the columns? No, thank you — no. Calculate, scheme, be afraid, love more to make a visit than a poem? Seek introductions, favors, influences? No, thank you. But . . to sing, to laugh, go lightly, solitary, free with a voice that means manhood — to cock my hat the way I choose. For a yes or no to show a fight. And if fame or fortune lie beyond the bourn — *never to pen a line that has not sprung from the heart within* — to say, *'Soul be satisfied with flowers, nay weeds, but pick them from no garden but thine own'* — not to climb high perchance, but to climb alone!"

I had known for years that too much of my energy was being used to attack ghosts rather than translating, discovering, interpreting my life and times.

I kept thrashing about in great emotional discomfort because

I knew I was guilty as hell of not being true to myself. But when I'd discovered it I no longer knew who that "self" was that I had to be honest to.

On this Sunday morning I'd taken my kids high up into the Malibu mountains. Katie and I had long argued about the children's upbringing. I had wanted them brought up in some religion — I didn't care which — but I felt strongly that they should at least know the form of some faith. Later they could change if they wanted. I knew that you can only change the form *if* you know the form.

Katie, on the other hand, felt that she did not want to impose any creed on the kids — they would choose one when they grew up.

I had given in. I was rationalizing that I was too busy forging out a career to fight her.

How easily we men slough off responsibility for our most important creations, yet accept it for far less significant ones.

Once the children were growing older, I felt it was important that they should commune in some way with God, or nature, or the life force, or even themselves. I used to take them out on Sundays to some lonely spot, either at the beach or to a mountain top, and ask them to just sit and think about anything they wanted to think about — preferably about God.

So we set out for a mountain in the Malibu ridge. It was warm autumn morning. We parked the car down on the winding road and hiked up the hill through the sagebrush and the mesquite. On top of the hill were several scrub oaks and tall laurel bushes. Each of the four kids chose a tree, sat beneath it, and stared out at the Pacific Ocean in the distance.

I looked over at my four children. The two older girls, Chrissy and Kathy, were seventeen and sixteen, respectively. Duncan was thirteen and little Vally was only seven. I wondered what was going on in theirs heads.

Vally was having great fun. She would break the silence every now and then, yelling that she had seen a squirrel or a lizard or a "flutterby." The other kids would "shush" her up. I loved them for making an effort to please their Pop.

The kids were very good about "playing the game." We had made a pact that I wouldn't ask them what they'd thought about

Thank God they didn't ask me. They were the only bridge I had to reality. I didn't want to disillusion them in any way.

"The boy" was happiest during those forays. He would choose a nice cool spot and nod his approval. But the little bastard would never let me get near enough to ask him what was still bugging him: why he refused to leave me alone; why I could never feel what I most wanted to feel — the love of another human being. I felt love *for* my children but I, in turn, was insulated against feeling their love for me. I felt love *from no one*.

I had talked myself into the fact that I had *never* been loved. There is no money, no possession, no accomplishment that has any meaning without that feeling of being loved.

I had the capacity, thank God, to give love — even if sometimes misguided — so why did I have no talent, no ability, no means of accepting love? Why did I have all the sending equipment but none of the receiving? I was a man sending out all sorts of messages and never knowing if they were being received or not. I was talking into a void.

But that Sunday, with my children and "the boy" sitting beside us, was somewhat successful. I had felt affection and approval, if not love, on that hill. The warmth I felt was enough for me to continue my fight for survival.

The secretary told me I'd have to wait, since the doctor had an emergency. I wondered what that meant for a psychiatrist. What does he do in an emergency? What instruments can he use? How does he dig out the buried block or the emotional bullet that is crippling you?

I sat in the outer office and leafed through magazines, looking at photos of pretty women, wondering which one was capable of saying, "I love you" and really meaning it.

After a while, the emergency case came out of the doctor's office. She seemed like a very nice girl. She was smiling. If one had seen her walking down the street one would have envied her apparent tranquillity. God, I thought, the only trouble with neurotics is that they are geniuses at hiding their pain.

The doctor motioned for me to enter the lion's den.

He put away the "emergency" folder and opened mine. I wondered if he had to refresh his memory. Oh, yes — Mr. So-and-so; age, such-and-such; illness diagnosed as inability to feel love.

"Well, how was the weekend?"

I duly reported a successful forty-eight hours. No suicide attempts, no drugs except one mild sleeping pill, no emotional outbursts except when my wife had looked at a painting I'd been working on for one month and said, "Oh, yes — your lunch is ready," and I had slashed the canvas to pieces. Nothing terribly important, just quiet desperation.

I told him about the time up in the hills with the kids. I also reported that "the boy" had been around and seemed to approve.

"Did you talk to him?"

"No, he didn't want to talk. He just sat there as if he were part of the family."

"Does he like the kids?"

"In different degrees. He identifies himself with Duncan. They both have that strange thing about not knowing what to do with their eyes. At first, it seems like shyness. But it's not. They're afraid to look into people's eyes because they see so much pain. They both have a tendency to look away. But 'the boy' looks on the girls more or less as sisters. He loves them but finds it difficult to identify with them. Besides, he knows he can never be number one with them, that he must eventually give way to a husband or lover. He's afraid to be vulnerable."

"Are you talking about you or 'the boy'?"

"I'm now speaking for both of us."

"Do you have a favorite among the girls?"

"Kathy reminds me of my grandmother in beauty and moral strength. Vally reminds me dangerously of myself. I say dangerously because we are both driven by gigantic 'wants' and must rely on our own breaks. I hope hers are better than mine. Christina is the most difficult to define because she hates the responsibility we saddled her with."

"You mean because of Christopher?"

"Yes."

"One day you started to tell me about the death of your first-born. Can you face that now, Tony?"

"Never. Please don't talk about it. Please."

"Will 'the boy' talk about it?"

"No, that is one subject on which we are in complete accord."
The doctor sighed and took another tack. "So tell me about
Christina."

"I guess she knew she was there to cement two people. It was
a big responsibility for a baby. Some of it was forced on her, some
of it self-imposed. Later she chose to change her identity by having her nose fixed. I was appalled. I could never have changed
mine. If anything, I used *all* my faults. I made them work for me.
I remember once when I couldn't get a job I blamed it on the
stars and I went to a numerologist to give me some advice. He
said I'd never get anywhere with a name like Anthony Quinn.
He said I'd have to change it to Bruce Quinn. For a while I even
tried writing under the name of Arthur Andretti. But I always
came back to the fact that I'd have to make it with the name I
was born with.

"Anyway, I thought it strange that a daughter of mine would
want to change her nose. It was a good nose. It was my father's
nose, my nose, my sister's nose. It was a good strong nose with
a certain air of defiance."

"Cyrano again."

"If you wish. But Cyrano wasn't only talking about his nose.
He just used that as a banner. It could have been racial, or political. It was just another kind of banner. When Christina changed
her nose she gave up the banner. She wanted to look like a thousand other girls. I know the value of daring to be different, making them accept you on *your* terms. I know Christina can never
recover from that operation until she finds a banner to replace the
nose she bobbed. Because of her problem I worry about her the
most. The others are making the best of their faults."

"You're a tough father."

"I don't feel that I am. If anything, I feel I'm too soft."

"But you had a nice weekend."

"Yes."

"You told me some amusing stories about the dance contests
but I was wondering about all the lives you were juggling. As far
as I can figure it out, you were boxing, dancing, going to school,
and working with Frank. What was happening to Aimee Semple
McPherson during all this?"

"You sound like my wife. When you are poor and growing up

it's amazing how much you *have* to do. First of all, while I wa
going to Poly High I was working with Frank. I had taken ove
a couple of automobile showrooms and offices. It was my respon
sibility to keep them clean and polished. I earned fifty cents an
hour doing that. Then occasionally I'd pick up a few dollars each
time I fought at a smoker. But I only had sixteen fights in two
years so I was hardly getting rich from that enterprise.

"As to architecture, I must admit the dream was fading. I had
to skip a lot of school to work with Frank or pick up odd jobs
The money Grandmother was getting on the sly from Mother
was not enough to run the house. Besides, I was dying to be the
sole support of our group. I hated being dependent on Mother
who I felt belonged to Frank and not to us.

"At Poly I was studying with a man named Baker, who had
halitosis. For some reason he had taken an intense dislike to me
and made studying a terrible bore. He taught by the book and
lived by the book. He left no room for any creativity. I remember
that we had to paint skies in gradations of blue. You started with
dark blue at the top and in seven steps of one inch apiece you
had to reach the light blue. I had never seen skies like that and
thought it was stupid. I liked to paint dark ominous dramatic
skies.

"I also knew even then that the world is made up of book
keepers and minor mathematicians who can be hired for smal
sums to work out details but who can't create worth a shit. I wa
anxious to get on with the big creative problems. Otherwise
knew I'd wind up being one of fifty guys in an office, bending
over a drawing board, for the rest of my life. I didn't want t
copy somebody else's dreams; I wanted to be the dreamer.

"The standardization of architecture drove me crazy. The fac
that doors had to be a certain height and a certain width, an
windows a certain measurement, drove me up the wall. I knew
that what they were teaching us was the standardization of man
I was totally against it. I liked the Greek concept of architecture
not building to the measurement of man but to his aspiration

"The only one who gave me any hope was Frank Lloyd Wright
whom I went to see one day. I had drawn plans for a supermarke
and won first prize at school during the eleventh grade. I called
up Wright's office and was able to obtain an interview.

"When I arrived, they told me he was too busy to see me. I had huge portfolio of drawings under my arm and started to leave. Then I saw this handsome man walk into the office. He was immaculately dressed and looked more like a movie star than a famous architect. The thing that struck me about him besides the ramrod, straight-backed walk, was his eyes. They were the most lovely eyes I'd ever seen, full not only of visionary dreams but great humor. Though he was not a tall man, he gave the impression of being a giant.

"I don't know what it was about me that drew his attention but as I started to move out of his path he looked at me with those marvelously dancing eyes and asked me what I had come for. I became literally tongue-tied.

" 'I — I came to see you, sir. I'd like to be an architect like you someday.'

" 'Like me, son? I hope you will be better than me. I want no one around who doesn't think he's better than me. It keeps me on my toes.'

"I wanted to tell him I was really Michelangelo, but decided against it.

"He motioned for me to follow him into his office. The walls were filled with drawings of projects in progress — hotels, houses, cities all over the world — in Japan, India, France, Italy. The man had the world in the palm of his hand.

"He asked me to show him my portfolio. While he glanced at my drawings he checked his calendar and corrected drawings his office workers shoved on his desk.

"I thought he barely looked at the drawings I'd slaved over. He didn't say a word as he glanced at them. When I had turned over the last one he went to a drawing board at one end of the room and made some notes and corrections. He seemed to have forgotten that I was there.

" 'My God,' he finally said. 'Who taught you to paint skies like that?'

" 'At Polytechnic High School. Mr. Baker says that skies should be painted like that.'

" 'Do you think all skies should be blue?'

" 'No, sir. I painted a stormy sky the other day and he gave me

**a** D. According to him all clouds should have diagonal line *never* horizontal.'

"He threw an eraser across the room. 'What the hell does th[ have to do with the measure of man? Why do you want to be [ architect, son?'

"I knew he didn't want any evasive shit. 'Because, sir, I thi[ human beings live wrong. I don't think we were meant to li[ in boxes. It's enough that we're going to spend eternity in a bo[ Why do we have to do the same with our lives?'

" 'That's good, boy. You're right. What else?'

" 'I want to build cities.'

" 'Whole cities, eh?'

" 'Yes, sir.'

" 'What kind of cities?'

"I had a thousand thoughts. I knew I was spilling over but [ couldn't stop. Wright seemed amused and I didn't know ho[ much time I had before we would be interrupted, so I want[ to get all my points in.

" 'Where are you from, boy?'

"He was the only one who had ever said 'boy' with affecti[ and not with a note of patronization.

" 'I was raised in Belvedere. That's on the East Side, sir. I n[ live in the Echo Park district.'

"He smiled. 'That's near Aimee's temple, isn't it?'

" 'Yes, sir.'

" 'I built a house near there.'

" 'I know.'

" 'What's the matter with your speech, boy?'

"He took me by surprise. I had never been aware there w[ anything wrong with my speech.

" 'Nothing.' I said defensively.

" 'Yes, there is. You talk as if you were tongue-tied.'

" 'No, sir. I'm nervous.'

" 'There's nothing to be nervous about with me. Open yo[ mouth and lift up your tongue.'

"He peered into my mouth.

" 'Uhuh, you have excellent teeth but your frenum is too thic[ You should have it out.'

"I didn't know what the hell a frenum was. He lifted his tongue and showed me the piece of skin underneath.

" 'That's a frenum. When that is too thick it keeps you from enunciating clearly. Being a good draftsman is not enough if you want to be a great architect. You will be meeting people and influencing their lives. You have to be able to enunciate your ideas and philosophy. They are not going to listen to you if you don't sound clipped and decisive.'

" 'Yes, sir.'

"I had never been aware of any speech problems, except an occasional stutter, but that was because my mind traveled faster than I could get the words out. Stuttering was a way of putting the brakes on my tumbling thoughts.

" 'Go and see a doctor. Tell him to cut that piece of skin under your tongue.'

" 'Yes, sir.'

" 'Then go somewhere and learn to speak — "trippingly on the tongue: but if you mouth it, as many of your players do, I had as lief the town-crier spoke my lines." '

"I nodded. I was wondering how expensive and how painful such an operation would be.

"I could tell by the way he hunched over the drawing board that the interview was over. I started for the door.

" 'By the way, boy,' he said over his shoulder, 'skies are not always blue and I like your ideas for a city. Come back and see me after you learn to speak.'

"I left clutching my portfolio. I felt I had been interviewed as an actor rather than as an architect.

"I had met a giant. He had posed a problem I'd never been aware of. Why hadn't anybody ever talked to me about it? I knew I spoke with a slight Spanish accent but I had *never* thought of myself as tongue-tied! It now became an obsession which I kept to myself. It wasn't until a year later, when I was drunk one night, that I confessed everything to the woman I was to fall in love with."

"Sylvia, at last?" asked the doctor, smiling.

I nodded.

# 14

BOY (*nodding toward the doctor*). He's waiting. Besides, you on
have a half hour to get all your licks in.

I turned to see the doctor waiting patiently for me to bri
him up to date.

BOY. He's not going to understand anyway. Just skip to the se
part so he can get his jollies.

I threw the kid a dirty look and began the story of Sylvia. (
course, it had a preamble, a curtain raiser — Evie.

"Some girl from Poly High invited me to a party. It was tl
first I'd ever been asked to. Heretofore, I'd always done thin
with Danny or one of the other guys. I've never had stage frigl
as I had about making an appearance at that party. I shined n
shoes five times and brushed my hand-me-down suit over an
over. As I neared the house, however, the self-confidence I ha
tried to muster evaporated.

"Through the window I could see the kids dancing to the ph
nograph. The laughter and gay sounds made me want to ru
away. How the hell do you walk into a room full of people? Wh
smile do you use? Where do you put your hands? I walked aroun
the block several times before I had the courage to go to the fro
door. I had prepared a self-deprecating smile, aloof but not sup
rior, a smile denoting sadness and a touch of arrogance. It w:
totally unnecessary. No one noticed as I entered.

"I held on to my frozen smile while I pretended to be bu
searching for someone. I saw a door and headed for it, only t
find myself in the backyard. It was enclosed, and the only way t
get out was to go back into the living room and brave anonymit
once more. I sat down on a rickety low chair, deciding on m

xt move, when a young girl came out. She had a glass of punch
 each hand. She held one of them out to me.

" 'You must be Tony. My name is Evie.'

" 'Hello.'

" 'Betty told me you were coming. She sort of invited me to be
 th you.'

"The girl had the largest brown eyes I had ever seen, and the
 ost disarming. Her red hair was cut short and framed her doll-
 ke face. She sat down pertly beside me, as if we'd known each
 her forever.

" 'Don't you like parties?' she asked.

" 'This is the first one I've ever been to.'

" 'Betty told me you were a lone wolf. You go to Poly High,
 n't you?'

" 'Only part-time.'

" 'What are you studying?'

" 'Architecture.'

" 'Oh, my mother wanted to be an architect. She's always plan-
 ng the perfect house. Do you have a perfect house?'

" 'At the moment I'm revising some plans for a supermarket.
 howed them to a big architect.'

" 'That sounds exciting. What's the name of the architect?'

" 'Frank Lloyd Wright.'

" 'Oh, my mother says he's the greatest. Maybe you could let her
 e the plans. She has some very good ideas. And after all, markets
 e for women mostly, aren't they?'

" 'Yeah.' I gulped the sweet punch, wondering what to say.
 e chattered on.

" 'My father is a painter. I mean he was. He used to do wonder-
 l paintings of the sea and fishing boats and things. But now he
 s a factory that reproduces paintings. My mother says it's better
 do one original thing than a thousand great reproductions.'

" 'Your mother sounds very deep.'

" 'Oh, she is. She's also a poet. When she's not drawing plans
 r her ideal house, she's writing poetry and strange mystical
 ories. I don't know how she does it with four kids to look after.'

" 'You're one of four?'

" 'I'm the second oldest. My sister Joan is eighteen. I'm sixteen.
 ert is fourteen, and Lenny is only four. Joan is the brains of the

family. She reads heavy stuff, like Dostoevsky and Tolstoy. I prefe
fairy tales.'

"I didn't know what to add so I tried my social smile on he

" 'Listen," she said, 'this party is icky. Would you take n
home?'

" 'Sure,' I said.

"When we reached the corner of Mickeltorena and Suns
Boulevard, she took my hand in silence and led me up the lor
winding hill leading to her house."

BOY. You were scared to death. She was purity. As you walked u
that hill, the fresh smell of her made you aware that yc
couldn't live up to her.

MAN (*squirming*). She was only sixteen.

BOY. And what were you? You were an acned eighteen and ha
just started to shave.

MAN. If she was so perfect, why did you screw it up for me? It w
the one time in our life we were number one. Maybe the on
time.

BOY. It got mixed up. If Sylvia hadn't come along, Evie woul
have been the answer. But you were in too much of a fuckir
hurry to make it.

MAN. I'm to blame for the whole thing?

BOY. Sure. When you saw Sylvia she was ready-made. With Ev
you'd have had to do the molding. She was a lovely piece
clay and you didn't know what to do with it. Sylvia was cor
plete, no building to be done, no interior decorating. She w
all ready to just move in.

I was silent for a long time. I wondered how to continue, ho
to tell about that first meeting with the woman who was to chang
the whole course of my life, to haunt me forever. The woma
who, even after her death, would never leave my side.

In retrospect, after all I've said about Sylvia, you'd think the
was thunder and lightning when we first met. Actually, she w
bending over, throwing some broken toilet seats into the hug
fireplace.

Evie laughed. "Mama, how embarrassing," she said.

Sylvia turned around. She was an older version of Evie, more
fined, statelier. She had a rich, throaty laugh.

"Well, these toilet seats are made of mahogany and walnut.
hey make a very lovely fire. Besides, what better use for such
undane objects?"

"Mama, this is Tony Quinn."

She held out her hand. She had a strong, firm grip. It trans-
itted assurance and warmth.

"Hello, Tony Quinn. We have some homemade brew that tastes
ke beer. Will you have some?"

I wasn't used to drinking but now that I was breaking into
ciety I felt it would be wrong to decline.

"Okay."

Evie ran out to the kitchen to get me the drink.

"Are you Spanish, Tony?"

Oh, Christ! Here it comes, I thought. Here comes the demand
r my pedigree. I remembered the time when I'd brought home
questionnaire from school. My father was supposed to fill it in.
the blank space after "nationality" he'd written: Turkish,
lian, Chinese, Hindustan, Japanese, Mongolian, Mexican,
sh, Aztec and Scandinavian. I had been called in by the princi-
l, who was furious. But my father had refused to budge. He
sented the question and said the principal should prove that
wasn't all those nationalities. I knew very well that it was more
shionable to be Spanish than Mexican.

"Mexican," I said.

She didn't blanch. "Oh, really? Where does the name Quinn
me from? Irish, isn't it?"

"Yes, my grandfather."

"What a wonderful combination. You must be at constant war
th yourself."

I was glad to be interrupted by Evie's handing me the drink.
on, some other kids came in, Joan, Bert, and a whole crowd.
ter a while, everybody gathered around the fireplace. Evie and
at on the couch. I felt like an outsider. Joan read something
om Walt Whitman and then somebody read Rupert Brooke —
mes that I didn't even know then. A tall willowy boy with loose
ists said, "Oh, darling, can you compare it, can you really com-
re it with Edna St. Vincent Millay?" There was a thin, hand-

some, crippled kid who was wonderfully witty. Every time  opened his mouth, everyone roared with laughter. They talke about painters, the Fauve period. . . . "Yes, darling, but wh about the Renaissance?" And so it went. I thought, what the he am I doing here? I was also beginning to feel the beer. Sylv seemed to sense my discomfort. She came over and put her ar around me reassuringly, saying, "Now don't be upset, don't be p off. Evie and I like you and that's all that matters."

They served a buffet supper around eleven-thirty. I didn't kno how to eat, which fork to use for what. Then I heard a convers tion from the kitchen, and the kids were laughing. I heard Jo say, "Did you see what my sister brought in? Well, that's Evie f you."

Evie heard, too, and gripped my hand. She laid out two plat for us on a little coffee table and we sat away from the others. watched her and ate as she did.

After a while, people started drifting away. Only Evie, Sylv and I remained. I wanted to go, but Sylvia said, "No, Tony, dor go, please. All that nonsense those kids were talking, they do know what they're saying. I want to hear about *you*. Wouldn't y like something else to drink?"

"I'd like some whiskey, please."

Evie brought me a highball, which I drank in one long gulp. five minutes I was drunk and started crying. Once the tears start I lost control. "Those bastards, those sonsofbitches, they thi they're better than me just because they've read a lot of books, a that's a lot of shit. What the hell do they know about painters? could be one of the best painters that ever lived. I could be N chelangelo if I wanted to. I feel as much as Shakespeare way dov inside of me. Have they ever read the Bible? I can quote t Bible."

I went into a long recitation of Ecclesiastes. I must have talk for an hour, saying things I didn't even know existed in me, e posing all the pent-up dreams, the yearnings for beauty, and sor of the poisons, too. When I'd finished, I felt wrung out.

"Tony," Sylvia said, "you mustn't stop coming here. Evie lik you and I like you, too. If you come back tomorrow night, I'll gi you some books, start you on some wonderful reading."

They both came down to the streetcar stop, about a block aw

om the house, and waited with me. I thought, my first time in a
ice, big, white home and I made a fool of myself. Finally, the
reetcar came. Evie reached up, kissed me on the mouth, and
ugged me. Sylvia kissed me on both cheeks and said, "Please
me back tomorrow night." I got into the streetcar and went
ome.

The next day was Sunday. I woke up with a terrible headache,
id a feeling of shame and regret. I got dressed and walked
round the park, then over toward their house. In the sunlight, it
oked gayer and even more remote, with its lawn and flowers. I
ought, am I being ridiculous even considering going back? They
ere just two very nice people who took pity on me. They prob-
ly didn't mean it at all. But I found myself walking up the
airs. Sylvia came to the door and was obviously glad to see me.

"I was taking a walk and I thought that I had made such a fool
 myself that I wanted to come back and apologize," I blurted
it.

"Evie went off to the beach with the kids," she said. "What a
ame. Of course, she wouldn't have gone if she'd known you were
ming. Come in and wait for her? She'll be back around five or
x o'clock."

So I went in. We sat in the parlor and I apologized again.

"You don't have to excuse yourself, Tony. I know the pains of
owing up, the hunger to be somebody. Maybe there is a Michel-
ngelo inside you, or a Beethoven — who knows? We'll just have
 find out, won't we?"

We were sitting on the couch. I was suddenly rocked by the
alization that I had come to see her and not her daughter. I
gan to look away and fidget.

She talked about how superficial mere knowledge was; it was
hat you did with it that counted. Her kids weren't really doing
nything with their education. She was sure that once I had suffi-
ent knowledge I would put it to good use. While she was talk-
g, I kept saying to myself, oh God, if she only knew what dirty
oughts I have, she'd throw me out of the house.

"All right, Tony, let's start. What do you like to read?"

"The only thing I know about is religion."

"Well, that's the most important subject of all, isn't it — at the
sis of everything. So, maybe we'll start with some metaphysics.

185

There's a philosopher I love very much, his name is Santayana. Why don't we start by reading Santayana?"

She took some books from a case. She had underlined her favorite passages and made marginal notes. It was as if she were telling me her innermost thoughts. That night I started reading Santayana, but he was too theoretical for me, not practical enough.

"Well then," she said, "we'll read Schopenhauer. He is certainly practical."

I liked Schopenhauer. His ideas fitted in with my background somehow. I liked his patriarchal attitude, and the clear line of definition between man and woman. And he said life was precious; you shouldn't waste time; you should spend every minute of your waking day advancing yourself.

Sylvia insisted that whenever I found an author I admired I must live as he preached for a week, or a month — as long as I could apply his thoughts to my life. And I did, with Schopenhauer, then Nietzsche, with Thoreau, and then on to Emerson. I suddenly found myself avariciously devouring philosophy and literature. I was like a boy who had been in a coma for eighteen years, fed intravenously. Now I awakened. I began reading books from morning to night, drunk with discovery. Sylvia made me keep lists — the books I had read, those I wanted to read. She made me put my thoughts, my impressions, into notebooks. I began to haunt second-hand bookstores and buy volumes on every subject — philosophy, science, literature. I read Fielding and Smollett, Baudelaire and Balzac, Dante and D'Annunzio. I read Ford Maddox Ford, Sinclair Lewis, Scott Fitzgerald, Wolfe, Hemingway. . . .

Sylvia turned it all into marvelous games. She would strew postcards of famous paintings on the floor.

"Who painted that one?" she would ask.

"Van Gogh."

"That one?"

"Gauguin."

"The one over there?"

"Del Sarto."

She would play music for me, selections I came to recognize, Bach, Brahms, Mozart, Beethoven. The names were reference points in this strange wondrous new world.

All the while, intoxicated as I was by this exploding world, I thought Sylvia was being nice to me because Evie and I were supposedly in love. Evie was still going to school. I had quit, and was working at various things, including architecture, but it had become very secondary. I only wanted to be with Sylvia.

I would go to the house when her kids were off at school and her husband at his work. She had married a man who seemed to have lost his youth and ideals, who had compromised with life. She confessed that she hadn't been in love with him for years, that she remained married to him because of the children.

One day, after a long walk through the Hollywood hills, we sat on a promontory overlooking the orchards and farms of the San Fernando Valley. Beyond we could see the snow-capped mountains.

I looked over at Sylvia. She was all flushed from the long climb. I saw tears in her eyes. Suddenly the difference of twenty years between us disappeared. She looked so young and vulnerable. I reached over and touched her shoulder. She leaned on me and took my hand. I wanted so desperately to kiss her, to hold her as a man. She got up and went to the edge of the cliff. I didn't dare stand up for fear she'd be aware of my desire.

"Tony," she said softly, "are you in love with Evie?"

Y. Why didn't you come out and say it? Why didn't you take her in your arms and say, "I love *you*"?

AN. I've asked myself that question a million times.

Y. Maybe it wasn't that simple. Evie was as worthy of love as Sylvia.

AN. I guess that's when you and I started to part. You wanted Evie and I wanted Sylvia.

Y. I wanted you to have more guts. One way or the other.

AN. You're right, it would have saved everybody a lot of pain. But I was afraid Sylvia would think I was some kind of degenerate, being in love with the mother of the girl I was engaged to.

Sylvia waited for my answer.

"Yes, I love Evie."

It wasn't a lie. I did love her. But it wasn't the same kind of love. It was kid's stuff. It was touching hands and playing games

BOY. Evie was a woman. She didn't go through any of that crap about "What are you doing to me?" — "I've never done it before." She was a woman giving herself to her man. The blood on the sheets was the greatest proof of love you could ever hope to see.

MAN. Must a man give up his life because he's broken a cherry?

BOY. How many cherries do you think are around, old man?

MAN. We've only known two.

BOY. And that's the only time we were number one.

MAN. No, that is your sickness, kid. You drove me crazy with the numbers game. I was number one in more important ways with a couple of others.

BOY. Who, for instance?

MAN. Sylvia, of course.

BOY (shrugging). Hell, you were about number four with Sylvia.

MAN (angrily). I was number one with her.

BOY. Have it your way. Who else? Who? Why can't you even say her name?

MAN. Because I know how you feel and if you say anything against her, I'll kill you.

BOY. Okay, we won't touch Saint Katharine. But then what the hell are you doing here vomiting all over this man's desk, you're so sure you were number one in her life?

MAN. She isn't the reason I'm here. It's you, you little sonofabitch, I'm trying to find out where it all started. Where you and I went different ways.

BOY. You know the hour — the day — the year.

MAN (holding his ears). I don't . . . I don't.

"Things got complicated after that walk, Doctor. Evie and I became engaged. Sylvia kept throwing us together more and more

"I began to sleep in the study downstairs, surrounded by books, records, reproductions of paintings, and my piles of notebooks. Evie quit school and I found less time to be alone with Sylvia except for what we called our study periods.

"She was doing everything in her power to make me commit yself to her daughter. She went so far as to suggest that Evie d I go away somewhere and find out if we were really well ated.

"The hotel I chose was hardly ideal for a honeymoon. It was e of those dollar-a-night fleabags in downtown Los Angeles. ie was not aware of the peeling plaster or the cracked furni- re."

Y. She wasn't there to look at the furniture or decoration. She was there to give herself to her man. Whether it was a palace or a cave couldn't have mattered less. God, the way she came to bed — so honest.

N. And we were so clumsy, kid.

Y. No, I was kind of virginal, too. I wanted to cry because even the blood didn't seem to bother her. It was her gift to me, as if we were lying on a bed of crushed red roses.

N (*kindly*). Why did you start to cry, kid?

Y. I don't know.

N (*gently*). Yes, you do. Because you knew that it was Sylvia you really wanted. You were full of guilts about that sweet creature in your arms. You felt unworthy of her. She was a fairy tale. Sylvia was reality.

"For a while it seemed that things would work out with Evie d myself. She began to behave like my woman, cooking for me, ving, mending my clothes. I would go out and work sporadically th my stepfather and hand the money to Sylvia for my board. via's husband was not too happy with my presence in the use."

Y. He was a shit!

N. No, he was a poor soul. In retrospect, I feel sorry for him. We made his life miserable.

Y. What about the time he called you a dirty Mexican?

N. He didn't know how else to strike out. But that's probably he reason I stayed there. It was an act of defiance against him.

"We were sitting on the front porch, not saying much, when heard Sylvia and her husband arguing in the kitchen. I heard hi say, 'If you don't get rid of that dirty Mexican, I'll throw him o bodily.'

"Evie knew I had heard it. I got up quietly and stood by t steps, deciding what to do. Then I turned around and said, ' right, Evie, I'm going home. I'll call you.'

"I started down the steps. Evie rushed into the house, screami at her father. She said terrible things to him.

"Sylvia joined in, 'She's right. Tony's one of the brightest b ever to come to this house, and you're too stupid to see it. You going to lose a daughter, talking like that.'

"I was halfway down the hill when I heard them coming af me, both Evie and Sylvia. I started running, because I knew wl kind of a scene it was going to be, but they kept calling anc finally stopped.

"Sylvia said, 'If you don't come back, I swear to you, you never be a man, Tony. The world is full of people like hi You've got to learn to face them. You must never allow that ki of stupid talk to affect you.'

"I didn't want to return and face a man who hated me beca I was Mexican. But when I looked at those two faces, those t lovely faces, I suddenly knew that my first great test had arriv I walked back up the hill and into the house.

"He was sitting in the kitchen. He was about forty-five ye old, a big man who could have gotten up, hit me, and thrown out of his house. I sat across from him while Sylvia and Evie ma me some supper. We all sat down at the table. No one spo Pretty soon he got up and walked away. Sylvia sighed. 'He sho have said he was sorry, or he should've hit you, but he should have just sat there.' "

I saw the doctor sneak a look at the clock. I stopped talking.

"What's the matter, Tony?"

"It all gets mixed up in time. I find it impossible to keep chronological."

"Don't worry about the storytelling. I'm really only interes in your emotional state. Go on."

I smiled. "I saw you look at the clock and I turned off."

"Goddamnit," he laughed, "I've got to learn how to do it more subtly. Excuse me."

He picked up the phone and called his wife and said he'd be late for dinner. So now I had no excuse. I had to continue.

"It was 1934. There was a ray of hope that the Depression would come to an end. Beer had been legalized and Roosevelt had made us all feel better by telling us there was nothing to fear but fear itself. Saroyan was preaching hope in all his books and things were looking up.

"I had now reached my full growth, at least physically. I was surprised one day when I stepped on the scales and found that I weighed a hundred and ninety pounds. Just a little more than a year before, I'd been boxing at a hundred and forty-seven pounds."

"Though the sun was trying to peer through the dark clouds of the Depression, there was still great evidence of the catastrophe that had overtaken the country.

"That summer, Sylvia took the kids and myself to live at Playa del Rey. What is now a luxurious yacht harbor was at that time a dummy backwash canal. The beach was littered for miles with shacks made from cardboard boxes, canvas, tin cans, anything to keep out the wind and the rain. It was one of many such communities dotting the countryside. These were called Hoovervilles, in honor of Roosevelt's predecessor.

"At night, the edge of the canal would be ablaze with bonfires. Though the thousands of people living there came from all walks of life, there was a great community spirit, a kind of picnic air. Many of our neighbors were teachers, doctors, scientists and artists out of work. We all had one thing in common. The will to survive.

"During the day we would go and pick clusters of mussels off the rocks or we'd scatter over the surrounding fields looking for edible plants. At night, we would all throw our findings into a huge pot. Neighbors would go down the line sampling everybody else's cooking. I can't remember anyone on that beach ever going without eating. After dinner, people would sit by the fires and play guitars and sing."

Boy. It *was* a great summer. It goes to show you don't need yachts and expensive resorts to find happiness.

MAN. That's not why you think it was a great summer. It's because of that night.

"Most people on the beach had gone into their shacks. Only few fires were still burning. In the distance someone was singing 'Here we go, singing low — bye, bye, blackbird. . . .' Evie and th other kids had gone to sleep in our improvised tent. Sylvia and sat by the fire.

" 'I guess we should be getting back to town soon,' she sai sadly. 'Bert and Lenny have to go to school. And I think you hav to decide what you're going to do with your life.'

"She threw her cigarette into the fire and lay back on the sand

" 'Look at all those stars,' she said.

"I lay down beside her to look at the heavens. The sky wa ablaze. I became aware of her hand clutching mine. Neither of said a word. After a time she reached over and pulled a blanke over us. Almost before I knew it, I was making love to her.

"Afterwards, I became aware she was crying. I tried to say som thing but she put her hand over my mouth. She got up an walked into the tent. The blanket smelled of her love. I fell aslee feeling her presence still beside me."

BOY. Evie knew that night, you know.

MAN. No, she had gone to bed. She was asleep.

BOY. She lay inside that tent knowing the two people she love most in the world were shoving a knife in her guts.

MAN. I don't think she knew that night, but she found out soo enough, poor girl. I did have the decency to move out of th house when we went back to Los Angeles. I rented an apar ment not far away from the house.

BOY. You and Sylvia were selfish shits. All you could think abou were yourselves. Did you ever think of what you did to that po girl and the rest of the family? Did you ever think of how h sons took it?

MAN. Stop being a moralistic creep. Sylvia opened up a whole ne world. She led us across the fucking barbed-wire fence that ha us locked in. We couldn't have made it with Evie. Evie wou have settled for us being a truck driver or a fruit-picker. Sylv challenged us to reach for the stars.

The doctor studied me for a long time. I felt uncomfortable under his gaze. I wanted his understanding. But for the first time felt disapproval.

"Did you sleep with Evie after that night on the beach?"

"I can't remember."

"Tony . . ."

Oh, boy. "Yes, Doctor, I did. For some strange reason I only felt complete having the love of the two women."

"It's not difficult to understand, is it, Tony? You had started that game as an infant, playing your mother against your grandmother."

"That's too simple. But I needed the feeling I got from Evie . . . that I would always be the first man in her life. I needed her innocence and her dependency. At the same time I needed Sylvia's worldliness — her wisdom, her experience. I could identify with her huge hunger for life."

"She was the extension of that phrase you learned from your father, where Villa said the ocean was too small to quench his thirst. How long did you go on with both of them?"

"Our *ménage à trois?*" I sighed. "Not very long. I finally had to confess to Evie I was in love with her mother."

"How did she take it?"

"She claimed she'd known it all along. Soon afterwards she started going out with another guy."

"Did it upset you?"

"Yes, but by that time Sylvia had become my woman and helped me understand.

"Sylvia helped me fix up my apartment. She'd come and do the housecleaning after she got through at her home. There was a great sense of liberation at not having to skulk around anymore. I began to study and work harder than ever. We were both intoxicated with dreams of the future. I don't know whether I had grown so much in the two years that I'd been with Sylvia, or whether our love had made her younger. Neither of us any longer felt the difference in years.

"I brought up the subject of marriage. At first, she scoffed at the idea. But I hated not to be with her twenty-four hours a day. Without her, loneliness would close in on me.

" 'The kid' had already begun to bug me with his numbers game.

Obviously, I had not been the first man in Sylvia's life. I dug int
the past and brought out all the ghosts. There had been thre
other men before me. I became pathologically jealous of them.
made her sit around for hours and help me destroy them. I wante
to grind them under, obliterate them forever. I began to hate an
one that bore the same names as her former lovers. Peter becan
anathema to me; so did Edmund. One night, during our discu
sion about painting, she brought up Peter Brueghel.

" 'Goddamnit, don't say that name!'

" 'Tony, dear, he was a great painter.'

" 'I can't stand hearing the name Peter. I can hear you whispe
ing that name while you're in his arms.'

" 'It was so long ago, I can't even remember what he looke
like.'

" 'But you were in his arms. You did go to bed with him.'

"Now in retrospect it was so silly, but it was to set a pattern th
affected my life and all my relationships with women. I had to d
out all the ghosts and blot them out. God, the wasted energy.
never succeeded in killing any of them. They all still haunt me."

The doctor laughed. "Christ! You must be fighting twenty-fo
hours a day."

I had to laugh too. "I keep hacking away but they're like eart
worms. You no sooner cut them in half than they get new hea
multiplying."

"When the hell do you find time to be free?"

"I don't."

"Tell me more about you and Sylvia. How did she handle yo
jealousy?"

"We were both on the brink of being demented by it. I used
create such scenes about her relationship with her husband, ev
though that was all over basically. God, I was so in love with h
I couldn't stand the thought of another man ever having touch
her or looked at her as I did. It reached the point where I'd on
take her places she'd never been before. I wanted to be the first
every way. She, of course, was everything to me — my sweethea
my teacher, my mother. I wanted to be her son, friend, stude
lover. I wanted each of us to be the other's creation.

"I had to make her my wife.

"She finally asked her husband for a divorce. The poor m

didn't put up a fight. He took off for San Francisco, where he had originally met Sylvia. Maybe he, too, went to search for ghosts. When the divorce became final, I couldn't wait to apply for the marriage license. We drove to the Santa Monica city hall, where we had to stand in line with a dozen or so other applicants. The clerk gave us forms. After we'd filled them out, he said we'd have to take a blood test and suggested a doctor around the corner.

"We paid him the three-dollar fee and went around to see the blood specialist. Once again, we had to wait with all the other applicants. When our turn came, he barely looked up. He picked my chart up first. I had stupidly put down my right age, twenty. He looked at me, then at Sylvia.

" 'Are you the boy's mother?'

"I could have reached across the desk and killed him. Sylvia shook her head. 'I'm to be his wife.'

" 'Oh,' said the baldheaded bastard, 'I'm sorry. The boy is underage and will need his parents' consent, but as long as you're here . . .'

"Sylvia turned and walked out of the office. I ran after her. We drove to my apartment in silence. Once inside, she fell on the bed and cried.

" 'That man looked at me as if I was something dirty.'

" 'He was an idiot. What does he know!'

" 'My God, Tony, you have to get your mother's permission — and I'm two years older than she is!'

"Then she started to laugh.

" 'If that doctor hadn't pointed it out and we'd have married, your mother could have had me put in jail for molesting a minor.'

"She was wrong, of course. My mother knew how much I loved Sylvia. Both she and my grandmother were tremendously grateful for what Sylvia had done for me. They had already learned to love her as part of the family.

"I tried to take her in my arms and tell her so. She got up and headed for the bathroom.

"When she came out she had removed all traces of tears.

" 'Tony, it was a silly idea to think we could get married. I'm eighteen years older than you are. When you're forty I'll be fifty-eight. We'll look ridiculous together.'

"I gripped her by the shoulders. 'Stop it, stop it. For me, life

doesn't exist without you. There's a whole world out there to dis
cover with you. I can't face it alone.'

" 'You must learn, dear.'

"She walked out and closed the door."

BOY (*unimpressed*). That's your version.

MAN. That's the way it was!

BOY. No, it wasn't. After Sylvia left, you went to the bed and sa
down. You started to play with a piece of lint on the cover and
you thought, so this is the way a love affair ends — playing with
a piece of lint. You made a mental note to use it someday — to
write about how love ends with someone playing with a piece
of lint.

# 15

TRY AS I MIGHT I couldn't get Sylvia to reconsider. She kept kid
ding that she wasn't going to marry me until I could do it withou
getting my parent's consent.

The change in our relationship was slight at first, but it wa
there. Fortunately, we still shared countless common interests and
this helped us get through a period of transition. We often amuse
ourselves toying around with the plans for the supermarket tha
I'd started designing at Polytechnic High. Now Sylvia made m
redo them. She called up Frank Lloyd Wright's office and was abl
to get an appointment for me.

As I once again walked into Wright's office, I saw that the sam
clutter existed, except that there were new drawings on the wall
and new mock-ups piled on chairs and the desk.

He was not in his office, so I had time to study the drawing
There was a stunning project of a city to be built in Persia. O
another wall were plans to buttress up the sinking city of Venice

I heard his clarion voice behind me. "Well, Mr. Quinn, we mee
again."

He gripped my hand. There was a friendly twinkle in his eyes. "A very persistent lady called and insisted I was passing up a reat talent."

I searched for my portfolio to show him my new version for the upermarket. He didn't bother to open it.

"Say: Peter Piper picked a peck of pickled peppers."

"P-Peter — P-Piper — picked — a p-peck — of . . . ," I stam-ered.

"You didn't do as I told you. Goddamnit, son, get that frenum ut! What kind of student are you going to be if you don't follow uy orders."

"Y-Yes, sir."

I started to pick up my drawings, but he stopped me.

"Leave them here. By the way, are you still painting skies in fferent gradations of blue?"

"No, sir, they are more like Vlaminck now."

"Good." He held out his hand. "Come back to see me when you un say: She sells seashells by the seashore — without stumbling."

A few days later, Sylvia took me to see a throat specialist. He fted my tongue and agreed that my frenum did need cutting in der to articulate. Unfortunately, the operation would cost a undred and fifty dollars, which seemed like a fortune.

I paid the specialist the three dollars for the examination and id I'd be back someday.

"You mean you can't afford it now?"

"No, sir, I can't."

"Why is it important for you to have it done?"

I told him about my meeting with Frank Lloyd Wright.

"Well, we don't want you to miss the opportunity of being a eat architect," he said. "I'll perform the surgery and you pay me hen you can."

It was a long time before I was able to speak after the rather mple operation. My tongue, not used to its newfound freedom, ipped around in my mouth. I couldn't control it.

Sylvia suggested that I take voice lessons. I found a drama hool in the yellow pages of the phone book. The ad specified ocution and speech. The school, on the corner of Cahuenga and ollywood Boulevard, was run by a former actress named Kath-ine Hamil.

Miss Hamil told me she had an opening in her busy schedul
and that the lessons would cost five dollars an hour. I had notice
that the place wanted a good sweeping out and that the window
needed washing. I haltingly suggested that I would be willing t
do the janitor work in exchange for elocution lessons. She agreed

The following day we started. My first exercise consisted of pu
ting a cork in my mouth and trying to pronounce tongue twiste
like, "How much wood would a woodchuck chuck if a woodchuc
could chuck wood," and "Theophilis Thistle thrust three thou
sand thistles through the thick of his thumb."

I often stood at the back of the rehearsal hall and listened t
the director, Max Pollock, lecture on the Stanislavski method. H
was a slight, eccentric man, a recent immigrant from Russia, wh
loved to say everything was a "jew-el."

Outside of a long stringy young man named Lang Hargrove,
thought the kids were wasting their parents' money. To most c
them it was glamorous to be "paht of the thee-atah." I noticed tha
they were much more interested in their weekend "pah-tys" tha
in what old Pollock was talking about. He kept reassuring then
that the play they were preparing, Noel Coward's *Hay Fever*, w
a "jew-el" and that each one of them would be a "jew-el" in it.

Miss Hamil soon allowed me to take the cork out of my mouth
She gave me exercises in Shakespeare. One night, after working o
Othello's speech — "Behold, I have a weapon; a better never di
itself sustain upon a soldier's thigh" — she asked me if I'd ev
thought of being an actor.

I didn't want to tell her about the disappointment when
didn't play the bear cub in that movie years before. I didn't te
her either about the period when I hired myself out at parties an
did imitations of Bing Crosby, Louis Armstrong, and Mauri
Chevalier. I used to hang a sheet up on a doorjamb, shine a lig
behind me, and in silhouette mouth the records I traveled wit
I'd get two dollars a night.

The act hadn't got me bookings at the Palace Theater so I le
it all unsaid. Instead, I told her I had no ambitions of being a
actor. As soon as I learned to speak, I intended to go back to Fran
Lloyd Wright and rattle off "Peter Piper picked." The subject w
dropped.

However, one day while I was reciting — "Tomorrow, and t

morrow, and tomorrow, creeps in this petty pace from day to day,
to the last syllable of recorded time" — I heard applause behind
me. It was Max Pollock, standing in the doorway.

"A jewel — a jew-el, my boy," he exclaimed deliciously, with
Slavic intonations. "I thought you vas chust a chanitor. I didn't
know you vas an actor."

Miss Hamil seemed pleased to have her suspicions confirmed by
such an authority. Pollock called her outside for a private conference. A few minutes later they both came in smiling. It seemed
that the young man playing the part of Simon in *Hay Fever* had
developed a real fever. The part of Simon was mine for the taking.
I couldn't figure out what a kid from my background had in common with the English Simon in Coward's play, but I was eager to
find out.

I think I had much more courage then than I have now, maybe
because I had less responsibility. In any event, I worked very hard.
I knew that Hollywood agents and producers came to see the
school productions and that *Hay Fever* would be reviewed by the
film trade papers.

I got rather good notices in the play. Sylvia, of course, came to
see me. That night when we went home, she said, "Tony, I think
that you have found your profession."

I was now secretly fired with the idea of being an actor. I kept
on at Miss Hamil's school, but I was very broke. Sometimes I'd
only have ten cents in my pocket, so it was a question of whether
I would eat a sandwich or buy a book to read, or a play to study.
Most of the time, literature won out and I went hungry. Rather
than spend money on a streetcar, I'd walk home, some four to five
miles.

Max Pollock asked if I would like to do another play with him,
Gorki's *Lower Depths*. Again, I got good notices. Encouraged, I
kept on. I began working with a group called the Gateway Players.

At that time I was introduced to something I had heard about,
but never really understood. As boys we used to kid about what
we called "lilies" or "pansies." At the Gateway Players one of the
leading men, who later became a movie star of sorts, was always
asking me to go out with him. Since he was already an established
name, I was flattered. He took me to a fancy restaurant. I thought
it was so "classy" when he ordered wine. We had a few glasses,

and after dinner he asked me for a nightcap to his house in Beverly Hills. Once there, however, he seemed to forget about the promised drink. He went into the bathroom and came out in his pajamas. He threw another pair at me and said, "Come on, let's go to bed."

I said innocently, "I'm not sleepy, I'd better go home."

"Come on, you're not going home. Relax and come to bed."

"But I'm not sleepy," I insisted. "Why the hell should I go to bed?"

He was a very big fellow, taller, heavier than I was, and he started to get mad at me. "Listen, what the hell did you come here for?"

"You invited me; you said you wanted to talk to me about my acting."

Then he told me he had been in love with me since the first time he set eyes on me. He was saying things that girls said; it was scary somehow. I didn't know whether to laugh, hit him, or feel sorry for him. I started to get up and he grabbed me by the shoulders and said, "Listen, you're not leaving!"

"Look, George, I'm leaving. I'm sorry, but I'm not like that."

"You fool," he said, "you can't be an actor without having experienced everything."

"I don't think that I have to experience *that* to be an actor. It doesn't interest me." I retreated and said, "Besides, I've got a girl." I thought that would dissuade him. "Well, I have girls too," he said, "but I'd much rather be with you." He started to grab for me.

I pushed him away. He fell on the bed and started to cry. Dawn was breaking outside, and I could hear the birds starting to sing. I could see the light starting to come through the windows, and thought, my God! What kind of nightmare is this? I felt I was in the wrong cast in the wrong play.

"Get out!" he shouted. "Get out of here! You'll never be an actor — you'll never be anything. I thought you had some class, but you have no class."

As I went to the door, he shouted something that sounded very profound, and to this day I don't know what the hell it means. "Don't forget," he said. "Life is two mountains and there is no valley."

When I got home, Sylvia was waiting. I told her about my experience. She didn't seem to be shocked.

"You know, the theater's full of people that are rather highly strung and individual," she said. "All the arts are. You mustn't have prejudices against homosexuals. You should try to understand everybody."

Her attitude struck me as rather remarkable. But there were no such incidents with homosexuals again for a while, so I didn't have to put the tolerance she recommended to the test.

One day, walking home after having spent a quarter on a book, I ran into a young man I had met while doing *Lower Depths*. His name was Feodor Chaliapin, son of a renowned basso. He asked me what I was doing. When I said I was looking for a job, he told me Mae West was in the market for Latin types to play gigolos in *Clean Beds,* a new play she was producing.

"You'd be perfect," he said. When I got there, a long line of actors was waiting to be interviewed. My turn finally came and I met a jolly, red-faced man. He'd been a prominent lawyer in New York and had fallen in love with Mae West after representing her in some case. He had given up his practice to become her manager. Now he was interviewing the actors and she was standing by, looking like a queen.

She stared at me for a minute and said, "Come over here, boy." I walked up to her. There was something tantalizingly and almost coarsely sensuous about her.

"What do you do?" she asked, on four different levels.

"I'm trying to be an actor."

"One of those, eh? Well, a couple of years from now, I'll take you on. Right now you're a little young for me."

I didn't want to argue the point. "Fine, I'll come back when I think I'm ready."

Later, everybody wanted to know what she'd said to me, because she hadn't spoken to any of the other young men. She would merely nod and her manager would either turn them down or tell them to stick around.

As I was walking out of the theater, I stopped and looked into the auditorium, where they were also casting different roles in *Clean Beds*. Up on the stage, an actor was obviously imitating John Barrymore, who had become my idol. From the back of the theater, the director shouted: "Thank you very much, sir." Another actor came up and he read, also imitating Barrymore. He wasn't very good.

"Why is everybody imitating Barrymore?" I asked a man who was assisting the director. "The author wrote *Clean Beds* with Barrymore in mind, but he's busy with his new wife and told the writer to go fuck himself," he said. "Also, the play prognosticates that Barrymore will wind up a drunk in a flophouse. They've sent it to Fredric March."

I asked the man if he thought I could read for the director. "You're crazy!" he said. All the actors reading for the part were much older. One later became a very dear friend of mine, a painter named John Decker, who looked amazingly like Barrymore. The man thought I was being silly, but he went up to Vladimir Uranov, the director, who looked toward me.

"Do you want to read for the part?" I nodded yes. "The character is an old man. How old are you?"

"I'm twenty-two," I lied.

He gave me a script. I had already heard some of the dialogue as I'd listened to the auditions. He rehearsed with me, then I walked through it. I don't know whether I had a fantastic memory or what, but I had learned most of the scene.

I entered from the wings and started playing the part, when I heard applause. I stopped. It was Mae West, standing in the back of the theater. She came down the aisle and said, "You're very good. Maybe I passed up a good thing."

She turned to the director. "I think the kid's pretty good. If I were you, I'd give him the part."

"But," he said, "the part's a sixty-five-year-old man. . . ."

"You can put makeup on the kid; he'll be sensational."

At first Uranov though she was kidding. He said, "Miss West, you know it's a very important production and we're thinking of going to Broadway."

"Look, I made a mistake a few minutes ago with him. The boy's got it." Since she was producing the play — though not appearing in it — her word carried the day. I got the part and started rehearsing.

One thing I had not learned at Katherine Hamil's school, or in the other plays that I had done, was makeup. Though the director

ept telling me I sounded well and managed the famous Barrymore camel walk, I still looked like a twenty-year-old imitation
f that legendary figure. I was in a quandary as to what to do
o make myself look sixty-five. I called up Feodor Chaliapin for
dvice, having heard that his father had been a genius at making
p for characters like Mephisto and Boris Godunov. Feodor told
me he'd bring a friend on opening night to help me.

I was at the theater three hours before curtain time, desperately
studying photographs of the Magnificent Barrymore Profile. It was
no use. I couldn't transform my Aztec-Irish face into any sem-
blance of the great actor.

Half an hour before the curtain was to go up, Feodor brought
in a cherubic-faced man, whom I immediately recognized as Akim
Tamiroff. In addition to being a very fine actor, he also was a
master at makeup. He took one look at me and howled in a deep
Ukranian voice.

"I'm supposed to make dis baby bwoy look sixty-five? True, I'm
great makeup man, but I am not God."

He was wrong. He almost was God. In a half hour he had aged
me forty-five years, and with a little putty had made me look like
John Barrymore's father. The rest was up to me.

As I was about to make my entrance, word arrived backstage
that Jack Barrymore had just walked into the audience. The director almost fainted. We became so concerned about him I didn't
have time to get my usual attack of stage fright.

After the show, there was a lot of applause. I think it was the
first time I'd really felt I'd had any kind of meaningful success. I
went backstage to my tiny cubbyhole. Uranov came in and congratulated me. Akim Tamiroff and half the Russian colony were
there. Mae West came back, hugged me, and said, "You lived up
to my expectations, kid. I hope someday you can live up to my
other hopes."

Pretty soon I could hear a rumble down the hall and I sensed
something immense was about to happen. Sure enough, there was
a knock on the door, and there stood John Barrymore. Nothing
can ever equal the impression he made walking into that little
dressing room. He glowered at me, and said, "You're a sonofabitch; you're a shit. You were marvelous out there. How old are

you?" By that time, I had pulled off my nose. "By Christ! You'r
a kid!"

"Mr. Barrymore, I hope you don't —"

"Ach! Christ, everybody's doing a takeoff on me, kid, wh
shouldn't you? At least you do it well. I live on Tower Road; i
you're ever around there, drop in and see me." He gave me hi
address.

A week later he came back to the theater. He saw the pla
again, came backstage, and said, "You sonofabitch, why haven'
you been up to see me?"

"I'm sorry, Mr. Barrymore; I thought you were just being nice.

"I'm never nice. Anyway, I came back because I didn't believ
you were that good. I thought it was first-night nerves that mad'
you look good. How about lunch tomorrow?"

Oh my God, to be invited . . . !

The next day I went out to lunch with Barrymore. I had to tak
a streetcar. I was earning ten dollars a week doing the play. Ma
West was very sweet to me, but she knew how to drive a har
bargain. My part was supposed to pay twenty-five dollars a weel
She had said to me, "Kid, this is great experience for you and
don't want to spoil you. As a matter of fact, you should be payin
me for playing the part, but I'm going to give you ten dollars
week."

So I took a streetcar and a bus, then walked up to Tower Roa
which was a hell of a long way. I was careful to arrive on time, bu
the gate was closed and I rang the bell. The caretaker came ou
I told him Mr. Barrymore had invited me to come to lunch. H
probably thought I was just another fan trying to get in.

"Mr. Barrymore never sees anybody," he said.

I started off dejectedly when I heard the famous voice: "He
shit face, where are you going?"

I stopped. My idol came to the gate, opened it for me, an
showed me into the house.

It was a huge, rambling place. As I walked in I stopped t
admire a magnificent suit of armor by the entrance. Barrymor
said, "Bobby Jones designed it for me for *Richard III*."

He stared at me. "You know, when an old bullfighter's about t
leave the ring, he usually hands his sword to a young bullfighte
coming up. It's called an 'alternativa,' kid."

I thought he was joking. He showed me around the house. There was some hammering going on, and he said, "I never stop building. If I stop building, I'll die."

He took me into a little den, right off the living room. About eight by nine feet, it was an incongruous room. The walls were cracked; there were some photographs on the wall; in one corner was a sink. He proceeded to it and peed. He said to me as I watched him relieving himself, "This is my favorite room. It reminds me of all the dressing rooms I lived in when I was traveling around the country."

He sat down in a huge armchair that was all tattered and torn, with grease spots. He yelled for his caretaker: "Bring us some drinks."

I didn't know that at that time he wasn't supposed to drink. His man brought him a vermouth and he turned to me: "Kid, what do you drink?"

I didn't drink in those days, but I said, "Oh, I'll have whatever you're having."

They brought me vermouth, too, which I discovered I didn't like.

Barrymore had an amazing quality. He could make you feel at home immediately, give you the impression that you were the most important person in his life. I've only met three other people who had that ability — Greta Garbo, Aimee Semple McPherson, and Katharine Hepburn. Of course, this was only if they liked you: if they didn't like you, all three had a remedy that Barrymore often talked about — closing the iron door.

That afternoon, as we sat in his little rigged-up dressing room, he again complimented me on what he had seen me do on stage. He asked where I had learned to copy him. I said I had seen most of his movies. He wanted to know all about me. I told him a bit of the story. He was intrigued by my involvement with Aimee Semple McPherson, whom he had gone to see at the Tabernacle. He agreed with me that she was one of the greatest performers he had ever seen. He said no actress had ever been able to hold the stage like she did, with the exception perhaps of his sister, Ethel Barrymore.

Then he asked me how I was, as he called it, fixed. Did I have money to get along with? I hemmed and hawed. He soon unde[r]stood that I was broke.

"Well, kid," he said, "I wish I could stake you, but at th[is] moment my advisers have a proclivity for keeping me one ste[p] above a beggar."

He used words magnificently. I remember that he used a phras[e] eleemosynary treat, which I recognized as one of the opening line[s] in Henry Fielding's *Tom Jones*. He was delighted when I tol[d] him I'd read the book.

He advised me strongly to go to England to learn to speak. H[e] regretted the fact that he hadn't gone there to study. It wasn[t] until he was in his thirties, when Hopkins, the great directo[r] asked him to do *Hamlet* and *Richard III*, that he had starte[d] working on his speech to eliminate a nasal New Yorker's accent.

He was very talkative that afternoon. I was fascinated by all th[e] stories he told me. He kept emphasizing that speech was the mo[st] important thing in the world for the actor, I suppose partly b[e]cause mine had not improved as yet. He told me about his fir[st] speech lesson.

He had reluctantly gone up to see Margaret Carrinston, wh[o] was married at that time to Robert Edmund Jones, one of th[e] great set designers of the theater. She pointed to a bowl on th[e] table and asked him to take one of the pieces of fruit in his hand[.] He wondered what the hell it had to do with the speech lesso[n] he'd gone for. He reached over and took an apple.

"Mr. Barrymore, what do you have in your hand?"

"I got a red apple."

"You have what?"

"I got a red *apple*."

"I'm sorry, I don't understand."

"You don't understand? I got a *red* apple in my *hand!*"

Then he laughed and said his speech lessons for the first two [or] three weeks consisted of making that apple sound like the juicie[st] reddest apple in the world. She wasn't satisfied until he ha[d] created not only the imagery, but the fullness of each word. H[e] said, "She taught me to make love to words. Don't get carrie[d] away with emotion, kid. Caress the word."

I didn't interrupt him, I just let him go on. He seemed to be i[n] need of someone to talk to. His wife, he told me, was out sho[p] ping, spending his hard-earned money. He seemed to be amused by all the scandal in the papers, and took it for granted that I knew about it.

He said to me: "Kid, I'm going to give you the greatest lesson in acting. The best way to learn to be an actor is to read Walt Whitman's 'Two Strangers from Alabama.' It's a poem about two birds that come to Alabama in the spring; the female bird has come to make her nest and lay her eggs, and the male bird helps the female make the nest. They are both terribly excited at making their little home and looking forward to the birth of the baby birds. Then one day the male bird goes out in search of food and that night he doesn't come back. After the little female waits all day for him, in vain, she goes out in search of her mate, flying about in the wet, looking for him. But she never finds him. It's a very painful poem of lost love."

And as he quoted it to me, his eyes filled with tears. I watched this phenomenal performance with awe. He had forgotten I was there. I must admit that I, too, had tears in my eyes when he finished.

When he saw that, he laughed sardonically and said, "Well, kid, if you can read that poem in front of a mirror while you're sitting on the toilet, you'll be an actor. Seated on your throne, naked, performing your maleficent duties, recite that poem. If you can forget that you're defecating and get lost in the beauty of the words, then you are an actor."

He would jump from one subject to another. He seemed to like me, to want to be saying something, but he could only say it through quotations.

"Have you read the Bible?"

"Yes, sir."

"Holy Christ, you're kidding! I guess it's just you and me, and the Pope, who ever read the Bible anymore. Do you know the Song of Songs?"

"Yes, sir."

" 'There be four things I know not of —' "

He stopped in midair, waiting for me to finish the quotation. I continued the rest timidly: " '— the way of the eagle in the air, the way of a serpent on a rock —' " But he finished the last two lines. " '— the way of a ship upon the sea and the way of a man with a maid.' " For at that moment he *was* a Solomon.

Just then the phone rang; he was annoyed by the interruption. He picked it up and shouted rudely into it.

"Hello!"

His whole countenance changed, and he said, "Of course, my love, yes, my love." I could tell that he was speaking to his new wife.

After he hung up, he asked me if I was married. I said no. He said, "Do you have a broad?" I nodded that I did. "Well, don't trust any of them as far as you can throw Fort Knox. They're all twittering vaginas." He spoke of his various marriages, to a Miss Harris; to Michael Strange, a poetess by whom he had a daughter named Diana. He spoke about Dolores Costello, whom I sensed he had really loved. He asked if I'd ever seen her in a picture and I said yes. He said, "Christ, isn't she beautiful?" She had remarried by then. Strangely enough, he said, she had married her obstetrician. He laughed cynically. "Too bad he wasn't her proctologist!"

He had absolutely no faith in women. I tentatively asked him why he had been married so many times and he seemed irked at the question. "Because, I loved the cunts." He used the latter word freely in talking about women. With men, he would use "shit" or "shit-face," and make it sound like a term of endearment. He only called people he loved "shits," like John Decker, W. C. Fields, Roland Young, Thomas Mitchell, and Gene Fowler. I was very happy when he included me among the "shits."

He kept coming back to the point, however, that I had acting ability; I should go to England and study speech. He mentioned that at one time his sister, Ethel, had been semi-engaged to Churchill, who was also a friend of his. I understood why both men had that resonant delivery of speech, both seemed to have a common reverence for language. He recited a list of words he particularly loved: eleemosynary, expectoration, defecation, glorious, wonderful. He stressed each word and you felt a whole world in them. Then he laughed that Satanic laugh of his and said old Roosevelt and Churchill knew how to use them: "They would rather make love to a word than to a woman; maybe that's goin bit far, but I do think it would be a dead heat. My poor brother, Lionel, uses words only to flog them. He makes them suffer."

Then he was off on another tangent, asking me what I read besides the Bible. I gave him a rundown, but left out Shakespeare. I knew I was in front of a man who knew every word Shakespeare had ever written. But he wouldn't let me off the hook. "Why did you leave out old Bill?"

"He scares me. I'll never be able to play him. Too many people have ideas about how he should be played. Besides, it's for people who speak good English."

He let out a huge, rude noise and said, "Horseshit. I shoved Shakespeare down their throats in London. Someday you should play Othello, kid. Othello is not English, though he's usually played by some English nancy; they play him like a Harlem Negro. Christ knows, the Harlem Negro has enough problems; why saddle him with Othello's as well? Besides, don't forget that Othello was an Arab, a Moor, a Moslem."

The telephone rang again. "Yes, darling, I'll be down immediately."

He got up and I knew the meeting was over. He very sweetly walked me to the door and asked me if I had means by which to go down the hill. I didn't tell him that I didn't need a car, that the meeting had given me wings.

As I started out the door, he said, "Kid, I would ask you to dinner, but unfortunately I'm married to a young girl who would probably immediately want to fuck you."

He laughed again that peculiar, sad laugh of his. I smiled feebly and started off.

He called after me, "I wasn't kidding, kid. Someday I'll give you that armor."

I never thought I would see him again.

During the run of *Clean Beds,* I had some difficulties with Mae West about my salary. I was hoping that I would become part of her company, and I said I would sign a seven-year contract if she would give me twenty-five dollars a week, but she turned me down, thank God.

Later, I met her one day, and she said, "Well, you're doing very well, kid, I'm getting all sorts of reports about you."

"Yes, Miss West, thanks to you and your letting me do th[e] play."

"Oh, kid, I don't want any credit." Then she said her famou[s] line: "Why don't you come up and see me sometime?" I nev[er] knew whether she was joking because everything she said ha[d] five meanings. I said I'd love to, just being civil, but she invite[d] me up that evening. At that time, she was living in a lovely b[ig] hotel in one of the most exclusive sections in Hollywood.

When I got there, the bellboy escorted me to the elevator an[d] right up to the top floor.

Mae herself came to the door, a most dazzling creature, wit[h] beautiful translucent skin, like white silk with a light behind i[t,] and soft lively eyes, and the blond hair worn loose. She wa[s] dressed all in white, a negligee that just barely covered her breast[s;] the cleavage was dizzying.

Everything in the apartment was white, not one drop of colo[r] but for her. She made me a drink and we sat down. "You kno[w] I take a very special interest in you, you're one of my boys," sh[e] said. "How do you like the hotel?"

"Oh, I think it's a lovely —"

"It's my joint. I had a boyfriend; he happened to be a Negro – do you know him, Tiger Jones?"

"Yes, of course."

"Well, one day I wanted to bring him in and they told me [I] couldn't do it; so I told them to go fuck themselves and I bough[t] the joint."

She served us supper, and we talked. She wanted to know if [I] had a girl friend, and I said yes, though I never had thought [of] Sylvia in that way. She started asking me a lot of personal que[s-] tions; I thought, maybe she feels very familiar with me becaus[e] I was in the play.

After dinner, she said, "I've got a great part for you in a ne[w] play. I'm thinking very seriously of taking you to New York wit[h] me. I'd like to see how you work it out, and if you don't min[d] I'm going to give you a little test tonight."

I was twenty-one years old, meeting this incredible woman, an[d] I felt awkward and unsure. "If you don't mind coming into m[y] boudoir, I have my script there," she said. So I slunk into he[r] bedroom. Again, it was all white; the only difference was that th[e] ceiling was mirrors. At the side of the enormous bed she had a pile of beautiful leather boxes. She rummaged around and brought out a script. "Turn down the lights, boy; they hurt my eyes." I turned down the lights and sat in an armchair across the room.

"Now, in this scene you play a kind of Lothario; I'm lying in bed." And she took a position in bed. "It's a hot summer night and I can't keep my clothes on because it is too hot, so I slowly start to undress." And with this, she started undressing; underneath she wore a little chemise, I could see right through it. "It's terribly hot, and I'm writhing in the heat." And she started writhing, and I was watching her like, okay, tell me the rest, tell me the rest of the story.

Then she said, "And suddenly what do I see but this young man who has been pursuing me, coming through the window. . . ." And I went over by the window. "He stands there, just like you're standing there now, and it thrills me, because he's been pursuing me for a long time, but I pick up my dress and cover myself. That doesn't stop him; he keeps approaching and I see this man and I'm beginning to realize I'm about to fall under his fascination. Come on, closer, boy, let me see how you're going to do the part. Now he approaches and he's standing beside my bed and it's so hot and I feel his breath coming down the point of my neck . . . bend over, bend over, boy! Well, I look at him for a long time and gaze into his liquid brown eyes and suddenly my mouth starts opening because I want him, I want him: I suddenly realize that this is the man of my life and I'm just lying there with mouth open and I feel him getting closer, and closer . . . get closer, boy."

So I got close and I was saying to myself, gee, this is a great scene. She went on. "Here you are, awfully close; now you can't resist me, you're bound to kiss me, and I know your mouth is going to taste so sweet. I know you're a young boy and you have to have a woman like me before you know what a woman can really be, and you're sensual and you start to. . . ." I was just leaning over the bed, fascinated, waiting to hear more. She paused and stared at me for a minute. "How do you like the scene?"

"I think it's a great — it's a great scene, Miss West!"

"Yes, it's a lovely scene, isn't it?" And there was a long silence, then she said, "Well, don't just stand there, boy, hand me that third box from the bottom." I did, and she opened the box and said, "Would you like one?" It was full of chewing gum. She took a piece and started chewing. I felt terrible, because I knew I had failed; I just couldn't do it. She said, "Well, I'm going to think very seriously about giving you the part," and she couldn't get rid of me fast enough. I never saw her after that, except in a nightclub.

While I was still appearing in *Clean Beds*, I went one day to see my grandmother, who had taken a turn for the worse.

"Tony, you're going to be a big star someday."

"Aw, come on, Grandmother, that's a lot of nonsense."

As far as I was concerned she was indulging in wishful thinking, and I was going through periods of doubt: although I was having a momentary success, nobody was breaking down the doors to offer me pictures, or any other plays, for that matter. Though Barrymore had said some nice things.

I didn't really have much hope for myself as an actor. I didn't have the ability to caress words.

But she said, "I will not die until I know for certain that you're on your way to becoming a big star."

I thought, well, that's a good sign, because she's going to have to wait; she'll be living a long time before I become a movie star.

Then I was asked to go for an interview at Universal Studios to see a director named Freidlander. He had seen me in the play and wanted me for a picture called *Paroles for Sale*. There was a young man named David O'Brien in the play at the time, and when he heard about the possibility of my doing a movie, he synthesized the art of movie acting by advising me that it was very simple. "All you have to do is keep your eyes moving." Perhaps I would have gone farther if I'd followed his advice.

The call finally arrived for me to report for work. I put on the only presentable pair of trousers I owned and an old sweater.

It was early in the morning when I rushed to the director. He said, "All right, go and get made up, kid. Wear your suit."

"What suit?"

"Kid, you're playing a very important gangster in this picture and you have to wear a sharp suit."

"I'm sorry, sir. I didn't know, I thought the studio would loan e a suit."

They rushed me over and tried to fit me, but were unable to nd anything adequate. The director said, "Kid, I'm sorry. I'll st have to take somebody else."

There was another young man standing around, looking very mart and sinister. "All right, you've got the part."

I started to walk away, disappointed, when the director called e back.

"Look, I saw your play and I thought you were wonderful. I'd ve to use you on this picture. This afternoon, we're doing a quence; it's not very much — you don't talk at all — but if you on't mind doing it, I'll tell them to give you seventy-five dollars r it." I accepted on the spot.

"Go over to the wardrobe," he said. "They'll give you a pris- ner's outfit."

That afternoon we shot a small scene: a bunch of prisoners ere watching a show. I was laughing in the middle of the show hen suddenly somebody shoved a knife into my back. In the iddle of the laugh, I fell and died. That's all I had to do. The irector was very sweet to me and shot it as a big close-up. The ene lasted about forty-five seconds on the screen.

Two or three months later, I heard the picture was going to be reviewed at the Pantages Theater. I mentioned it to my grand- iother, who insisted she had to see it. I told her what the scene as about. "There's nothing to it," I said.

She was adamant. "I've got to see it. I have to know before I ie if you are going to be a movie star like Ramon Novarro and ntonio Moreno."

She was hanging onto life by a bare thread, living on hope, nd I couldn't refuse her. I borrowed a car, and she and my sister nd Sylvia and I went. She was so sick that I had to carry her a my arms to the balcony.

The movie wasn't bad, but it wasn't the most memorable pic- ire of all time.

My sequence came on. The camera panned around the group f prisoners. When it swept past me, I could feel her tighten up. he grabbed my hand as if to say, now let's see what you can do. he camera started moving in on three men, and then it froze on a big close-up of me watching the show, smiling and laughing

I had made up a whole story, of course, about the man I was playing; he was stupid and like a child; he reacted like a child to whatever was said: when everybody else laughed, he laughed; he wasn't a very nice man; the reason he was going to be killed was that he had ratted on another prisoner.

There it was now on the screen. In the middle of the laugh we saw a man sitting behind me make a gesture and shove the knife into me. The laugh froze and I seemed to wonder: Why did you kill me? How can I possibly die in the middle of the laugh? Why?

That was all — forty-five seconds on the screen. I felt so sheepish — to have come all the way from across town, to be with the stars of the movie, the director, the producer, and everyone. They had seen me carry in my grandmother, and I thought, oh, my God! For forty-five lousy seconds! I kept saying to my grandmother, "Let's go." I was afraid the lights would come up and everybody would see me there. But she wouldn't budge.

"I don't come on the screen anymore, Grandmother. That's all."

"I know, I know," she said. "But I want to watch the rest, to see how you fit into the whole picture."

Soon it was over. The lights came on and I was afraid to look up because people were passing by in the aisle. I tried to hide; my grandmother still held my hand. I was dying of embarrassment. A very nice man leaned over and said, "Very good, kid."

Somebody from the publicity department rushed over and asked, "Well, what did Jimmy say?"

"Jimmy who?"

"That was Jimmy Starr who stopped and said something to you."

Of course, I knew who Jimmy Starr was, quite a famous movie columnist. A good word from him meant either success or failure. The director stopped and said, "I thought you were very good." The more people complimented me, the more flustered and self-conscious I became. I thought everybody was pulling my leg.

After the crowd had walked out, I carried my grandmother down to the car and we drove home, and she made coffee. You would have thought I had come straight from a great performance of *King Lear*, or some other majestic role. To Sylvia, whom my

214

andmother liked very much — although she was confused by
e relationship — she said, "Well, Tony has a very big career."
I was annoyed at her. "Come on, Grandmother, cut it out. No
ıe is ever going to remember that I'm in the damn picture. It
as just seventy-five dollars, that's all it meant to me."
"No, Tony, I don't agree with you. You were excellent." I
ʊuldn't talk her out of it. Since we had discussed it, she knew
ıat reviews would appear in two trade papers, *Variety* and the
ɔllywood *Reporter*. She said she wanted to see what they said
ɔout me.
"Grandmother, for God's sake, nobody's going to say a damn
ɔrd about me. It was just a bit. Nobody will remember it."
"I want to see the papers," she insisted. Early the following
orning I had to go out and get them for her.
I opened *Variety* and read the review: *Paroles for Sale* — good
elodrama, et cetera, et cetera. Alan Baxter, very good, so and
ɔ. . . . And then, I didn't believe my eyes; there was a little
ɪragraph all about me. It said: "We didn't catch the name of
young man we saw on the screen: he didn't say anything, he
ıst laughed, but I think it is a face that we're going to hear
ɔm. I called the studio to find out who he was and they told me
s name was Anthony Quinn."
I thought to myself, somebody must be paying for publicity:
was very suspicious, wondering whether the studio had exerted
essure, or maybe Sylvia had called somebody. Then I opened
ıe Hollywood *Reporter* and it, too, mentioned me favorably:
There was an excellent bit part played by an unknown young
tor . . . we didn't catch his name. . . ." I knew they were
lking about me.
I rushed home to Grandmother because there it was, in the
ıpers, and she said, "Now I can die in peace."
The dear soul died about two weeks later.

# 16

KATIE HAD TAKEN the kids to visit her parents at the big hou
on top of the hill. They were going to stay there for the usua
Sunday night dinner. I knew I couldn't face the ritual of he
father's cutting the roast beef and doling out the portions. Be
sides, the big house had so many memories, so many pains assoc
ated with it. I knew "the boy" hated it there. He'd never fe
accepted.

I had begged off and driven up along the coast. Several time
I'd parked the car and walked along the beach trying to find th
answer to the doctor's question after our last session: "What d
you think of death?" It had been asked about my grandmother
passing away. When I said I did not believe in death as a fina
act, it didn't satisfy him. Now I stared out at the endless ocear
I felt the boy sitting beside me, waiting. He had followed n
silently all day. I thought of Katie and the kids. Life had bee
so full of promise. Where in hell had I gone wrong? What wa
the lie caught in my throat?

It was dark when I headed back toward our house on the Pal
sades. The boy, sitting beside me, could hold it in no longer.

BOY. She was the greatest.
MAN. Who?
BOY. Grandmother. She loved only one man.
MAN. One man at a time, you mean. First there was Grandfathe
then Father, and later we came along.
BOY. There you go, with the endless numbers game.
MAN. I got the bad habit from you.
BOY. So what's the answer?
MAN (annoyed). Who the hell knows? I'm looking.
BOY. That doctor wants you to kill all the ghosts. He wants yo
to bury them — Father, Grandmother, Sylvia, and all the res

MAN (*in pain*). I know, but I can't. I wouldn't know what to do without them.

OY. We don't hang around just to make you comfortable. We don't put up with all your shit to make you feel protected. You promised us all something and you fucked it up. You got screwed up with the "wants."

MAN. Listen to who's talking about wants. You had the biggest "want" in the world.

OY. But for important things, big things — not collecting nuts like a squirrel.

MAN. You little prick, I remember exactly the day you got screwed up. You even had me believing it for a while. It was that day when Mrs. Tanner was talking about Michelangelo and Florence. I saw your face. You and your crappy little chicken-scratching. You thought you were a reincarnation of Michelangelo. Come on, you even got me believing it so that for years I read everything about him. Of course, you wouldn't let me really try because you were afraid I'd fail and your childish fantasy would come to an end. Later you had me go to that Theosophist group because they believed in all that crap about the aura and the seven stages of reincarnation.

OY. That was just dreaming, to get away from the smell of the privy and the stench of hunger. Was it wrong to think I might have been somebody someplace?

MAN. That time I wanted to go to Florence and you found all sorts of excuses for me not to go. Why? Because it was all a lie, and you'd find out you were not Michelangelo, or even the guy that carried his bags. No, kid, you are no undiscovered genius, and neither am I. I've done my best. I will keep on doing my best, but I tell you now, either you join me, or I will kill you. Because I can't live with you on my back. I can't have you destroy everything I've done. I have other responsibilities besides you.

OY. I'm the most important to you.

MAN. No, boy, I have kids of my own. I hope it's not too late, but I don't want them to grow up emotional cripples, just because you have some crazy notion about being Michelangelo, or Napoleon, or Lincoln. One of these days you might want to

be Jesus Christ, and I'm not about to be crucified for you
I will give my life for many things — but not for *you.*

BOY. You want me to leave you alone? Just say the word and I'
disappear.

MAN. Don't give me that. Without me, you'd still be back ther
in that stinking two-holer. You'd still be back there, terrifie
of the old man with his two poor women, both frightened t
sneeze in front of him. You had me twisting and turning o
the doctor's couch the other day, trying to explain how you fel
the day our father died.

BOY. Shut up!

MAN. I'll tell you. You were secretly happy that he'd left.

BOY (*screaming*). That's not true.

MAN (*stops the car and grabs the kid by the shoulders*). Yes, it
true. You were finally number one and you had all the wome
to yourself. (*The boy squirms in the man's arms but the ma
holds him hard.*) Yes, it is true. That's what you had alway
wanted. And that's what you keep bugging me for with all tha
numbers shit. You loved that feeling of being number on
even if it was at the expense of the poor man's death. Yo
didn't have the balls to take him on. But I did, kid. I've gon
the full ten rounds with him and he doesn't scare me one bi
He was just a twenty-nine-year-old guy with all the crazy d
sires of youth. I've been through his pains and hungers. I'v
known them all. And if you really want to know, I think I
took the easy way out. What do you think of that? You wer
both fucking cowards. But me, kid, me with my Mexican-Irish a
hanging out; me, taking all that shit and insult and indignit
I didn't hide behind your fucking Mexican machismo and yel
from across the fence. Me, I went out and took them all o
the real ones and the ghosts you saddled me with. I fought the
all. And you, little prick, someday I'll kill you if you don't la
off me. (*The man is choking the boy. He feels him go lim
under his big hands.*)

FATHER. "Elephant!" (*A man's face peers through the car wi
dow.*)

FATHER. "Elephant! Are you all right?" (*The man eases up on th
boy. The tall young man walks away as if satisfied that the b
is safe. He is holding a guitar in his hand.*)

218

OY (*looks up at the man sardonically. He rubs his neck*). You were saying, sir?

AN. That sonofabitch is something, isn't he?

OY. How would you like to live with *that* all the time?

AN. I do. I've got him *and* you on my back.

OY (*after a pause*). Doesn't he know any fear himself?

AN. The poor guy is so scared he can't see straight. Remember that time the panther almost killed him?

OY. I can still remember Mother and Grandmother crying. He could have been something great.

AN. Kid, he was a janitor for a bunch of animals at the zoo.

OY (*surprised*). I thought he was a cameraman!

AN. Do you think he was going to come home and announce to his son, I've got a job wiping up elephant shit?

OY. But what about the panther? Tell me the story of the big black cat.

AN (*stroking the boy's head*). All right, one day a black panther got out of the cage and everybody ran for cover. They called *him* and told him to get the cat back into the cage. It was a big she-cat. The sonofabitch walked over and made some noises at the panther and the big cat walked up to him and nuzzled against his leg. He just reached over and patted her and started to walk her to her cage. She followed. When they got to the cage he went in ahead. As he was backing up he inadvertently leaned against the cage door next to it, the one that held the male cat. The male jumped at him and was clawing him to death when the she-cat jumped to his defense. He was caught in the middle. They found him on the floor half dead beside the dead male cat. The big she-cat died a few weeks later. He had been in the hospital and the she-cat had refused being fed by anyone else but him.

OY (*almost in a whisper*). She was in love with him?

AN (*amazed at the silly question*). How the hell do I know?

OY. Jeez, now I understand your hang-up about panthers.

AN (*shrugs*). So now you understand.

OY. Remember all those cats stalking Fifth Avenue when you got sick in New York?

AN (*laughs*). Yeah, the whole damned city became a cage. There were thousands of black cats roaming the streets. They were in

the house, in restaurants; they even came to my dressing room
many a night. They'd really howl.

I dutifully reported the scene at my Monday-night session. The
doctor seemed amazed. "The little bastard is relentless, isn't he
But you didn't answer my question about your grandmother
death."

"I thought I had. You'll just have to believe me when I say
don't believe in death. I can't accept the death of people I lov
As long as one is remembered, one is not dead."

The doctor made a helpless gesture. "But you're carrying s
much dead weight," he laughed. "I didn't mean that as a pun.
mean one has enough problems living one life; why take on the
responsibility of others?"

"Doc, maybe when you hand me my diploma we will have
solved that problem. For the moment, I enjoy living with the
idea that the ghosts are around, still real. The only one I can
deal with is the kid. The rest of them are good companions—
certainly much more pleasant than most of the living people
know. But I guess you're right. I refused at the time to accept the
fact that Grandmother wasn't around. She had always been the:
to catch me when I fell. I didn't have to live up to any condition
to deserve the love."

In spite of my grandmother's assurances that I was on my wa
to stardom, nothing had happened besides a couple of bit par
in gangster pictures. I was a long way from deserving the alte
nativa promised me by John Barrymore. Notwithstanding Sylvia
admonitions, I decided to go off somewhere and find out what the
hell I really wanted to do — without hanging on to her apre
strings.

Sylvia's oldest son, Bert, and I had become very close. He w
the younger brother I'd always wanted. One day, I told him
my plans to hop a train and go out and see the country. He aske
if he could go along. He seemed so eager, I couldn't refuse him

"When do we leave?" he asked.

"Tonight."

Bert ran home to pack. A few minutes later he showed up wi
a very distressed Sylvia at his side.

"What is this I hear about you two taking off?" she said.

"You've always talked about gathering experience," I said.
We're going to have some."

Reluctantly she gave us her blessing.

I had thrown the barest necessities, plus my theater notices,
into a small handbag. I had also packed a Bible and the hobo's
handbook, Harry Kemp's *Tramping through Life*. I was completely prepared for any eventuality we would encounter, or so
I thought.

As we got to the yards in downtown Los Angeles, we saw a
long line of freight cars pulling out. I gave Bert quick instructions on how to board the train, then ran out ahead to illustrate.
We were on our way like Don Quixote and Sancho Panza in
search of adventure.

We had decided to play it by ear, go wherever chance took us.
Secretly, I had it in the back of my mind to get to New York, the
Mecca of theater and culture. But then we had wound up in a
little town in the southern part of Texas.

We met a Negro hobo, who said, "It's a bad town, it's bad for
me and Mexicans, kid. Get out."

Being forewarned, we tried to avoid the center of the town,
skirting around the edges to the other side to catch another
freight. On the outskirts we saw a farm. We hadn't eaten all day
and I decided to chance it and ask for a job at the farm.

I sent Bert in because he was blond and very tall. He looked
like a nice clean-cut American boy. I had taught him to wash his
shirts like I did and he was very clean and proper-looking.

A woman of about thirty-five opened the door. She looked as
though she herself could go out and do a man's work, riding a
horse and rounding up cattle. I was standing under a tree as Bert
talked to her. He motioned to me to come over to the door, and
the woman looked at me rather peculiarly. I guess she saw that
I was Mexican, and she said, "Well, we're kinda low on hired
hands at the moment. Can you boys ride horses?"

We had to admit we couldn't.

"Well, what the hell can you do?" she asked.

Bert said, "We can cut wood for you; we can do anything else
you want."

She looked toward me and said, "Well, there's a room back of the barn, if you boys don't mind sleeping there. I'll give you three squares a day, room and board and twenty dollars a month for both of you."

We went over to the barn and there was a charming room, with a private bathroom. Bert and I, who had been sleeping in flop houses and Salvation Army dormitories, were delighted by the place.

After a while, the gong rang. We had washed up and made ourselves presentable, thinking there might be other people for dinner. As we walked into the house, which was simple but very tastefully done, I saw a huge library right off the dining room with hundreds and hundreds of books. The woman — her name was Mrs. Harris, she told us — saw me looking and asked if I liked to read.

"Yes, I do."

"What do you read?"

I laughed and took out my own collection of pages torn from books I had read on the road. My pockets were stuffed full. She was impressed.

"Isn't it a shame? I've no time to read and these books are going to waste. While you're working here you can use the library. Now, let's go and have dinner. We'll come back later and you can browse around."

During dinner, she told us her husband had died a few years before and left her with this farm. She said she was having a rough time trying to make it work. She lived by raising a few head of cattle, fruit trees, and a small vegetable patch.

After dinner she said brusquely, "All right, boys, tomorrow we have a hard day's work ahead of us. I'm going to go to sleep. Breakfast at six-thirty." And she gave us a rundown of our chores.

During the following week, we worked hard. She wasn't too communicative, but one day, while I was hoeing the vegetable patch, she drove up in her Dodge pickup truck.

"I have to go into town to do some shopping. Would one of you boys come with me? I hate to drive at night."

Bert said, "Yeah, I'll come with you."

"Do you drive?"

"No, I'm sorry."

"What about you, Tony?"

"Yes, I drive."

"Well, that's fine. You come with me, Tony. And Bert, you can watch the house."

When we were out on the road, she relaxed.

"I thought you were lying about knowing how to drive."

"It's my Irish side that knows how to do things." I couldn't resist needling her.

She just stared ahead.

When we got into town it was obvious there really wasn't much shopping she wanted to do: she bought a few things in a drugstore. As we drove back, she was peculiarly quiet and kind of nervous. She smoked a lot.

"I've bought you some things," she said finally. She showed me cologne, shaving soap, razor blades and other toilet articles. "One of these days you'll have to come into town and get a haircut. You need one."

I was disturbed: she'd already begun treating me like something that belonged to her.

When we arrived at the farm, she asked me if I'd like a cup of coffee. I was reading when she came into the library and set down the coffee. She didn't say much. After we had finished our coffee, I got up. "Well, I guess I'd better go to sleep; there's a hard day's work tomorrow."

"Do you feel sleepy?"

"Not particularly."

"I don't either," she said. "I feel so awake. Why don't you sit here? You can sleep late in the morning if you want."

"But you're not paying me to sleep . . ."

"Now come on," she said. "I'm certainly not treating you like a boss. We're friends; I'm enjoying just having you around. You're not punching a time clock or anything. Please, why don't you sit around and read? I want to go and take a pill so I can go to sleep later. Keep me company. I hate to be alone."

"Fine."

"I spend so much of my time alone."

Pretty soon she came in dressed in her negligee. She sat across from me on the couch. She stretched out and said, "Oh, I feel so tired, and suddenly so relaxed, so good. I could go to sleep right here."

I played along. "Would you like to hear some music?"

"No, no. All that winding of the machine, and changing th records. You know what I'd love? I'd love for you to read to me Come over here and read to me."

So I sat down beside her.

"Read softly, because I want to go to sleep. You have such nice voice, Tony. I took that pill and I think it's beginning t work."

I knew the poor woman was trying to find an excuse to get m to bed with her, and that she was embarrassed. I was pretty sur that she had been without a man since her husband had died.

As I was reading, her hand fell on my knee. I could feel th pressure of it. I watched it as it went up my thigh. Her eyes wer closed and I was reading to her and pretty soon, her hand wa between my legs. Then she moaned as if she were asleep. She kep pretending she didn't know what she was doing. Although sh had my penis in her hand, I was afraid of making an overt mov Still pretending to be asleep, pretty soon she took my hand an put it on herself. Suddenly, she pulled me down and she wasn faking sleep anymore.

After she had spent herself, again, and again, she said, "I thin I'd better go to bed. Come and read to me in bed."

I took my clothes off and really made love to her. It was ph nomenal, because this woman just didn't seem to get enoug After a while, she started talking to me, telling how the first tim she had seen me, something had happened to her, something sh didn't understand. She had watched me through the windows I worked in the garden. My body had glistened in the sun, an she had had these strange feelings.

"You know, having grown up in Texas, I've never really looke at a Mexican before. Suddenly, here I found myself being a tracted to you. I almost sent you away tonight. When I took th drive into town with you, I was going to tell you that you mu leave. And then, I don't know. I remembered the stories you tol me about yourself and the reading you do. I realized that yo were an unusual young man. And you've taught me a lesson. hope you like me, that you'll stay."

I still called her by her surname. Here I was, sleeping with h and calling her Mrs. Harris.

"Mrs. Harris, you know it's going to be embarrassing because
I'm working for you and I. . . . One of these days, I hope you
don't hate me because of all this."

"How could I hate you? I've never been so happy in my life.
No one has ever made me feel like this."

She said she hated living there alone; she was thinking of selling the place, of moving into a town, maybe New York. If she
sold the place, maybe we could both go to New York, she said,
and started to make plans right away. She was going to be part
of my life.

Every night thereafter was a repetition. Bert, of course, was
delighted. He lived vicariously and everything was wonderful to
him. "How was she?" he would ask me.

"Bert, there's going to be trouble here. I know there's going to
be trouble, soon, with this woman."

"Aw," he said, "she's lovely, she's wonderful, and she's crazy
about you."

I said, "Yeah, that's the trouble; I don't want to stick around
here."

After we'd been there a month she called me into the library.

"Tony," she said, "I'm embarrassed because your month is up
and I have to pay you."

"Yes, Mrs. Harris."

"How do you and Bert work?"

"Bert gets half and I get half. That's ten dollars apiece."

"Well, here's an envelope for Bert and here's one for you."

I went back to our room. Bert was lying on the bed, reading,
and I gave him his envelope. When he opened it there was fifteen
dollars in it.

"Jesus, she gave us more, she gave us five dollars more!"

Bert was thrilled. Then I opened mine. I saw five crisp twenty-
dollar bills.

I ran into the house.

"Mrs. Harris, I just opened my envelope."

"Yes?"

"You gave me too much."

"What do you mean, too much?"

"I said I'd work for ten dollars. I haven't earned a hundred
dollars this month."

"Listen, Tony, I can't treat you like a common laborer; you're not a common laborer."

"But I'm working here, Mrs. Harris."

"Tony," she said, "you're not working here; let's not use these stupid phrases."

"What am I doing?"

"You're here because I want you to be here."

"No, you hired me as a laborer; I'll accept ten dollars for that because I think I've earned it, but I don't want the rest. If you're paying me for anything else I've done, you're wrong."

"Tony, please, I'm very embarrassed, but what else can I do for you?"

I handed her the hundred dollars. "Give me my wages and my tip," I said.

She went to her room and came back with a ten-dollar bill.

"Thank you," I said. "Now I can take you out to dinner tonight."

"Where would we go?"

"We'll go into town."

She stared at me for the longest time. I was good enough to fuck but was I good enough to be seen socially?

"All right, Tony, fine."

I went to my place and put on one of her husband's suits which she'd given me. An hour later I came back. She looked lovely. As we drove to town I asked her which was the best restaurant. She said the best food was served at the country club. She told me how to get there and I drove to this very fancy place.

As we walked to the table, people turned to look at us. Apparently, some of them had known her husband.

We had a charming dinner. After a while, the orchestra started playing and I asked her if she would dance with me.

We got up and moved out to the floor. They played a slow rumba. Then people began moving away, just watching us: suddenly, she and I were dancing alone. At first, she was very embarrassed; I held her respectfully but firmly, and said: "It's very easy."

"I don't know how to dance to this music."

"It's very easy," I repeated. "It's just a box step, one-two-three ne-two-three. . . ." I talked to her very softly and she followed magnificently. She had a charming little body and she looked delightful. After the orchestra finished playing, everybody broke into applause. As we walked back to our table, she said, "My God, you're really a good dancer, Tony."

I think the whole evening, dinner and everything, had cost me eight dollars, practically a whole month's wages. On the way home that evening she said, "Tony, that was stupid."

"No, it wasn't," I said. "I wanted to do it, Mrs. Harris; you've been wonderful to me. Don't worry about it. What the hell do I need money for? Once a month I'll take you out to dinner."

"How much longer are you going to stay?"

So I told her more about myself and how I had started this trip to have experience and so forth. She asked if she was just an experience for me.

"No, Mrs. Harris. But right now I don't know where I'm going, or what I'm going to do. Eventually, I'll have to decide what to do with my life. I don't think I was born to be just a gardener."

She leaned over and kissed me. "No, I don't think you were."

There was something desperate in her voice as she put her head on my shoulder. "Do you really like me, Tony? Do you really like me?"

"Yes."

"Don't you think I'm a silly old woman?"

"No, you're very attractive." I didn't tell her that I still loved a woman older than she was.

"I'll sell the farm," she said, sitting up. "I can get fifteen, maybe twenty thousand dollars for it. We can live in New York. I'll help you get anything you want."

I drove along silently for a while.

oy. You could see yourself going to New York with her and spending her twenty thousand on an apartment and snappy clothes. You thought you had it made because you could fuck a red-neck's wife.

AN. She wasn't bad. She looked like Katharine Hepburn.

oy. Miss Hepburn has guts. Mrs. Harris just had a tight ass. Tell your shrink what she did to you finally.

I hung around for a few more weeks. I knew I was falling into a comfortable pattern. I'd do a day's work, then we'd all have dinner together. I had already read half of her library and besides, sex was good with her. But I began to hate her possessiveness.

One day, I reread page 551 from Wolfe's *Of Time and the River*. It triggered a decision in me. Suddenly it became clear that I would have to commit myself to something besides a woman's body. I had been avoiding things long enough. I decided to leave.

A few nights later, as she lay in my arms, satiated, I told her. She became a tigress. She accused me of having used her, of having taken advantage of her. The more I tried to placate her the more furious she became. Finally, she tried another tack and began demeaning herself. She begged me to use her body in any way I wanted. She was prepared to go to any limit to keep me there.

"It's nothing to do with that; it's something to do with me, with the fact that I must make a life for myself."

Next morning when I woke up she was sitting in the breakfast room having coffee; something had happened to her. She had hardened, she was the boss again.

"When will you be leaving?"

"In the next couple of days. There's some work to be done yet." I had been building a little house for the chickens, rabbits and other animals that she kept. I told her I'd leave as soon as I had finished that.

Later that day, she asked me to return the clothes she'd given me, two suits and some shirts, from her dead husband.

I took them down and handed them to her. She pointed at some books under the bed. "I want you to return those books and anything else you've taken from the house."

"Fine," I said. I quietly started picking up the books. She knocked them out of my hand.

"I've made a fool of myself because of you. You've humiliated me. I knew I shouldn't trust a Mexican. Everything they say about them is true."

I got mad. "Look, you bitch, I wasn't a dirty Mexican when you wanted to fuck me, so let's not get into that horse-shit. I can b ice up to a point but you're just making a goddamned fool of ourself saying stupid things like that."

"How do I know what you've stolen from me and hidden away?"

"I haven't stolen anything from you," I yelled at her. She turned and left in anger. Pretty soon I heard the car leave.

I was lying in bed, smoking a cigarette, when Bert walked in. I told him what had happened. He was scared.

"Let's get the hell out."

"No, she'll be all right tomorrow. I'll talk some more to her. I don't want to leave her like this."

We had just gone to bed when suddenly we heard cars drive in, and then three policemen walked into the room with their guns drawn.

"All right, get up, you dirty sonsofbitches." Mrs. Harris stood in the doorway. "Which one is it?" one of the cops said.

"That one," she said, pointing at me.

"All right, hand over all the stuff you've taken from her."

"What stuff?"

"She says that you've been stealing money from her."

I turned to her. "Mrs. Harris, now you know that's not true."

"It is true; you've stolen money from me. You've been robbing me blind for two months. You're always asking for money to fix this and do that."

"Look," I said, "I asked you for money to buy paint, to buy bricks, cement and things for the garden, but never for me."

"How do I know you bought those things?"

"Well, you can see all that's been done," I said.

The policeman interrupted: "Never mind, you lousy greezer. None of you sonsofbitches can be trusted. Just come on."

Bert jumped to my defense. "Hey, something's wrong here; this woman —"

They didn't let him finish. "You too."

They took us to jail. It was full of winos, drunks and mostly bums. Since I'd been living an idyllic life for two months, I'd forgotten what the other side was like; to be back in the vomit and the shit and the smell of piss in the cells was depressing.

Next morning, they took me to see the magistrate, or judge, or

whoever he was. He said, "We have a report here that you stol
money from Mrs. Harris, where you'd been working. . . ."

"It's not true, Judge," I said. He seemed a nice man. "I don'
know what to do. I hate to say anything against the lady, but sh
kept us there and she was talking about marrying me and all tha
sort of thing."

"Who are you? Where do you come from?"

"Los Angeles."

"What are you doing?"

"I've been hoboing my way around and I'm trying to make m
way to New York." I still had my little medicine kit with me.
opened it and said, "You know, I'm not just nobody. I work i
movies and I've worked in the theater." I showed him the re
views. He read them and then saw my Bible.

"Why do you carry that around with you?"

"I used to be a preacher and I like to read it."

He looked at me peculiarly. "All right, I'll see what I can d
Do you know anybody in town?"

"No, sir."

He motioned for the policeman to take me back to the cel
Apparently, he called Mrs. Harris and questioned her closely. Sh
couldn't keep up the deception.

The judge later said he informed her I could go to prison fo
two years if she pressed charges. She had started crying and saic
"No, I don't want to . . . forget it . . . I don't care about th
money, anyway." And then she asked to see me.

The guard showed me into a small, dirty office next to th
judge's quarters. When she came into the room I realized
couldn't stand her anymore. She looked at me and started to cr
"Tony, I'm sorry; you know why I did it. It's too late, I've done i
and I know I've ruined it, but I just went crazy. I was even sill
enough to think that at least if you were in jail, here, maybe
could convince you eventually to stay with me. Now I realize tha
you'll hate me."

"Yes, I do. Are you going to press charges?"

"No."

I called the guard to take me back to the stinking cell.

Many hoboes didn't mind going to jail because at least the
could eat three meals a day. The jails were often so crowded wit

agrants, hoboes and minor offenders that it was expensive to keep them, a drain on the taxpayers. Some towns had an ugly way of letting you know you weren't wanted around after you were released. People would line up on the street and you had to run the gauntlet while they threw rocks at you. It was a warning never to step into their town again. About seventy-five or eighty people lined up and started to heave rocks at me. It was a big, festive day for them.

BOY (*disappointed*). Somehow it doesn't tell as well as it happened. Or maybe you're just a lousy storyteller. One rock hit me on the side of the head and I thought I was going to pass out. I didn't dare go down because I knew those sonsofbitches were dying to kill themselves a Mexican greezer, so I kept on running with blood streaming down my face.

The doctor was asking a question and I asked him to repeat it. The kid had interrupted.
"Is being a Mexican a great part of your problem?"
I laughed. "It's never been a problem to me, Doc. As far as I'm concerned, that's your people's problem."
"You still insist on identifying me with the red-necks?"
"No, I'm sorry, I didn't mean that. It's just that I don't go around consciously thinking of myself as Mexican or Irish or Chinese or Hungarian."

BOY. Maybe the old boy is right. Maybe it is your problem.
MAN. No, that's another load you saddled me with. You were afraid to go it alone. You were afraid of not belonging. I don't give a shit about belonging. I just want to be . . .
BOY. Be what?
MAN. Myself — without any labels. You fucked me up that time back there. That time there was going to be a rumble down on the banks of the Los Angeles River.
BOY. There were so many rumbles. Which one are you talking about?
MAN. The one between the Mexicans and the Irish kids.
BOY (*sighing*). Oh, yeah. I remember. Walter Kelly came and asked

us if we'd join his side fighting against the spics because our name was Quinn.

MAN. Yeah.

BOY. So I said okay, I'd be there to fight that afternoon, beside the Kellys, the Chandlers and the MacLaughlins — against the Mexicans.

MAN (*laughing*). An hour later, Carlos Ramirez and Ernie Fuente came and asked us if we'd join the Mexicans in their fight against the lousy micks.

BOY. Even old Solomon couldn't divide himself in half. (*The man nods in agreement.*) Why did we choose to fight on the Mexican side, man?

MAN. I don't know, boy. We had every right to fight on either side. I suppose I could go into a lot of shit that we were heroes and we were on the side of a minority, and all that. I don't know kid.

BOY. I do.

MAN. Why, then?

BOY. Because we need windmills. Because we need mountains to climb. Because we like to jump into a cage of lions and fight our way out. Because we wanted to fly the banner and say, "We are Mexican and if you don't like it you can go and fuck yourselves." We would have called ourselves Hungarian if it had served the same purpose.

MAN. Or Negro.

BOY. That's right. We tried that bit.

MAN. So what's the point, kid?

BOY. We need banners.

The doctor brought me back for a résumé of my hoboing adventure.

I saw a lot of open country, many beautiful sunsets. I saw many dawns from speeding freight trains. I met ugly, mean people and some marvelous, kind ones. I learned that people were people with all their faults and all their insecurities, but that basically everybody was waiting around for someone else to make it better. That's why I fell in love with Romain Rolland's Jean Christophe

He spoke of the magnificent courage of the artist in his search for new horizons. That's why Thomas Wolfe had such an influence on me when he spoke of the artist being the tongue for his inarticulate brothers. I saw many emotionally tongue-tied brothers on my journey that year. I yearned to be able to speak for them. However, I still hadn't found the way.

While waiting for a job in Ensenada, Mexico, on one of the fishing ships that occasionally pulled into port, I picked up a discarded Los Angeles paper. I read an article that said that C. B. de Mille was having difficulty casting a picture called *The Plainsman*. He couldn't find enough authentic Indians to play some important parts called for by the script.

That night, Bert and I thumbed our way north to the American border. We were picked up by a fat, jovial truck driver. He asked me where I was headed. I decided to impress him. I told him I was an actor and going back to Hollywood to start a picture. He asked me what it was called and I said *The Plainsman*.

When we got to Tijuana he said that was as far as he was going. As we got out, he reached into his pocket and pulled out a fifty-cent piece and handed it to me.

I started to refuse but he closed my hand over the coin, saying, "Kid, I think you're going to make it. When you do, don't forget about us. That's what that coin is for."

He drove away. I was left staring at the coin in my hand.

Next morning, we got off a freight in Glendale. I went to a gas station and shaved with that harsh soap they have in men's rooms. It burned the hell out of my face. But I wanted to be clean. We took a streetcar and then walked the last lap to Sylvia's house. Bert was terribly sad. He was praying to God that I wouldn't get the acting job, so we could hit the road again.

# 17

AFTER GREETING EVERYONE, I changed my shirt and hurried to Paramount Studios, where the casting office was full of people looking for jobs.

"Will you please tell Mr. Joe Egley that I am here?" I told the receptionist.

"Who are you?" she asked.

"Tell him Anthony Quinn is here," I said. I gave her some clippings that I always carried with me, reviews of the plays I had done. "Tell him that Mr. Cecil B. de Mille wants to see me," I added.

She looked surprised but went off. After a while she came back and said Mr. Egley would see me. Joe Egley was a big, jovial, good-hearted man, with a slight stutter.

"What's this about de Mille wanting to see you?" he asked.

"Well, I understand you're looking for a young Indian. I'm an Indian and I came to apply for the job."

"What do you mean, you're Indian?"

"I'm Cheyenne."

"Kid, I saw you in that play; you were great, but you didn't sound like a Cheyenne to me."

I refused to be put off. "Listen, Mr. Egley, I speak Cheyenne fluently."

"Say something," he said. "Say something in Cheyenne."

"Ksai ksakim eledski chumbolum."

"Are you sure that's Cheyenne?"

"Of course it is. Would I make it up? How could I make it up?"

"Jesus, wait a minute." He picked up the phone and called de Mille's office. "Is C.B. there? I want to talk to him." A moment later he said, "C.B.? I think I've got a great find for you. Y'know that young Cheyenne Indian you want? I've got the guy. He's sitting here with me."

De Mille said to bring me right over. As we walked out of the office, Egley said, "Listen, don't tell the old man that you know English. Pretend you can't speak it at all. I promised to find him a real Cheyenne."

In de Mille's office was a "technical adviser" that he had hired, a Mexican I had seen around. I nodded to him. Joe introduced me to de Mille: "Here's the boy that I think can play the part."

De Mille impressed me as a man who wanted to make you feel uncomfortable somehow. He stared at me for a long time; he walked around, looking at me as if I were a horse that he was thinking of buying. He did everything except open my mouth and look at my teeth. Finally he said, "Yes, he looks right for the part. Is he Cheyenne?"

Joe said, "Oh, yes, one hundred percent."

De Mille turned to the Mexican fellow and said, "See if he can talk Cheyenne."

The Mexican looked at me and made some sounds: "Xtmas ala huahua?" Clearly phony, so I said, "Xtmas nana ellahuahua, heriota hodsvi." He turned to de Mille and said, "Oh, yes, he speak good Cheyenne."

De Mille asked me to please wait outside while he and Egley discussed casting me in the film. When Egley came out, he had a smile on his face.

"Well, kid, the old man likes you, but you must be very careful. I told him that you were a Cheyenne and you must never put me into a position where I'm caught in a lie." I didn't see how that was possible, because I naturally wanted to play other parts besides Indians; at that moment, however, the only thing that mattered was getting whatever money there was from a job. Joe told me it paid seventy-five dollars a day, a fortune to me. He said it would probably run two or three days, which meant possibly earning two hundred dollars or so.

"Do you ride a horse?" he asked, as an afterthought.

"No, I'm sorry."

"Don't all Indians ride horses?"

"Well, er, yes," I said, "but on the reservation where I was raised they didn't have horses."

"My God, Tony, you're going to have me in a hell of a spot

because the scene calls for you to ride a horse. How are we goin
to do it?"

"Well," I said, "if you advance me ten or fifteen dollars, I'll g
out to the San Fernando Valley and take riding lessons."

"Are you sure you can learn in one week?" he said in panic.

"Look, I'll ride a horse, I promise you. Just give me the mone
to hire a horse."

The poor guy was in too deep and reached into his pocket. H
took out twenty-five dollars and gave them to me. Next, he sen
me over to wardrobe to be fitted for the part. Then I was taken t
the "technical adviser," who was really a very sweet old man, eve
if his knowledge of Cheyenne wasn't very extensive. They aske
me to go over the script with him. My part was four or five page
of solid Cheyenne talk: I realized I had probably bitten off mor
than I could chew. Inwardly, I panicked. How does one study fiv
pages of a language that sounds like gibberish?

When Joe Egley came by, he saw my confusion. "What's th
matter?" he asked.

"This is a different kind of dialect from the Cheyenne I'm use
to," I said.

"Listen, kid, I'm one of the most important casting directors i
Hollywood. If I say somebody can do something, they can do it."

"Mr. Egley, don't worry, I'll have this down. I'll work on it wit
the technical adviser here; I'll get it down."

When Egley left the room, I said to the man, "Now, tell m
about the part."

His eyes glowed with excitement. He was a frustrated directo
"Well, it's one of the greatest scenes in the history of motion pi
tures and you're very lucky to play this part. This young India
warrior is inciting the Indian nation to go to war against th
frontiersmen, who are usurping the West. All the tribes are gath
ered together: the Cheyenne, Sioux, Blackfeet, Apache, they ar
all there. This young warrior gets up and makes his impassione
speech against the white man and arouses all the nations to g
to war."

I could already see the scene — thousands of Indians on th
plain, ready for the charge. I saw myself climbing very slowly u
on top of a huge rock looking over my people, then beginning th
speech. I saw myself slowly building, getting the rhythm of th

speech — inciting the crowd, exciting them — until I finally cried,
"WA-A-A-R!" And they would shout, "War! War!" It would be
like a congregation for me, just a little bigger, perhaps, than before. This time I was going to have ten thousand souls to hypnotize.

Then I improved on the scene — I'd be on a horse when I made
his speech; I'd ride up to the rock on my horse. I could see myself
standing there, feeling the people's tension, waiting until they
were all quiet, then starting slowly: "We have been discriminated
against; this country belonged to us, this was our land, and now
strangers have come among us to take it. At first, we thought they
were our friends, we thought they were with us, we welcomed
them with open arms. But they have taken advantage of our
generosity. Now we must drive them out, we the redmen. . . ."
And now I would build: "We that have stood for such and such
. . . we that have. . . ." And I was tremendously excited; I
couldn't wait to get out of the office to go away and practice.

I had arrived by freight that morning, and here I returned
home in the afternoon with a big movie job. I told Sylvia and
Vie about it. They were in an uproar, of course. My career had
begun, I was going to be a movie star!

That same afternoon, Bert and I went out to the San Fernando
Valley to a stable near Warner Brothers Studios. It was run by
a former boxer named Ace Hudkins.

"A lot of actors have the same problem, and we teach them," he
said. "If you're willing to spend eight hours a day, I guarantee
that in a week you'll be a good rider."

Ace was a nice man, and gave us two horses for the price of one.
Bert and I used to go out and ride over the hills for hours. I
would practice my speech. Bert became the ten thousand Indians
for me. He would ride down and wait in the valley for me. I
would stand on a height and yell the speech: "Cosa oja kiso neva.
Ja mahaj osi avist. . . ." It was a matter of associating all sorts
of images with the words. I didn't even know whether my pronun-
ciation was correct, but I didn't think anybody was going to
bother. After all, how many Cheyennes would go and see the picture? All I knew was that I had to *sound* like a Cheyenne.

At night, Sylvia and I would go over the pages and I'd start
panicking again. I'm not going to remember! My God, five pages

of gibberish. Finally, about the fifth or sixth day, I had it down t
where I could say the whole speech off the top of my head. It mad
such an impression on me that to this moment I can still remen
ber a great deal of it.

The big day was near; I was ready for it. Joe Egley called an
asked about the riding lessons. I said modestly, "The horsebac
riding is fine."

"Listen, kid, they're going to shoot the scene Monday. De Mill
is concerned. He asked me again today if I was sure about yo
Are you sure you can ride?" I again said yes. "Great, kid. No
what about the speech?"

"Do you want to hear it?"

"No, no," he said. "But you do know it all?"

"Yes," I said.

"Okay, fine. Monday morning report for work, eight o'clock i
the morning. Be there for makeup and costume."

You can imagine what kind of a weekend I had. I was doing
picture with Cecil B. de Mille, starring Gary Cooper and Jea
Arthur! I must have gone over that speech at least a hundre
times. Monday morning, I was up at six o'clock. Sylvia gave m
breakfast. I was a nervous wreck, and she said, "Look, hone
don't be nervous, you're going to be fine."

I arrived at Paramount early. I had a little room that they ga
to bit players. I remember seeing all the stars begin to arrive -
Carole Lombard, Gary Cooper, Bing Crosby, Bob Burns, Mauric
Chevalier, Cary Grant — they were all making pictures at th
same time. Just to be in that atmosphere, to be part of it, w
intoxicating. I thought, goddamnit, today I'm going to show then
I'm going to show them I can act!

I went to the makeup department. I was supposed to wear
certain kind of war-paint. Wally Westmore, one of the leadin
makeup men of that time, who only made up big stars lik
Dorothy Lamour and Carole Lombard, was to make me up. Ga
Cooper was also waiting. Nobody bothered to introduce us, b
he saw me being made up and he said, "What are you doing, kid

"I'm working with you today, Mr. Cooper. I'm in the T*
Plainsman."

"That's great," he said. "I'll see you down on the set."

"By the way," I said, "what kind of a director is Mr. de Mille

"He's a nice guy, but he's tough. Just be sure you know your stuff," he winked.

And that scared the hell out of me. As he was going out, I said, "Mr. Cooper, excuse me, but please don't tell Mr. de Mille that I speak English." He asked me what I meant and I told him the whole story. "So when I meet you on the set and I don't speak to you in English, please forgive me," I ended up.

"Fine, kid; don't worry about it," he said, laughing.

I asked the "technical adviser" what Gary Cooper was doing in the scene and he said, "Cooper is an American who has come to try to make peace with the Indians. He makes a speech to them saying, 'Let us live like brothers . . .' and so forth. When he gets through, you get up and you say, 'This man is a liar because he's a white man . . .' and you start your speech."

"Oh, I see." I wondered what the hell that had to do with the ten thousand Indians I was supposed to address. I said to myself, gee, I've got to hate Gary Cooper by nine o'clock. Well, he probably hates Mexicans and no doubt he. . . . I started building a case against Gary Cooper so that when he went on the set and he made his speech, I could really murder him with mine.

I went to my little dressing room and waited to be called to the set. I ran over the speech in front of the mirror. I liked what I saw. All that was missing now was my magnificent costume.

In a few minutes, the wardrobe man came and delivered it. When I saw it, I said, "Hey, wait a minute, there must be some mistake." He had given me an old torn shirt, a loincloth and moccasins. "Maybe you haven't got it right; I'm playing the chief."

"What chief?"

"Well, er . . . how can I speak to all those Indians in a loincloth and this old shirt?"

He looked at me like I was crazy. "That's what they told me to give you and that's what you put on. Now go on the set. You're almost late. De Mille is very punctual and he wants you on that set at nine o'clock."

"But I can't go on the set in the wrong outfit."

"That's the right outfit, now get moving!"

I walked across this huge lawn with the fountain. All the movie stars were being picked up in their limousines to be driven to their stages and here I was, almost naked in the loincloth. My behind was showing. I went inside Stage 7. It was enormous. I looked around for the Indians that I was supposed to address, but there weren't any. I thought, gee, maybe we're going to rehearse here and then shoot the scene out in the valley.

The "technical adviser" — Armando was his name — came up and looked me over. "That's fine."

"But I think they made a mistake, Armando; they gave me the wrong outfit."

"What's the matter with this one?" he asked.

Just then de Mille walked up and I had to hush. He studied me and called the wardrobe man. "Mike, I don't like that shirt. It should be in tatters, like it's been burnt, and get the makeup man to put a wound on his shoulder."

I thought, Wound? . . . Burnt? . . . What's going on? But I couldn't speak English, so I turned to Armando and in garbled Spanish I said, "What the hell's going on? Tell Mr. de Mille I want to talk to him." He tried to shut me up. "No, tell him I want to understand what I'm doing."

De Mille said, "What's he saying?"

Armando said, "Oh, nothing. Boy's just nervous."

De Mille said, "Look, I don't want any nervous actor. The scene is difficult enough. I don't want any nerves today."

Armando said, "No, he's not nervous, he's just asking questions."

De Mille said, "What does he want to know?"

I said in Spanish, "How is he planning to do this scene? Where are the Indians that I talk to? How far away are they from me?" I could see that Armando was embarrassed, and de Mille was fuming, "What the hell is he saying, what's he saying?" I wanted to speak to de Mille, but everybody was standing around; Joe Egley was there now and everybody was terribly nervous because de Mille was not someone that you discussed anything with.

Armando was refusing to translate because now he knew he was in trouble, that he might lose his job. Finally, Chico Dey, a young Mexican assistant director, said, "Mr. de Mille, he wants to know where the ten thousand Indians are."

De Mille said, "What Indians?" and Chico Dey said to me, "What Indians are you talking about?"

"Well, I was told that in the scene I was addressing ten thou-
nd Indians."

De Mille said, "What kind of a nut do we have here? He's talk-
g to Gary Cooper."

Suddenly, everything that I had been doing for one week, every-
ing that I had planned, was for nothing. I wanted to kill that
echnical adviser."

De Mille saw the panic in my face and said to Chico, "What's
e problem? Doesn't he know his speech?"

I said in more garbled Spanish, "There's no trouble, no trouble
all. I just had an idea that maybe I was talking to some other
dians."

Finally, de Mille said, "All right, let's have the rehearsal." And
walked over on the set. They had built a kind of forest of
out twelve pine trees. They put on the lights and de Mille said,
ll right, you go and get on your horse, and you lead the other
rse. You ride down, there's a path there, and when you get to
at tree over there, you turn and you see the fire. You get off your
rse and go to the fire, and that's the first cut."

This was translated for me, and off I went behind the rock to
t the horses. But the horses didn't have saddles. I'd never ridden
thout a saddle or a bridle. I went back and I prayed, "All right,
od, this is a disaster, please help me, make me an Indian, make
e an Indian right now for the next two hours." I suddenly felt
peculiar kind of peace. I think it was "the boy" who stood there
d said, "You can do it, you can do anything you want." I think
anybody had spoken to me at that moment in Cheyenne I would
ve answered him.

I stood up on a rock and got on the horse; it wasn't as difficult
I thought. I took the reins of the other horse. De Mille was be-
ming impatient, "What's the matter back there?"

I yelled something that sounded positive, in gibberish. After a
tle more yelling back and forth, with translations both ways, I
de the horse out and everything was perfect. I arrived in front
here he wanted me, I got off the horse, and went to the fire.
e Mille turned to the "technical adviser" and said, "Where's the
ng?"

Armando shouted, "Yes, why don't you sing the song?"

"What song?"

"The song I taught you to sing!"

My God, I was in the middle of a nightmare. "What song am [I] supposed to sing?"

"What the hell is going on?" yelled de Mille. "The kid com[es] in, he wants to talk to ten thousand Indians, he doesn't even kn[ow] the song, what is going on?"

The adviser said, "He not a movie actor, he Cheyenne India[n] he just off reservation and he pretty stupid; we explain things [to] him."

De Mille abruptly called Joe Egley. "Get somebody else, [get] somebody else," he told him. Then he went over and sat down [in] his chair, his secretary started running around, and everybody w[as] in a panic.

Just then Gary Cooper walked in and de Mille said, "Sit dow[n,] Gary. We're going to have to wait awhile. I don't think the ki[d's] going to work out."

And Gary, I'll always love him, said, "Give the boy a chan[ce.] Maybe he's confused, it's his first picture, why don't you give h[im] a chance."

"I don't want to waste your time, Gary."

"I don't mind," said Gary. "I saw the boy in the makeup roo[m] and he seems like a nice kid. Give him a break."

De Mille stood up and said, "All right, we'll try it again. T[ell] him to sing anything he knows, nobody's going to know the diff[er]ence, just so it's in Cheyenne."

Chico said to me, "Sing a song as you lead the horses."

I took the reins and got on a horse and told myself, "All rig[ht] so I'm a Cheyenne, I'll sing a Cheyenne song."

De Mille yelled, "Action!" and out of me, I don't know fro[m] where, I heard this voice singing. There was an Indian in me [I] sang defiantly. In gibberish I was singing, "To hell with y[ou] white men, you're not going to make me embarrassed, you're n[ot] going to take away my dignity, we are the Cheyenne people, [we] will be victorious." I thought, well, if he's going to fire me and [if] he thinks I stink, at least through my Cheyenne song I'll tell h[im] to go fuck himself. And for the first time, I saw C.B. smile. "We[ll,] that's more like it."

He turned to Gary and said, "Maybe the kid will work out. D[oes] he know his speech?"

I realized that the speech, the way I had rehearsed it, was completely wrong and that my mind had to go into a different gear. Gary winked at me. Some people there in the company already understood that I was not a real Indian and they were going along keeping the secret from de Mille.

De Mille said, "All right, will somebody please explain to this boy what the scene is? He arrives, sees this fire, and he's standing here when Gary Cooper comes from behind the tree with a gun. The boy puts his hands up and starts his speech."

The interpreter mumbled a translation.

"Let me hear the speech now," said de Mille. So, immediately I made up a different story for myself, and started my speech. The boy has just come back from a battle. He's telling the white man, "We beat you, and even though you kill me now, you can't get away because the countryside is full of Indians and you will die. If you save my life, maybe I will save yours, but it doesn't matter if you kill me because now I know that in the end my people will not be conquered!"

All my anger at de Mille, all my embarrassment at the indignities that I had suffered all morning, I was expressing in this speech.

After about thirty seconds, de Mille asked, "How does it sound?" Gary spoke up, "It sounds pretty good, C.B. This kid sounds great."

De Mille seemed pleased now, and started setting up the lights. I went into my cubbyhole — there was only a chair and a little dresser there. I had to reconstruct the whole story for myself. This young Indian had just come from a battle; he had seen carnage; he had seen two huge armies, the white army and the Indian army, come together; his grandfather, his father, his uncle had died in the battle; they were all fighting for something, for the Indian nation to survive. And they knew that the white man was stronger and this was their great effort to throw the white man off their land, the land they loved. And now he had seen the white man beaten; although he knew he would come back with more soldiers, the Indian nation had won the first battle!

An assistant came to the door and said, "You're on; we're going to go for a take."

As I walked out of my dressing room and went to get on the

horse for the first take, I saw a girl talking to de Mille. She wa:
dark-haired, with beautiful skin and the most piercing eyes I'v
ever seen in my life. She looked part Indian, and I thought it wa
a good omen that I had another Indian there; I thought perhap
she was also in the picture. Apparently, de Mille had been talkir
about me.

She looked over my way, and as she did, I realized who she wa
— the great man's daughter — Katherine de Mille. I had seen he
in several pictures, among them *Viva Villa* and *The Call of th*
*Wild*. I felt an immediate rapport with her, perhaps because sh
played in *Viva Villa*, which I could relate to my life. As she looke
over, I felt she understood about me. I liked the fact that she wa
there and I was going to show her what a good actor I was.

I think I saw a flicker of an encouraging smile on her face, bı
her father said something, and she looked away from me.

As I went back to get on the horse, she was fresh in my minc
now I had a reason to give a good performance. I had been alon
the only person I had to keep me company was "the boy"; he ha
no doubts; I think my grandmother was there, too. She had con
back from Heaven or wherever she was to watch me act. My fathe
was there; he was not so sure; he was kind of sitting there sayin
"All right, kid, let's see if you really can do it." They were a
sitting there, watching; I could feel them out behind the camer
sitting there. And with them was this dark-haired girl. She wa
alive, she was the only one that wasn't a ghost. She was the one c
whose face I would see approval or disapproval. It became ve
important for me to show off for her. It seemed interminable, tl
time I was back there, sitting on the horse.

There was a globe hanging above me. When the light went o
I was supposed to start singing, lead the horse down, and get c
the horse. I watched that globe; when that light went on, either
would fail or my life would start. The light flashed. I heard myse
singing. I forgot everything except that I was an Indian, a youn
Cheyenne. I looked over at the fire. Then I did a strange thing -
I suddenly saw the fire and jumped behind a tree. De Mille yelle
"Cut! What the hell is that sonofabitch doing? What the *hell*
that sonofabitch doing?"

And, again, a harried conference, secretaries running aroun
people all terrified. Everybody surrounded me, saying things lik

Why did you do it? It was such a beautiful take." "You're supposed to stay there by the fire until he says cut."

I said in Spanish to Chico, "You tell him I don't agree with this scene. I think he's making a mistake; tell him I don't like the way he's directing it."

And Chico said, "Tell that to de Mille? Shut up! Don't be an idiot."

I looked over and there was a man dressed just like me with the same makeup. Chico said in Spanish, "They've got another actor here who will do the part if you don't shut up." I knew if I said one more word, they would replace me. I felt lost. Then I looked over and saw this girl sitting there quietly. I could see that she was sorry for me, because her father was yelling at me and calling me all sorts of names: that I was stupid, an idiot. He was blaming Joe Egley, he was blaming everybody. I saw a slight smile come to her face as if she wanted to say, "Do it; do it the way he wants you to do it."

So I said to the assistant director, "Tell him I'm sorry and I'll do it the way he wants me to, but tell him I have another feeling." He said to C.B., "At that moment at the fire, he jumped away because it was too hot."

De Mille said, "All right, if the fire is too hot, to hell with it. Just tell him to stand there and I'll cut before it gets too hot. But I need some footage on him, because I have to cut back to Gary Cooper. Let's start once more." And he made it very clear that I was going to get just one last chance. "Tell him to get back on the horse, tell him it was wonderful the way he sang the song — I love it. I like the way he got off the horse and walked up to the fire; everything was perfect, except that the sonofabitch shouldn't move away."

So I took the horses back and waited while they fixed the lights. I was looking at the globe and saying to myself, why do you do these things, Tony? Why? Just do what he says, that's all you have to do. But there was something in me that didn't like the scene, though I found it difficult to say exactly what.

The globe went on and again I was singing the song of victory, and by now I was beginning to enjoy the song, because the more they got mad at me, the more defiance I put into it, the song got more crazy, more wild. And as I was singing, I saw the fire and this

time I did something different; this time I looked around, li
tened, got off my horse very quietly, walked very carefully so
not to make any noise, and stood by the fire for a second. Then
looked around and suddenly I turned and ran behind the tree!!

Well, if the first explosion of de Mille had been something, th
was the atom bomb. He began to cuss, to say the most filthy thin,
about that "idiot sonofabitch" and, "Forget about it . . . forg
about it . . . forget about everything."

People started saying, "Mr. de Mille, it was wonderful," and th
cameraman, whose name was Milner, said, "My God, that w
exciting! It was marvelous the way the boy got off that horse ar
looked around. I forgot I was doing a movie; I just watched th
boy. It was life. And the way he walked to that fire, cautiou
apprehensive, you could really feel the boy knew there was a
enemy around. We can use it, C.B., because he stayed there abo
two seconds."

De Mille screamed, "I wanted him to STAND there, STAN
THERE! NOT move away!" And people were saying, "Look, i
the boy's first day and maybe he's —"

"I don't give a damn what the boy says," shouted de Mill
"He's not directing this picture, *I* am directing this picture! P;
him and send him home."

I looked over at Katherine de Mille but she wouldn't look
me. Everybody was terribly embarrassed. And now, for the fir
time, I figured everything was lost, it was all over, so I said, "M
de Mille," in English.

He turned as if somebody had cracked a whip over his hea
"So, you speak English?"

"Look, you fired me, you've sent me away and it's all right. Yc
don't like me, okay, but I am not an idiot, and I am not a stup
Indian. I know what I am doing, I am an actor. I have done mai
stage plays and I am not just coming here to earn your fuckii
seventy-five dollars — you can shove them up your ass. I dor
want money for something you think I'm not doing well, but I
me tell you that I think you're doing this scene wrong."

There was a hush. He walked over to me and stared up at me
moment before he said, "I am doing w-h-a-t?"

"You're directing this scene wrong. What kind of Indian wou
I be? Is that a white man's fire or a redman's fire, there?"

246

"What fire?"

"The fire that I'm standing in front of, where you want me to and for five fucking minutes. Did an Indian build that fire or d an American build that fire?"

"Gary Cooper built the fire."

"And he's a white man, isn't he? I know when I walk up to that e and the fire is still burning that someone's got to be around mewhere. You think that I, as an Indian, don't know the differ-ce between a white man's fire and an Indian's fire? If it had en an Indian's fire, I'd stand there for fifteen goddamn min-es, but I am not going to stand here in the open, in front of a e that's been built by a white man who I know is still hiding ound somewhere. I'm not going to stand there and let him shoot e. I'm going to hide and protect myself!"

A hundred and fifty people — the crew, the girl sitting over ere, Gary Cooper — held their breath as de Mille and I stared each other for what seemed an awfully long time. He suddenly rned around and said, "The boy's right. We'll change the setup. l right, you can hide behind the tree." And there was a sigh of lief from everybody. I did the scene my way.

It had been such a horrible day for everybody that when I had iished my four-page speech in one take everybody broke out in plause.

De Mille came over and shook my hand. He was very sweet. Thank you, and I am sorry about all the confusion. People ouldn't have lied to me. Even if I had known you weren't eyenne, I would have hired you, because you were right for the rt. We wouldn't have had to go through all this. I think it is e of the most auspicious beginnings for an actor I've ever seen my life. I hope you will come back and see me in a few days; l like to talk to you about putting you under personal contract. have a picture that I am planning to do next year. I've been nsidering other actors for the part, but if you will do a test for e, I'll consider you, too."

He called over Joe Egley and said, "Look, I think this boy has future. Pay him for three days, anyway, because he saved us all at time; we would have had to come back tomorrow and maybe e next day — so pay him for three days' work, and I want to do est of him next week."

We shook hands and I went back to my dressing room. On the way, people were very complimentary. Chico Dey was walking with me. "Gee, Tony, it was great. God, I can't tell you how excited the old man was about the film and what he got with you today."

"Listen, that girl, she is his daughter, right?"

"Yes."

"How can I get in touch with her?"

"What for?"

"I want to talk to her. She helped me today, she helped me this scene, and I would like to thank her."

"Well, just write her or something."

"No, I'd like to thank her personally."

"Well, don't get any ideas, kid," he said, "because she's going South America in a few days to marry somebody." And my heart was broken. In my moment of victory, my heart was broken because I was sure I was in love with that girl.

A few days later, I was called by Joe Egley, who asked me come over to the studio; de Mille wanted to talk to me. He was shooting some scenes with Gary Cooper, and Gary was very sweet saying he was really thrilled for me. De Mille said, "Kid, I just saw the rushes, and I'm going to nominate you for a special Academy Award. I think they should have awards for bit parts for the most outstanding debut."

Of course, I was in seventh heaven. He added, "By the way, the night when I got home, my daughter scolded me. She said I'd been very nasty to you, but I think you understand the pressure I working under."

"Of course," I said. "If people hadn't come between us, if hadn't had to lie to you, everything would have been fine."

"Well, you made a great impression on my daughter. She thinks you have a great future, and I do, too. I'd like to shoot a test you this afternoon, just photographic. You can do anything you want. I've only seen you dressed like an Indian, so if you go over to the wardrobe department, they'll give you some clothes. Get nice suit or something, or do you have one at home that you can wear?"

I had hardly a pair of jeans to my name, so I said I'd go wardrobe. By then, the whole studio was buzzing about me. Eve ody had seen the rushes, and they knew that de Mille liked me.

In wardrobe they gave me an old suit of Cary Grant's; it was too nall, but it was the only one they could find for me. I felt awk-ard when I walked out on the set. De Mille was very nice about , said it didn't look too bad. We went over to a barn set, where e had me sit on some bales of hay. The plan was to photograph simple interview.

While they set up the camera, I sat there, suddenly scared stiff. s an Indian, the Indian took over the part; but as Anthony uinn, I didn't know where to put my hands, what to do with yself. I had nothing to rely on. De Mille started the questions. What is your name? Where were you born?" Then he said, "Can ou do a scene for me?"

"A scene?"

"You said you did some plays."

"Yes, but I can't remember any speech." The camera was still lling.

"Well," he said, "think of one, I don't care if it's a poem, any-ing you can do."

I took out a cigarette and lit it slowly; I felt like a gangster, but had no gangster dialogue. Then I remembered a speech from thello:

> Behold, I have a weapon;
> A better never did itself sustain
> Upon a solider's thigh. I've seen the day,
> That, with this little arm and this good sword,
> I have made my way through more impediments
> Then twenty times your stop —

For some reason, the crew broke out in applause as de Mille id, "Cut! What was that from?"

"That was *Othello*."

"Do you mean you improvised?"

"Yes. That's the only speech I could think of. I probably chose dly, Mr. de Mille. When the camera was grinding, I couldn't ink, but if you want, I can do *Hamlet* for you, or *Cyrano de ergerac*." He said no, he was more than content with what I'd ne.

249

Just as I was walking away from the test, Joe Egley called m
over and said the head of the talent department wanted to talk t
me. His name was Lesser. I went to his office and it turned ou
that there was a lot of excitement about me on the lot. They o
fered me one hundred and fifty dollars a week. It was a tremen
dous amount of money, and I don't know what made me say, "I'
think about it." I guess I was already beginning to think in the
terms.

I was leaving the studio when I saw a gloriously beautif
woman, the epitome of sophistication, loveliness, charm, ever
thing. I had seen her in several pictures; her name was Caro
Lombard. She was also famous for being very outspoken. She cam
over and said, "You're the young boy they're all excited about.
hear you told C.B. to go fuck himself." She had a way of sayir
the vilest things in the most enchanting way.

"It's all straightened out."

"Well, I'm making a picture next week and there's a marvelo
part for you. Would you like to play it?"

"With you?"

"Yes, with me," she said.

"Oh God, yes."

"What have you been doing in there?"

"They offered me a contract."

"How much?"

"A hundred and fifty dollars a week."

"That's a lot of shit! Tell them to go shove it up their ass, ar
I'll get you the part with me."

I went with her to her dressing room. She made a phone call
the director — his name was Mitch Leisen — and she said, "Mitc
I've got the boy to play that Panamanian part. His name is A
thony Quinn."

Apparently, he knew the story; he had been de Mille's designe
and he was amused. He asked her to send me over. I went rig|
away.

"Well, old Carole thinks you're quite something — and do |
careful of Carole because she'll seduce you, you're just her typ
Now let me tell you about the part. The role is important -
though you don't speak English."

"What's going to happen to me in pictures?" I said. "Am I only going to play Indians and foreigners?"

"It's a nice part," he reassured me. "Carole Lombard has been turned down by Fred MacMurray, and she meets this attractive Panamanian. She thinks for a moment maybe she'll fall in love with him. Then Fred MacMurray comes back and there's a fight. I think it is a very interesting role for you at this stage."

"Well, I've a big decision to make because the studio just offered me a contract and Mr. de Mille has offered me a contract, and I frankly don't know what to do."

"How are you fixed for money?"

"If you really want to know the truth, I have very little. I've just paid back a lot of debts I had." I told him about my operation, and so on.

"Wait a minute, I know where there's a wonderful part." He called another director, named Frank Tuttle, and he said, "Frank, you're making a picture about Hawaiians, aren't you? There's a boy in my office you've probably heard about." Sure enough, he had heard the story of the young boy who had dared to tell de Mille where to put the camera. I was something of a *cause célèbre*. When I went to see Mr. Tuttle it turned out that he had seen me in *Clean Beds*.

"Of course, son, I'll give you this part," he said to me. "It's not a big one, not sympathetic either, but the picture is with Bing Crosby, Bob Burns, Martha Raye and Shirley Ross. It will be wonderful exposure for you. Tony, will two hundred dollars a week be all right?" Since that was more than I was being offered by de Mille, of course it was all right. "Okay, you've got the part; I'll go ten weeks." Ten weeks! That was two thousand dollars, and Mitch Leisen had offered me two hundred dollars a day for the other part, which would last about five or six days, so that was three thousand dollars I was going to make.

Later, Joe Egley called, quite enthusiastic. "Things are happening, kid. I'm delighted. Everybody's crazy about you, and I understand you've already got two pictures." I said that was true. "Well, what about the term contract?"

"I think we'd better wait with that," I said.

It had been a fantastic week. Overnight, my life had done a flipflop. I wasn't ready to make any move until I caught my

breath. I was on my way to fame and fortune, I thought. It a[l]
looked so easy then.

# 18

KATIE AND I were sitting on the terrace, which I had recent[ly]
added onto the house. From down below came the timeless soun[d]
of the ocean, making both of us contemplative. I looked over [at]
her, at that face which had put up with so much for twenty-od[d]
years. She had weathered all the storms and come out more beaut[i]
ful than ever, changing along the way from a rather chubb[y]
bosomy starlet into a stately woman. Even her voice, which ha[d]
once been a husky whisper, was now perfectly modulated, its ton[e]
that of a lady who had survived pain with great dignity.

I had done my best to live up to her expectations, but I felt a[n]
utter failure. There were so many ghosts to dethrone and I wa[s]
running out of strength. My energy was going out in a fight [I]
knew I'd lose unless "the boy" and the doctor could help me.

I wondered where the children were, and Katie reported tha[t]
everyone was out to a movie, except for Vally, who was upstai[rs]
doing her homework. Katie got up and went to the cupboard.

"Would you like a drink, dear?"

"No, I'd better not."

"Come on, it might relax you."

"Do I seem up tight?"

"Aren't you?"

I hated questions. I was so tired of questions. The doctor aske[d]
them, the kids asked them, "the boy" asked them, the whole fuc[k]
ing world asked them. Everybody wanted answers. I started [to]
get up.

"I think I'd better go for a drive."

"Please don't run away. We have to talk. I have to know wha[t's]
going on."

"I'll let you know when I find out," I said sharply.

I started to put on a jacket.

"Tony, do you want me to go and talk to the doctor? Maybe can help him find the answer for you."

"You don't have to go to the doctor," I shouted. "Just kill the hosts for me."

"Oh, God, are you still on that? We've had twenty years of it, ear. We've had five children together. How can you allow those tupid ghosts to haunt you? Are you sure you're not using them s an excuse?"

"An excuse for what?"

"Because you can't commit yourself to love. You're afraid of iving yourself so you find all sorts of reasons why you shouldn't ove."

"That lets a lot of people off the hook, doesn't it?"

I started to reach for the door.

"Would it have made that much difference if I had been a irgin?"

"It's too fucking late to find out, isn't it?"

"Did it make any difference with Evie?"

I stared at her.

"I've known so many things. Believe it or not, I've even prayed aany times that maybe you'd found the perfect woman. I have arried around guilts for years that perhaps I was the cause of our insane jealousy."

"And you don't think you are?"

"No, I don't think so. I think it started way before you met me. ylvia once told me of the terrible scenes you put her through. he warned me."

"You two must have had a wonderful time comparing notes ehind my back."

"We didn't compare notes. We both loved you and wanted to elp you."

"Sure, she loved me so much she turned me down."

"She was right. It wouldn't have worked out. Tony, she'd be xty-five years old now. You're still a young man. How do you aink I felt coming into your life knowing the love you'd felt or her?"

"I had gotten over it by the time I met you."

"You used to talk about her incessantly."

"She had become my dearest friend by then, the dearest frien
I've ever had."

I found myself sitting on the bed. I was surprised that I wa
playing with a piece of lint. I remembered the other time, mor
than a quarter of a century before, when I had watched love wal
out the door while I toyed with a piece of lint.

Katie stood silently for a long time. I could feel her eyes o
my neck. "I can imagine what you're going through. But I hav
four kids who need me. I don't have the strength to fight an
more. When we were young I could help you. But I'm no long
a young girl. I want some rest, too."

I longed to take her in my arms and reassure her, but I coul
hear "the boy" pacing outside the house. I hurried out to fac
him.

MAN. What the hell are you doing here?

BOY. I saw you start to give in. She can twist you around so easil

MAN. I love her.

BOY. So did I, once.

MAN. What the hell did she do to you?

BOY. She shouldn't have gone to South America after that fir
time we met.

MAN. She didn't know you from shit. You were just some hung
young actor fucking up a good scene.

BOY. I had fallen in love with her. She looked like Grandmothe
Did you ever notice how much they look alike?

MAN. They have the same strength. They don't really look alik
She has her own style which is rather formidable. Maybe w
can't handle it, boy. Maybe that's why we want to quit.

BOY. She wants you to put on the slippers and sit by the fire.

MAN. Well, it's been a long fight.

BOY. You never beat them. Christ! You never even tied them.

MAN. I lost to a lot of them, but which one are you referring
particularly?

BOY. Father, for one. Then all the big boys we were going
challenge.

MAN. That was a childhood dream. You weren't alone. Everybo
dreams of taking on Shakespeare, Hemingway, Gauguin, N
chelangelo. It's all part of growing up. It's the carrot th

dangle in front of you so you'll keep reaching for the sun. (*puts his arm on the boy*) Kid, we've come farther than we ever dreamed. The world thinks we've got it made.

OY. Fuck the world. Do you think you've made it?

IAN (*wearily*). I'm willing to settle.

OY. I'm not.

I saw him run down the hill toward the beach. For a second hoped he'd fall over the cliff and disappear forever.

It was too late now to go for a drive, and besides I was afraid 'd run into him again.

I went into the house. Katie was already in bed; she was read- ng Krishnamurti. That was her way of escaping to never-never and. I was even jealous of him. He could bring her the peace could never supply.

She looked up as I started to get into my bed. "You didn't go or a drive?"

"No, I ran into the boy."

The mention of the boy annoyed her. She knew how he felt bout her. She was as helpless with him as I was with Krish- amurti.

"He's going to drive you crazy. He'll never let you be. Forget im. You have two boys of your own who need you. You have hree daughters who think you're number one. Even if I have ailed you, think of them."

I picked up a magazine and leafed through it, not seeing a hing.

She reached up and turned off her light.

"Good-night, dear. By the way, have you decided to accept that icture in Europe?"

"I think so."

"What kind of a character is it?"

"A painter — Paul Gauguin."

"Oh, he left his family and went off to Tahiti to paint, didn't e?"

"Yes."

"He died a lonely man, riddled with syphilis."

"Yeah, but he painted beautiful pictures. He captured beauty ith the grappling hooks of his own art."

"I wonder if at the end he found it worthwhile?"

"It was better than being cooped up in a bank, adding and subtracting all day long. The world would have been a hell of a lot less if he hadn't painted those pictures."

"You may be right. Sweet dreams, dear," she said, already falling asleep.

After a while I turned off the light and listened to the sea. I wondered if the boy was down there frolicking in the dark waves.

The next day the doctor asked me about my early days in movies. After thousands of silly interviews I was tired of telling the story. I asked him if we couldn't skip it, but he said he was on the track of something and had to see the whole picture before he could pinpoint where the boy and I had started pulling in different directions.

I laughed. "You're sure you're not just a movie fan and want to hear all the dirt about the glamorous movie stars?"

He smiled. "I must say working with you makes it a bit more interesting. The cast in your life is rather impressive. Where else could I have met Aimee Semple McPherson, John Barrymore, Greta Garbo, Chaliapin, Carole Lombard and Mae West?"

So I went back to my early days at Paramount Studios.

The picture was called *Swing High, Swing Low*. Carole Lombard had kept her word and I reported on the set to work with her. I guess I had a slight crush on her. She was so sophisticated and frank, so honest, you couldn't be phony with her. But I didn't know how to behave. Between takes I didn't know what to talk to her about. I thought movie stars must all be terribly cultured, incredibly wise. When I suddenly found myself near this goddess I felt lost.

So I took a wild stab. "Ehm, I'm just reading *Tom Jones*, by Henry Fielding." I thought, well, that should impress her, now she knows I'm not without some culture myself.

"Henry Fielding?"

"Yes," I said, "I like him, don't you?"

"What studio is he at?"

I thought she was kidding me. "No, he's dead."

"And he wrote a script called *Tom Jones?*"

"No, he wrote a book called *Tom Jones*. It's one of John Barry-
ore's favorites."

"Oh, Jack. Do you know Jack?" she asked sweetly.

"Yes, I know Mr. Barrymore quite well." And I told her the
ory of how I'd met him.

"Oh, that sonofabitch, he's the greatest shit in the world, isn't
?"

I had made a booboo with Fielding and I tried several other
cks, mentioning Mozart, Brahms and Santayana, but she began
look at me like I was kind of crazy. Much to my amazement,
ter work she invited me to her dressing room for a drink. She
ld me she was in love with a star and was waiting for him to get
divorce and marry her. "I sit at home at nights because I can't
out in public with him. Would you take me out?"

"Of course, sure," I smiled inanely.

"Well, you sonofabitch, ask me to go out with you."

"Miss Lombard," I said, "will you go out with me?"

"You're damn right, Tony. But call me Carole. When?"

I hadn't been paid yet so I couldn't afford to take her anyplace.
Vell, er . . . right after I finish the picture."

"You've got a date, kid."

In three days I finished my scene with her. Everybody seemed
be happy with my work. Carole had complimented me several
nes and occasionally, when she thought I could do better, she
uld say to Mitch Leisen, "Let's do it again." She was protecting
e. Every night she'd invite me in for a drink, and she kept say-
g, "You're going to have a big career, kid."

Now that I'd finished my part in the picture, she said, "All
ght, we got a date, kid? We go out tonight and do the town.
ere's my address. What time will you pick me up?"

I told her I'd pick her up at eight-thirty. I rushed home to dress.
hen I got there I realized I had nothing to wear. All the money
at I'd made had gone to pay debts. I had relied on the studio
rdrobe for my clothes for the picture and had only a few pairs
patched pants in the closet and a few old sweaters. This was
rdly the garb for an evening out with the fabulous Lombard.
sides, since I hadn't received my check for *Swing High, Swing
w* I had about seven dollars in my pocket. I ran around trying
borrow money. By the time eight-thirty rolled around I had

only been able to scrape up six dollars. I couldn't see myself tal
ing Carole Lombard to a cafeteria so I never showed up for ou
date.

About a week later, Paramount called me again and I starte
another picture, *Waikiki Wedding*. As I was walking across th
courtyard of the studio I heard a blast of obscene language; sh
had the worst tongue in the world. "You sonofabitch, you littl
shit, you bastard, you fucking little . . . I've never been stood u
in my life before, you little prick." A lot of people stopped
listen to the scene. I was terribly ashamed. "Miss Lombard, pleas
I can explain —"

"Fuck you, you no-good shit, you just wanted the goddamne
job!" She walked away into her dressing room. I followed an
knocked on the door. "All right, come in, you sonofabitch." Ther
she was, so beautiful; she had such lovely skin, long blond hai
and those marvelous penetrating eyes.

"Miss Lombard, I have a terrible confession to make. I kno
that it's going to sound silly to you." And I told her the who
story.

She had tears in her eyes when I finished. "Is that the truth,
that why you didn't come?"

"It's the truth, I didn't have any money. Now I have some; I'
cashed the check, and if you want to go out, I'll take you an
where you want to go."

"All right," she said. "You're the only man that's ever stood n
up and gotten away with it. By the way, there's a great part con
ing up that I think you should play."

"I'm busy now doing a picture."

"Oh, that's shit. I know what you're playing, some Hawaiia
character in that musical. Horse-shit! You don't have to pl
Hawaiians and all that nonsense. There's a great part in this pi
ture and they want George Raft, but I know George doesn't wa
to do it; he doesn't want to take second billing to Gary Coope

She picked up the phone and called the director, Henry Hat
away. "Henry," she said, "there's a boy here in my dressing roo
who should play the George Raft part in *Souls at Sea*. His nan
is Anthony Quinn."

When I walked up to his office, he shook my hand. "I und
stand you've made quite a stir here in the studio. They say you

ery good in the picture that you made with Carole. Mitch Leisen
ays you're a good actor. As it happens, we're having trouble with
George Raft; he might not do this picture, and I'd like to test
ou. Take this script, read it, and see what you think."

Gary Cooper's agent was Jack Moss. Hathaway called him and
aid, "Jack, there's a boy in my office who'd be perfect for the
Raft part in *Souls at Sea*. He's twenty-one or so, and it'll be more
nteresting for the picture to have someone young idealizing the
haracter Gary plays. If you and Gary agree, I'll test him."

Cooper, who happened to be in Moss's office, said he liked me
ery much and by all means to test me.

I took the script home and read it. It was a great part.

The test was set for the following day. One of the contract play-
rs on the lot did the part opposite me. It was a long five-page
cene in which my character was declaring his love and affection
or the character Cooper was to play. Gary's kindness to me dur-
ng the filming of *The Plainsman* had endeared me to him for-
ver. So I found it very easy to tell his substitute of my undying
oyalty and affection.

As I walked off the set after the test, Carole Lombard was wait-
ng there. "How was he?" she asked Henry Hathaway, who was
alking beside me.

"He was great, absolutely great."

"Well," she said, "is he going to get the part?"

"As far as I'm concerned, I don't have to see the test; he's got
he part."

Carole took me into her dressing room and poured a couple of
ig drinks. "Tony," she said, "you're going to be a big star. I hear
he talk already; it's in the bag. Don't let them kid you, you get
qual star billing with Gary Cooper; after all, they were going to
ive George Raft star billing, you demand star billing."

"Miss Lombard, I just want to play the part. I don't care about
he billing. I love the part and I'll do it for whatever they want
o give me."

"Actors are dumb bastards; they should never talk business.
Have you ever heard of an agent named Charlie Feldman?"

I had been around Hollywood enough to know that he was the
iggest agent in town. "Of course, I know who Charlie Feld-
an is."

"All right," she said. "Do you want him to handle it for you?"

"My God, yes. But he wouldn't be interested in me."

"He's my agent and I'll tell him to be." She called him and told him about the test. He said he'd be right over. I realized suddenly that maybe I would be somebody. The most important agent in Hollywood, one of the biggest stars in the world, the most prominent directors all cared.

We sat there, Carole and I, waiting for Charlie. She had been overly generous pouring drinks and I was drunk — not only from liquor, but because Carole Lombard was my friend and Charlie Feldman was going to be my agent. On top of which I was probably going to make quite a bit of money.

Feldman arrived and went right to the point. "I'm your new agent. Let's go to the front office."

So we went to see the head of the studio, Adolph Zukor. The minute the secretary said "Charlie Feldman is here," all the door opened. We went in and I saw this tiny man, Adolph Zukor, a shrewd businessman. I was dressed in everyday clothes, a sweater and a pair of pants, and Adolph said, "Oh, my God! Have you got to him already, Charlie?"

Charlie had never seen me work; he didn't know a thing about me, but he said, "This boy's going to be one of the biggest stars in the business. I want to tell you that I've already got offers for him from Metro and Warner Brothers. I talked to Mitch Leisen and he says the film on this kid in *Swing High, Swing Low* is out of this world. De Mille can't say enough about him, they even want to create a special prize for him because of what he did in *The Plainsman,* and Frank Tuttle says he's excellent in *Waikiki Wedding.* This kid is going to be one of the biggest stars. As you know, he's just made a test for *Souls at Sea.* Henry Hathaway says it's fantastic."

Zukor nodded. "Yes, I spoke to Hathaway and he's quite pleased about the young man. But he's too young, Charlie. We can't give him a part that George Raft was going to play."

"I don't care whether you give him that one, there'll be other parts coming along, and this kid's going to be a big star."

"Well, we'll see. We'd like to have him under contract. Tony we offered you a good contract the other day and you turned it down." Before I could say a word, Charlie jumped in.

"Are you kidding? You offered him a hundred and fifty dollars
week. How much do you pay George Raft? You pay George Raft
vo thousand dollars a week, and you're paying this boy a hun-
red and fifty? That's crazy. This boy can wipe the floor with
eorge Raft. Adolph, you're talking to Charlie now, you're not
ilking to one of my leg men, you're talking to Charlie himself."

"Well . . . well, I admit . . . well, we thought we'd train
im —"

"The boy doesn't need any training. He comes from a great
neatrical background." I had told him on the way to the office
iat I had done a play for Mae West, and that I knew Barrymore.
harlie went on: "Mae West says this is one of the greatest talents
ie's ever seen. Barrymore can't wait to do a picture with him.
nd you're talking about a hundred and fifty dollars a week!"

"You got me, Charlie," Zukor said. "What do you want for
im?"

"I want fifteen hundred dollars a week for him."

The sound of the figure made me dizzy. FIFTEEN HUNDRED
OLLARS A WEEK! My stomach contracted.

Adolph laughed. "Charlie, the boy's unknown; nobody has ever
eard of him. Sure, he's done a couple of bit parts. Yes, they talk
out him. De Mille says he's good, but it's bit parts. I don't
now if he can carry a starring role. How do I know he can carry
lead? You know there's a difference."

"Talent is talent, Adolph."

"I'll tell you what I'll do, Charlie. I like the boy. I like him and
aybe I'm crazy, but I'll give him five hundred dollars a week."

I was holding onto my legs and my nails were digging in. I
uld almost feel the blood gushing out. I was playing: Oh, my
od, Charlie, take it. Please, Charlie, take it, take it.

And Charlie said, "Adolph, you're a hard man, you're a tough
an. I'll tell you what I'm going to do, tell you what I'm going
 do, Adolph. Give him a forty-week contract — no options. One
ar, a forty-week contract, no options — a thousand dollars a
eek."

My head began to swim; the numbers were getting me drunk.

"Charlie, how can I go to the board meeting and say I'm going
 pay this boy a thousand dollars a week? They'll take my job
vay; they'll say the Old Man's gone crazy. I tell you what I'm

going to do, I'm going to give you seven-fifty, right now, a fort[y] week contract, no options."

There was a long pause. I said to myself, well, that did it. No[w] I know Charlie's going to jump at it and I will get seven hundre[d] and fifty dollars a week. The two men stared at each other. [It] was a game between the two great traders. Then I heard Charl[ie] laugh. It was the most costly laugh of my life. I wanted to scream[,] I wanted to yell, "Give me five hundred . . . just give it to me!" I could see the money going out the window.

Charlie was laughing. "You're tough, Adolph. Boy, no wond[er] they call you the Emperor of the Industry. I can see why; you'[re] one of the greatest businessmen in the world. Seven-fifty you'[re] offering me for this great talent. Let's face it, this boy, in one yea[r] is going to be bigger than George Raft. He's going to be anoth[er] Rudolph Valentino, he's going to be another Gary Cooper. Th[is] boy is one of the big talents; all the big stars are dying to wor[k] with him. Carole Lombard can't find a picture fast enough to d[o] with the boy. And you want to get him for seven-fifty! Adolph, [I] tell you what I'm going to do. I'm going to give you this boy f[or] *nothing!*"

For nothing! They've just offered me seven hundred and fif[ty] dollars and now I'm being given away!

"I'm going to give him to you for nothing," he repeated. "Yo[u] give him *Souls at Sea*. You don't pay him anything, but if you pi[ck] up his option, you pay him two thousand dollars a week. Okay[?]"

Adolph said, "It's a deal."

It's a deal? . . . And I am going to play the part for nothin[g.]

As we walked out of the office I was terribly depressed. Charl[ie] saw that I was low. "What's the matter, kid?"

"Mr. Feldman, he offered you seven-fifty for forty weeks."

"Kid, you got to play for the whole thing, you gotta go for th[e] whole hog; if you're going to be with me, that's the way we're g[o]ing to play. Look, Carole Lombard didn't become a star ove[r] night. There's a place for agents, and that's the way I want to pl[ay] it with you. Do you believe in yourself?"

"Yes."

"Then they'll give you two thousand dollars a week. I promi[se] you on my soul that inside of eight weeks you will be earning tw[o] thousand dollars a week, for forty weeks — that's eighty thousand dollars a year, kid. Isn't that worth gambling for?"

"Yes, sir, but I don't have any money now."

"Well, do you need some?"

"No, sir, not at the moment, but . . ." And he took out a checkbook and wrote out a five-thousand-dollar check. "That's yours. That's how much I believe in you. You play it my way and in eight weeks you'll be getting two thousand dollars a week."

"Yes, but that depends on if I play the part."

"You'll play the part."

I went back to see Carole and told her exactly how it was; she almost died laughing. "That's Charlie for you — and he's right, Tony, he's right. They could have bought you for five hundred dollars a week, but what the hell is that? When it's money, go for the big one, go for broke. Either you're going to be the biggest, or go back to digging ditches!"

"He gave me this five-thousand-dollar check."

"Go and cash it, right away. He did it as a gesture, but you go and cash it and put it in the bank. Now he'll have to work for that five thousand."

So I had five thousand dollars in the bank, I was doing *Waikiki Wedding*, for which I was getting a very good price, and they called me and said I had the part in *Souls at Sea*, starring with Gary Cooper. And Adolph called Charlie and said that was a stupid deal they made. We went to his office again.

Zukor said, "I've changed my mind. I'll give the boy a thousand dollars a week." And the whole negotiation resumed and I was going crazy in the middle of it again.

Charlie said, "I don't want a thousand dollars. You had your chance. You could've had him for a thousand dollars. I told you fifteen hundred dollars a week and you turned me down, you started haggling with me. I've just paid him five thousand dollars and I'm taking the gamble on him. He will be there, Monday morning, to work with Gary Cooper, and after you see the first rough cut, you can tell me if you want the boy. If you don't want the boy, you've had him for nothing. If you want the boy, he's going to cost you two thousand dollars a week." That was that.

So, all week, they fitted me out with marvelous navy uniforms;

I was supposed to play a lieutenant. It was a terrific part, and by now I knew the whole script backward and forward.

I arrived Monday morning and they had a star dressing room for me, right next to Carole Lombard, which she had gotten for me. It was a small one, but it had a sitting room, a bed, a refrigerator and a stove — it was a complete little apartment. Twenty-one years old and I had arrived! No more going to wardrobe — the wardrobe came to me.

Well, I sat in my dressing room, I waited and waited, and nobody came. So I called Wally Westmore.

"Shall I come along to be made up?" I asked.

"Erhm, er, Tony, no, no, you stay there in the dressing room and I'll call you."

"Fine," I said, and called Joe Egley. "Joe, I'm sitting here in my dressing room; Jesus, I've got to be at work at nine o'clock. No one has brought the wardrobe to me."

"Kid, haven't you talked to Henry Hathaway?"

"No."

"Hasn't anybody been over to talk to you?"

"No, Joe, why? Did they change the call?"

"Well, I think there's been a little change . . . er . . . wait I'll be over to see you." Pretty soon Joe came in.

"Kid, didn't they tell you?"

"No, tell me what?"

"Look, why don't you go over to see Henry Hathaway on Stage Nine?" Joe walked me over to Stage Nine.

I asked him to come in with me, but he wouldn't. As I walked in, there was a hush. I looked over and Henry Hathaway was there and George Raft was playing my scene. It was the same scene I had done the test for. I turned around and walked out.

I went to my dressing room, and called Charlie Feldman.

"Who is it?" a secretary asked.

"It's Anthony Quinn."

"Just a second." And I heard whispering in the background.

Pretty soon the secretary came on again and said, "I'm sorry, but Mr. Feldman is not here at the moment. Can I have him call you, Mr. Quinn?"

"Yes, I'm in the dressing room, I'll wait here." I waited all day. I must have called Mr. Feldman ten times, but he was never in.

And finally, Carole came back to her dressing room; I saw lights and knocked on her door. She let me in and asked me to sit down. She poured me a stiff one. "Tony," she said, "those things happen to everybody; they happened to me. Take it like a man."

"I don't care, Miss Lombard. The only thing is I could have had a contract for five hundred dollars a week. Mr. Zukor ended up offering me a thousand dollars a week, and now I've got nothing."

"What do you mean, you've got nothing? You've got the five thousand dollars that Charlie gave you, and you've got me for a friend. All right, so you've missed the big time this time. Maybe you won't miss it next time. By the way, I have some good news for you: de Mille saw that test you did for him, and he's thinking seriously of you for the lead in *The Buccaneer*. I talked to the Old Man and I think you've got a hell of a good chance." She picked up the phone and called de Mille. "Listen, are you really considering Tony Quinn for that part in *The Buccaneer?*"

C.B. said yes.

She said, "Fine. As you probably know, he's just had a big shock. George Raft came back and Tony lost the part. I think he's got unusual talent, and as you know, Paramount has offered him a big contract, but I advised him not to take it. So, if you're really considering him . . ."

C.B. cut in. "Are you his agent?"

"Charlie Feldman is his agent," she said, but I made signs to her, and she smiled. "All right, I'm his agent, C.B. I'll be his agent."

C.B. laughed. "What do you want for him?"

"Five hundred dollars a week," she said. Then she hung up. "It's in the bag. He's going to run the tests. Tomorrow you'll know."

The next day, Joe Egley said he had been to de Mille's house the night before. In addition to friends, the de Mille children were on hand: John, Richard, Cecilia and Katherine, who in the meantime had come back — she had decided not to marry the man in South America.

After dinner, de Mille had announced, "Ladies and gentlemen, I want you to help me make a decision. I've tested several actors for the lead in *The Buccaneer*, the picture I'm going to

make next, and among them is a young man I'm thinking ver
seriously about; I think he's got possibilities. I would like you
opinion."

Everybody marched into the projection room, where a motio
picture was run, and after that, several tests.

The lights went off, he gave the signal for the projectionist, and
my test came on. Afterward, there was silence in the room.

De Mille said, "Goddamnit! I like him, there's something abou
the boy. He's got some qualities that are marvelous for Jean La
fitte."

His oldest daughter, Cecilia, said she thought I should get th
part, that it would be great to go with an unknown. He ha
turned to Katherine, who said, "Yes, he's good, he's interesting
but how can you trust a picture like that to an unknown boy? It'
too important to you, Father. After all, Jean Lafitte had been
pirate for many years, and this boy looks twenty-one or twenty
two years old. I think you should try to get Clark Gable for th
part. He's right for it; I mean he *is* Jean Lafitte."

The rest of the family and friends agreed that if Gable wa
available, of course, he was the right man for the part.

The next day, I got a call from de Mille. "Tony, I ran the test
last night. I want to tell you, there was great excitement abou
you. You made a big hit with my family. But, after much thinking
I have decided to go with Fredric March. I called Clark Gabl
this morning; he isn't available, but I think I have to go wit
March. However, there is a part you can play. Not a big one, bu
it runs all through the picture. If you will accept it, I'll talk t
Paramount and get you a contract."

I should have listened to Carole Lombard, but I was hungry.
was relieved and happy that the bargaining and suspense wer
over.

Then, I was working one day on the set and I saw the girl wit
the beautiful, enormous eyes, and the fantastic face. I knew tha
she had voted against me, but I walked over to her, and said, "D
you like Thomas Wolfe?"

"What? Do I like who?"

"Don't you know Thomas Wolfe?"

"He's a writer but I haven't read him."

I was dressed in a pirate's outfit, which must have made the co versation doubly incongruous. "Will you do me a favor, and read *Of Time and the River?*"

She shrugged. "Why should I read it?"

"Because if you like Thomas Wolfe, you'll like me, and if you love him, you'll love me, and you'll marry me." She looked at me with a strange expression on her face. Several days later, she was back. I was doing a scene and I could feel her eyes on me. It was while I was doing a scene with Fredric March. We were standing by some bales of cotton, on a dock. He was saying something about being careful because the authorities might discover the contraband. I could feel the girl watching me and I suddenly became very inhibited. There was a new ring in my voice as I yelled some commands to the pirates aboard the ship. De Mille said, "Print. That was very good." Fredric March turned to me and said, "Where did you learn to act?"

"I've been acting in a little theater."

"What have you done?" I told him. He said something I'd done had disturbed him because it was different from the way I'd rehearsed it. He looked at me for a long time and said, "You're either going to be one of the best actors around or you're going to be the biggest flop." Then he walked away.

I, in turn, walked over to Katherine and asked if she'd read the book. She handed it to me, saying she had.

"What did you think?"

"I think he's crazy."

But I saw a new look in her eye. We would never agree on Thomas Wolfe. She tried — God knows she tried. His quenchless thirst and his thrashing around were too alien to her own dreams of happiness.

# 19

AFTER I STARTED WORKING in pictures I felt that Sylvia had breathed a sigh of relief. She had charted the course and launched the ship. Her job was done. She still loved me but had steeled herself against what she considered to be inevitable, my finding a younger woman.

There was a big overblown Slavic girl who had become a close friend of her daughter Joan. She was tall and quite beautiful in a larger-than-life way. She didn't walk through life, she ran as if she were being pushed by a gale. I found out that she'd become Sylvia's disciple. Sylvia had begun putting her through the same course I'd taken. I suppose Freud could explain it very well, but Sylvia decided that the girl and I were ideally mated. And why not? We knew the same books, music, painters. We both had gigantic appetites and the same puppeteer was pulling the strings.

Actually, the girl's voracity offended me, but Sylvia kept insisting that we get to know each other better. It was inevitable that we at least make an attempt.

Sylvia was delighted, or so it seemed, when we told her we were going on a trip to the Big Sur together. We stopped at a seaside motel at Pismo Beach. We had no sooner entered our rented cabin than my newfound partner got down to the case in point as if she were doing research for a biology test. God knows how much, or how little, honest emotion was involved, but her groans and gyrations scared the hell out of me. She behaved as if she had found the secret of perpetual motion.

Sometime around three in the morning, I tried to get a little rest by talking. Music came up and we began discussing de Falla's "Fire Dance Suite." I saw her get glassy-eyed. Then she let out a long howl: "I love the 'Fire Dance'!"

She sprang out to the middle of the floor and illustrated the effect it had on her. As she reached a crescendo, she jumped into bed and swamped me once more.

Next day, I said I had to check with the studio. After the call I announced sadly that I'd have to get back to Hollywood because a very important job had just come up.

When I reported the debacle to Sylvia, she laughed. She thought I hadn't given the poor girl a chance. I could imagine nothing more frightening than living with that whirling dervish, forever doing the "Fire Dance." I knew it would have consumed me.

But the important thing was that Sylvia, in a peculiar way, had divorced herself from me. Perhaps that's all she'd been trying to do.

Though I was now under contract to a studio, I still worked in little theaters that existed all over town. I knew I had a hell of a lot to learn about acting and I wasn't going to rest on the laurels of a contract.

I joined a group called the Contemporary Players. Most of them were former members of the famous Group Theater in New York. At this time, they were casting *Waiting for Lefty, Bury the Dead* and *Golden Boy*. Because I was under contract to the studio, I couldn't accept a part but they let me study with them.

In the group was a very attractive blond girl named Janet Lawe. She was unusually intelligent but high-strung. Someone told me that she came from a very prominent South Pasadena family and had been disowned by them because of her theatrical aspirations.

One night after a rehearsal of *Waiting for Lefty* I found myself walking beside her. I asked her if she'd like to have coffee. She said yes, and we stopped off at a little café. She told me she was living in a dingy room with three other girls. She was unhappy with this arrangement because apparently they were call girls. I asked her why she stayed. She said she had paid a month's rent in advance and couldn't afford to leave. She told me the story of her parents and said she'd rather die than ask them for money.

"Have you ever gone hungry, Tony?"

"Many times."

"There's a kind of aesthetic beauty about it, isn't there?"

"I think it's ugly. Knut Hamsun wrote about it magnificently and so did Saroyan. It's good to read about but it's demeaning to experience."

"Do you know this is the first thing I've had all day?" she said, pointing to the cup of coffee.

"For Christ's sake, why didn't you say so?"

"I thought it would be unladylike."

"You're crazy. Come on, order something," I insisted.

"No, thanks. Where do you live?"

"A few blocks from here."

"Do you have a kitchen?"

"Yes."

"Do you have some food in the icebox?"

"Some eggs and things."

"Okay, let's go there and I'll cook something."

With the first money that came in from the studio contract I'e rented a comfortable apartment in the Silverlake district, not fa from Sylvia. I was still afraid to be away from her.

After Janet had cooked herself some supper, we sat aroune talking about plays and our ambitions. Her mind was very precis and incisive. She had a great sense of social and political con sciousness. Though Sylvia had made me aware of the classics ane philosophy, she had not put them into the perspective of th times. Janet made me aware that general learning was of no us unless it illuminated what was going on in the contemporar world.

I had found a new teacher, a younger Sylvia, except that i wasn't confused with romance and emotion, at least on my part.

When Janet saw the couch in a small anteroom I called a study she asked if she could stay there for the night. It would be luxurious change from the fleabag she was living in. She had aske in a very matter-of-fact way, with no romantic overtures, and agreed.

The next morning I got up to go to work at the studio and t my amazement she had breakfast all ready for me. In the evenin when I came back she was waiting for me with a sumptuous mea on the table. She no longer asked if she could stay. She had a ready moved in.

I was delighted with the arrangement. She kept the apartmen immaculate, asked no questions about my comings and goings. Sh was there whenever I needed someone to talk to. For a month o so it was like having a sister or a close relation living with me.

One night after having read for an hour in bed, I turned th light off to go to sleep. I heard her get up in the other room. Sh came into mine and climbed into bed with me. Until now, sh had never in any way indicated that she was romantically inte ested in me.

"Tony," she said softly in the dark. "It's ridiculous for us t live together like two neuters. I'm a woman and you're a mar We should be grown-up about it and enjoy each other."

"Janet, you don't have to sleep with me out of any sense c

duty or gratitude. I love having you here. You're great company. . . ."

"But don't you want to fuck me?"

It was the first time she'd used language like that. I thought, my God, she's from South Pasadena, she's in the social register, and she talks about fucking like everybody else.

"I'm just afraid that things might change if we do. I like it the way it's been."

"Tony, this is 1936. Haven't you read Havelock Ellis or Karl Marx? A woman is no longer some porcelain china doll. We have our wants and biological needs, just like a man. We like to fuck just as much as you."

Not wanting to offend Havelock Ellis, and lest I be thought a fascist for turning down Karl Marx, and to fulfill her biological need, I accepted the offer. She was a thoroughly liberated young lady.

Next morning at breakfast she announced that the experience had been satisfying and that her id was no longer bothering her. She did want to assure me, however, that I was not to interpret the episode as a prelude to romance. Nothing had changed. She would still do the housework and be my intellectual companion in exchange for the board and room I was supplying. That suited me.

Her id was apparently not too active. She visited me only rarely for her biological needs. While we still attended classes together I lived much of my own life away from her. In a relaxed fashion, I pursued my career.

After my meeting on the set of *The Buccaneer* with the girl whose eyes haunted me, I began to feel strange coming home to Janet. Katie had had the same impact on me that I'd felt upon meeting Sylvia. I knew that I would move heaven and earth to make her my wife. The only obstacle was the fact that she belonged to Hollywood royalty. But screw that, I thought. In America we were all potential kings. I, too, could get a crown. If that's what she wanted I'd get it for her. Thomas Wolfe wrote that America was a place where miracles not only happened but where they happened every day. Weren't miracles happening to me already? Besides, if Katie were destined to be my woman, she would be the kind of woman my grandmother had been. She would be like my mother, who had followed her man into battle. If she

loved me, she could learn to live on beans and tortillas. Love re
fused to recognize walls, fences, social barriers, language, econom
ics. Love was enough unto itself.

MAN. Kid, was that you talking, or me?
BOY. You took the words right out of my mouth.
MAN. Yes, boy. That first night we went out to dinner she started
the dialogue we had longed to hear all our lives.
BOY. Yeah, she had me sold.

Katie and I had lingered a long time over dinner. I'd purposely
taken her to an unfashionable place to have some Mexican food
I had to find out that first night where she stood. I talked inces
santly about what my life had been. I even threw in a few cus
words to see where she stood on that score. I told her everything
including the fact that I loved her and wanted her to marry me
I watched her while she toyed with two forks, trying to balance
them on a toothpick on the edge of a glass of water.

"Look," I added, "I'm under contract now, but God knows i
it's going to work out. I don't intend to play Indians and Hawai
ians for the rest of my life. If I don't think I'm going to make it
I'll go on to something else. I know you come from a rich family
but if you marry me you leave everything behind. Where I go
you go."

She smiled. "I know the Book of Ruth too — 'Whither thou
goest, I will go; . . . thy people shall be my people, and thy God
my God.' "

MAN. That was pretty heavy stuff, kid. You never expected to
hear that.
BOY. I've already said she was good back there.
MAN. And how about when she said, "I don't care if you succeed
as an actor or not. I don't care if you shine shoes or sell news
papers, because I know that whatever you do you'll do the best
you know how. If you want me to marry you, I will.
BOY (almost in tears). Words, just a bunch of words, probably
from some movie script she'd read. (the boy starts crying. The
man reaches out to pat him but the boy rushes out in tears.)

"When did the kid turn against Katie?" the doctor asked.

"I don't really know. Although he denies it now, it was the rst time he had really loved completely. Evie he had romanti-zed — it was a pink-cloud kind of infatuation. He had loved Syl-ia for awakening him to a new world, but he started to dig into er past to find an excuse not to commit himself completely. I ust say in his defense — and God knows that after all these years f the tortures he's put me through I find it difficult to defend im — that he did have his own peculiar sense of honor.

"He would have gone through the marriage with Sylvia if e had not become frightened at the last minute."

"Would it have worked out?"

"I think we would have had a great ten years together. Her fluence would have made me reach out for a bigger, more mean-igful life. That is, if he's been able to forget the ghosts."

"Would he have been faithful to her?"

After much digging inside me and trying to be completely hon-t with the doctor, I said, "Yes. You see, sex *per se* wasn't that nportant to the boy. Sex was almost dirty to him if it didn't in-ude the mysticism of souls coming together. He really believed the phrase 'making love,' in the mystery of two people sharing common magical experience. That's why that night under the ars with Sylvia was so perfect for him. There had been no aware-ss of bodies as such. It had taken place quietly, surreptitiously, you wish, under the stars.

"Because of his early dreams of being a priest and later a eacher with Aimee, the boy really was searching for a kind of sembodied love. I tease him now because he found it offensive hen people used four-letter words that had to do with bodily nctions."

The doctor seemed surprised. "He seems to use them quite fre-uently now, from what you tell me."

I nodded. "Believe it or not, up until I started working with u there were two words in the English language I couldn't say."

"What are they?"

I found it difficult to formulate them. Though I'd used them ten in our discussions, the words stuck in my throat.

"What are the words, Tony?"

I finally blurted them out — "Fart and snot."

His laughter filled the room. "Two good Anglo-Saxon words

"I'm not Anglo-Saxon," I reminded him.

"Could you say them in Spanish?"

"No, they were offensive in Spanish, too."

"But you told me of the boy's dissertation on the fart. I though
that was very funny."

"I'm glad you liked it. I must say that I was quite surprised t
his liberation. After that session I felt maybe we were beginnir
to break through. You have no idea what a victory that was, ju
to be able to utter those two words."

The doctor got up and walked about the room. "I'd have
difficult time explaining that to the next psychiatrist's conve
tion. My great breakthrough — I got a man to admit that far
and snot exist. Tony, maybe the kid is right. Maybe there's a ne
philosophy based on the ability to say fart and snot with aplom
After all, the word shit has always been an expletive, but, as yc
explained it, it can also be used as an expression of endearment

The doctor went back to his desk and made some notes in h
folder. "Tell me more about the boy and Katie."

"I had always met Katie away from her own environment.
thought the problem was making her adjust to mine. I took h
on several tours of the East Side, where I had grown up. I eve
showed her the exact spot where my father had died. I'd taken h
to meet my mother, Sylvia, Evie. We had gone to the Angel
Temple together. It was as if I wanted her to share every drop
my experience. I wanted her to accept me completely and u
conditionally.

"The only thing I hadn't done was show her where I live
Janet had suddenly decided she was in love with me and w
making demands. I hadn't solved that. I found it difficult to e
plain to Katie that a girl was staying at my house.

"One day, I went to the apartment, packed all my belonging
and left a note for Janet. I explained that what had started o
as a practical and comfortable arrangement, had gotten out
hand; I had never intended it as a romantic relationship; as f
as I was concerned, she could stay in the apartment as long
she wanted, and that as long as I earned money she needn't worr
that I would provide for her. She had been of great help to r

ut I was not in love with her. I had fallen in love and intended
o get married.

"I took a house way out in the San Fernando Valley. I felt that
ow I had broken the umbilical cord with Sylvia and would face
ay new life away from the comfort and protection of the old
eighborhood.

"The day came when Katie decided it was time she introduced
1e to her family and her background.

"For some stupid reason I was totally unprepared for the shock,
or the impact of that elegant house on the hill, the long circular
rive and the vast grounds, the attending butlers and maids. See-
1g Katie surrounded by all that wealth seemed so foreign to me.

"As I waited by the front door, I wanted to run away. I prayed
would be she that opened the door. When I saw the butler
anding there asking who was calling, I became tongued-tied.
hated his look. I despised the fact that I had to have his approval
efore I could see the girl I had begun to think of as my woman."

OY. She didn't belong in those surroundings.

KAN. They weren't hers. She came from the same tough background we had known. She had been left an orphan and had
been adopted at the age of eleven by the de Mille family. It
wasn't her fault that they were rich. If they hadn't adopted her,
you might never have met her.

OY. We didn't belong in that house. We had nothing in common
with it. That's when you started to compete for "things." That's
when you became obsessed with the big houses. You allied yourself with the wrong army. You tried to compete with the muscle-
your-way-through-life boys, the doers, the big go-getters.

"I was ushered into a cavernous entry hall and from there into
baronial living room. The fine Persian rugs and the brocaded
urniture scared me. The boy turned around and made a dash for
1e door. I stayed.

"Katie must have been aware of my discomfort. She did every-
1ing to make me feel at home. It was impossible. I had no refer-
nce point. I had never imagined I would ever be in a real castle.
"he only castles I'd seen were replicas on movie stages. This one
as real.

"Mr. de Mille and I had had an excellent relationship. I ha
developed a great respect for him, even a secret affection. He ha
seemed to have a sincere respect for my work. Often during th
shooting of the two pictures I had done with him he'd spoken t
me with great encouragement.

"Now, when he saw me in his house as a potential son-in-law,
sensed a change. I was no longer the actor but some kind of
threat, an interloper into his close family circle. No doubt h
thought his adopted daughter could do much better than marr
ing a struggling young actor whose future was still a big questio
mark.

"Mrs. de Mille, on the other hand, was most gracious. She di
everything to make me feel welcome. She no doubt remembere
when her husband had been an unsuccessful actor, struggling i
stock companies all over the country. She no doubt recalled h
own insecurities, his fears that he would never be equal to h
playwright brother, Bill de Mille. I was sincerely sorry the bo
had left, for he would have liked Mrs. de Mille and she woul
have liked him.

"The rest of the family sitting around at dinner gave me ve
little thought. Katie had brought other young men to dinner wh
had eventually disappeared. They wondered how many dinne
I would survive.

"After dessert the butler went around the table setting the dem
tasse service for coffee. I had ignored the small cubes of suga
since I didn't know how to extricate them without using my fii
gers. In front of the small coffee cup I saw a small receptacle co
taining what I thought was sugar. There was a tiny spoon at th
side. I reached over and spooned it into my cup of coffee.

"I saw Katie looking at me. I didn't catch the warning. I smile
back and drank the brew. I had poured salt into the coffee.

"Apparently, other members of the family had witnessed m
*faux pas*. Nobody said a word.

"I drank the coffee and smiled desperately, hoping I wouldn
vomit all over the doilies and the highly polished table.

"Katie later admitted that after the incident she definitely d
cided I might be worth marrying.

"The boy had been waiting for me outside when I finally le
the big house. He wanted to know everything that had happene

told him, including the coffee incident. He wasn't amused. He
id that was to be my fate, to always drink the bitter brew in
at house.

"I told him to go to hell. I wasn't going to hold it against Katie
at she'd been adopted by a rich family. Her name was really
ester, not de Mille. Her mother had been Italian, which was
ose enough to our background. She knew the Latin rules of
an and woman — "One man and a wall three feet wide for the
st of the world." She believed in Ruth's 'Whither thou goest.
. .' But the boy had been frightened."

ʏ. I wasn't frightened. I saw the prison you were taking us to.
ᴀɴ. You were afraid to take on her father. You were scared shit-
less because you'd have to fight him for the crown. I fought the
fight all alone.

"I was too committed to Katie to tell her of my doubts. I refused
tell her of the boy's reaction. She herself must have been going
rough endless questions, whether I was the right man to give
erself to forever. She was too honest to enter into a marriage
at she didn't believe would be permanent. She, too, needed a
ome she could call her own. She, too, was tired of being an
lopted member of a family.

"I decided to bring up the one circumstance I'd left out of the
count of my life. I told her about Janet Lawe.

" 'Are you in love with her?'

" 'No.'

" 'Were you in love with her when you met me?'

" 'No. As far as I was concerned it was a practical arrangement.'

"I was having a hell of a time explaining.

" 'But you did sleep with her.'

" 'Yes, but it wasn't what you think. Janet is a liberal.' I blurted
t, as if that would explain everything.

" 'You mean she's one of those people that preach free love and
arx?'

" 'Exactly. She says sex doesn't have to be complicated by love.
e says one should save those emotions for causes, or mankind in
neral.'

"Anyway, it was out of the bag and I felt relieved.

"Katie finally shrugged. 'Well, I guess one woman more or le[ss] in your life isn't going to make that much difference. It was dif[fi]cult enough for me meeting Evie and Sylvia. I suppose I shou[ld] have guessed there were others!'

"Her sophistication intrigued me at the same time that [it] frightened me. I knew the boy would not have been so tolera[nt] about those ghosts.

" 'There is one thing that worries me, Tony,' she said, takin[g] my hand.

" 'What?'

" 'You're twenty-two years old and I'm twenty-six.'

"I laughed it off. 'God, a year before I almost married a woma[n] twenty years older than myself, so what difference could four yea[rs] make?'

" 'Maybe a lot. . . .' She began, but I stopped her."

BOY. You should have let her continue. It would have saved us [a] lot of trouble.

MAN. Perhaps. But she had been so gallant, so understanding [of] my confession, I had to kiss her.

BOY. And you never found out till later, but I knew, I sensed [it.] I tried to warn you but no one could have stopped you. Yo[u] were blind, deaf.

MAN. I was in love.

"So the boy tried to warn you?" asked the doctor.

"Yes, but I felt I was now a man. I thought it ridiculous [to] listen to the advice of a silly kid. He spoke of the big house as [a] prison. I saw it as a challenge. The kid wove dreams by the hou[r] and they kept changing constantly. I tried to make his dreams [a] reality, my own reality."

BOY. Was that wedding your idea of reality?

MAN. I agree that was a slight mistake.

BOY. A slight mistake? All that horse-shit with those limousin[es] and the police escort. Guests sitting in the church, not becau[se] two people were promising to love and obey each other foreve[r] but because it was their duty to make an appearance for the o[ld] man. Were all those photographers there to record love eve[r] lasting or merely to shower the country with pictures of the peasant who had married royalty?

ᴀɴ. But she had nothing to do with it.

ʏ. Who made out the list for the wedding guests?

ᴀɴ. It was her wedding. Besides, Mrs. de Mille had made up most of the list.

ʏ. Why wasn't Mother included? Why wasn't my name on the list, or Elsie's, or Evie's, or Stella's, or Feodor's, or even Frank Bowles?

ᴀɴ. Maybe it was my fault, boy. Maybe I should have insisted.

ʏ. But you didn't.

ᴀɴ. No, I didn't. I remember seeing you across the street from the church in your torn pair of pants and the glee club sweater. I called you but you turned away.

ʏ. I couldn't take it. All that recorded music starting and the big fat-assed cops keeping the gawkers away. They would have clamped Mother in jail if she had tried to break through to see her only son getting married.

ᴀɴ (*defenseless*). I saw you heading down Santa Monica Boulevard. You followed those train tracks heading East. I knew they didn't go anywhere.

ʏ. I knew you weren't going anywhere either.

I found myself with a huge lump in my throat. I couldn't swallow, I couldn't even pass spit into my gullet. The doctor saw my discomfort. "Something wrong?"

I gestured helplessly to my throat. He quickly got me a glass of water. It hurt as I swallowed. Then I gave way to tears. I lay down on the couch and cried while the doctor stood silently over me, hoping the lie in my throat would now disgorge.

I couldn't stop sobbing. I was reliving our wedding night, and the terrible shock when I learned that my wife was not the Shulamite of the Bible. She was not undefiled.

The ghosts had sat around the bed and laughed at my surprise. The boy had joined them. Othello, overcome by jealousy, had had the strength to kill his Desdemona, to kill himself. I didn't. I could only wave my sword in anger, striking at ghosts who were untouched by all my empty thrusts. Their laughter grew and grew. My madness had begun.

"Go on," said the doctor.

I couldn't even reply. At the following session I still couldn't go into it directly. I had to edge into it very gradually.

# 20

I WAS CROSSING the courtyard at Paramount Studios one day when I heard, "You shit!" I turned around and there was the glorious mad, Satanic face of Jack Barrymore. "What's become of you, you sonofobitch? I understand you've become a movie actor, another clown they've bought and put in a fucking cage. You've sold your soul, son," he said. "They've bought you, haven't they?" I felt ashamed, because he was right. "You didn't go to England, did you?"

"No, sir."

"Don't you sir me, you shit," he said. "Only my enemies sir me. My friends call me Jack."

He took me by the arm and led me to his dressing room. He explained to me that he had just signed his soul away to do a series of B pictures based on Bulldog Drummond.

"I had to take it, kid. The cunts have eaten me out of house and home. Don't ever marry. There is nothing more tenacious and difficult to get rid of than a woman. Scurvy you can find medication for, leeches you can pluck out, but a woman is worse than a tapeworm. She is not happy until she's devoured your entrails."

I hesitated to tell him I had been married just a few months before.

"Oh, Christ, of course," he roared, in that wounded lion way of his. "You married Bianca."

"No, I married a girl named Katherine."

"I know who you married, but she played Bianca when I did Mercutio to Leslie Howard's Hamlet. God, she was a beauty, and the boss's daughter to boot, eh? I knew you had talent, my boy, but now my admiration is everlasting for your courage at taking on that *ménage*."

I didn't tell him I was more than aware of what I had walked into.

"Are you in loo-ve?" He stretched out the word as if he didn't believe in it but desperately hoped that the miracle of love did exist.

"Yes," I said simply.

Katie and I had taken a modest apartment near Westwood Village. I had been forced to go on a strict budget. Janet had threatened to sue me for breach of promise. I wanted to go to court to fight what I thought was an unjust action, but Paramount thought it was bad to have one of their contract players involved in a scandal. No doubt the fact that I had married the daughter of their most important producer had something to do with their decision. They made a settlement of five thousand dollars on the young lady. It took me two years to work it off.

Katie had been very understanding and handled the difficult situation as best she could.

I myself was going through a rough period at the studio. It was inevitable that everyone in town thought of me as an interloper, the guy who had married the boss's daughter to further his career.

ROY. Didn't you?

MAN (*angrily*). You know better. I married her in spite of it, not because of it. I was a twenty-two-year-old kid who thought he could conquer the world. I wasn't the first peasant who had ever dreamed of marrying the princess and taking her away to his hut to live happily forever and ever.

One day, driving out of the studio, I ran into Carole Lombard. She wasn't her usual gay self.

"How's it going, Tony?"

"Tough." I shrugged.

"You took on a tough one, kid. It'll take you a long time to dig yourself out."

"Meaning what?" I asked edgily.

"Sons-in-law have a rough time in this town. First there are the

ass-kissers who will try to use you to get to the Old Man, and the
there are the guys who will try to knock you down to get even wit
him. You're going to get it coming and going."

She was right. I became supersensitive. The very mention of
de Mille's name sent up the antenna. Many times I got into fis
fights because I sensed a note of derision.

Once, on location, I had taken my box lunch and gone to s
under a tree. The rest of the crew and the other actors were a
sitting at a long table. Someone called over and asked if the son
in-law of C. B. de Mille was too good to sit with the commo
people. I rushed over and made for the man's throat. I woul
have strangled the sonofabitch if they hadn't pulled me away.

It was inevitable that the word got around about my sensitivit
So naturally I became the butt of all the son-in-law jokes. All tha
was trivial, however, next to the emotional upheaval of our wec
ding night.

I looked up at the doctor. "Doctor, I know some of this soun
insane."

"That's *my* job, Tony. That's up to me to determine."

"I know, but my sitting here twenty-odd years later telling yo
about that night in Carmel, the pain I felt, the jealousy, the i
sanity that overtook me, embarrasses me. After all, it's the twer
tieth century. Life, morals, values, have changed. What the he
has a small broken piece of tissue in a woman's vagina to do wit
accepting her or not?

"The look on that poor girl's face as I slapped her when I foun
out I wasn't the first man. I felt betrayed, I felt cheated, I fe
lied to.

"Not only could I not make love to her, but I wanted to ru
away. All the love, all my dreams had turned into a nightmare

"The poor, frightened girl packed her things and ran out o
the hotel. She said she'd take a train to Reno and get a divorce.

"I was left there in that room all alone. I looked at the be
where an hour or so before I thought all my childish dream
were about to come true, and now the girl was off in the night o
the way to Reno to get a divorce."

"How did the boy feel?"

"Peculiarly enough, he was relieved. He had taunted me at fir

say terrible things to my new wife. He had wanted me to stran-
gle her, punish her for her great sin. Once she had walked out, he
felt relieved. He had gotten even with her. He now had me all to
himself again."

"What did you say?" asked the doctor.

"I said now he was happy because we were alone."

"I see."

"What the hell does that mean?"

"The boy seems to be happy with you when you and he don't
have to rely on anyone else."

I tried to figure out what the doctor meant, but then he urged
me to tell him the rest of the story about our aborted honeymoon.
I decided to get it over with and relieve myself of the pain.

"I sat there on the bed for an hour. I tried not to think of the
girl who'd left me there alone. I tried to tell myself through my
sobbing that it was all for the best. I tried to conjure up all sorts
of evil images of the girl, but I couldn't. There was something
about her sad, beautiful eyes that haunted me. I saw the vulnerable girl who had lived in an orphanage for two years waiting for
someone to give her a home, now on a train feeling guilty because
she had dared to look elsewhere for happiness. I knew that if I
didn't rush after her I'd never be a man.

"As I threw my stuff into a bag, the boy tried to talk me out
of it. He swore he'd never leave me alone, that he would haunt me
the rest of my life. I took him by the throat and strangled him
until he went limp. I thought he was dead.

"I ran out and got into the car. I drove over those tortuous
winding mountain roads all night, racing to get to Reno before
her train. Fifty miles outside of Reno, the train had come to a stop
at a siding to let some freight trains by. I boarded it and looked
for Katie's compartment. As I burst through the door, she barely
looked up. She was sitting there in silence. She had been crying.

"I picked up her bags and told her to follow me. She didn't say
a word until we were in the car and the train was pulling away.

" 'Are you sure that you can live with it?'

" 'I have to,' I said, throwing the car into gear. 'You are my
woman. I have to learn to be your man.' "

"Did you?" asked the doctor.

"I tried for twenty years."

283

"Did you ever forgive her?"

"I'm paying you fifty dollars an hour to help me learn to forgive. I've read all the right things; I've searched everywhere for the answer. I no longer know whether I can blame the kid for everything. I have to bear some of the brunt. I can no longer accept or tolerate all the pain I've caused everyone. I want desperately to believe in 'forgive us our trespasses as we forgive those who trespass against us.' I want to believe Kazantzakis when he says that a woman is like a beautiful stream you come upon in the desert; you drink from it and you don't destroy it simply because someone has drunk from it before you. It sounds so nice in print. I still can't accept it as part of my belief, but I want to."

"What kind of life did you have with your wife?"

"The only way we could survive was to destroy all evidence of her past. I refused to have anything to do with her old friends. I avoided going to any place where she had been before. I tried desperately to become the center of her life."

"Did you succeed?"

"No, I was never able to feel number one. I often thought of running away from Hollywood and starting all over again somewhere else."

"Would she have gone with you?"

"Yes, but I knew that the ghosts would follow me. The only way was to take on the ghosts on their own terrain."

"Did you beat them?"

"Most of them."

"Not all?"

"Most."

"Did she acknowledge the ghosts?"

"For her they didn't exist, she said."

"But you didn't believe her?"

"No."

The doctor stood up and stretched. He paced about the room. "That time when the women's drama club honored you, they certainly felt you were number one. Certainly there have been very few people who can point to three major motion pictures and a play simultaneously playing on Broadway, and yet you couldn't accept their word. What more proof do you need that you have arrived, that you are accepted, that you have whipped the ghosts

I knew the answer. It sounded so simple. I felt my body heave
ith the need to cry — that lost, hopeless feeling, the gnawing at
y guts knew the answer.

"I need the boy's approval. I need *his* love."

# 21

ᴇᴄᴀᴜsᴇ of my self-inflicted pain, because of my self-torture and
dless flagellations, I found it difficult to communicate with most
ople. I identified with Thomas Wolfe and his lengthy descrip-
ons of his tortured relationship with Aline Bernstein in *The*
*eb and the Rock* and *You Can't Go Home Again.* I knew and
d lived through every experience of Othello's. I found comfort
the cynicism of Barrymore and his group. I sat for hours listen-
g to them berate and flagellate the word love. And yet I never
et a group of men so desperately wanting to believe in it. Jack
ould often insist that we close an evening by going to a night
ot on Sunset Boulevard to hear a whiskey-voiced woman sing,
alling in love with love is falling for make-believe." It was his
vorite tune. Somehow he found solace in the fact that he was
t alone in his aborted experiences with that great mythical emo-
on. I, in turn, loved him and wanted to emulate his offhand
anner on the subject. I admired the fact that he could scoff at
and yet face life with such dauntless panache.

For instance, the night Gene Fowler, John Decker and I went
Earl Carroll's nightclub on Sunset Boulevard. It was famous
having the most beautiful women in Hollywood as entertain-
s. It had a huge seating capacity, perhaps twenty-five hundred
ople.

Barrymore was hardly dressed for a nightclub; he hated to wear
rmal clothes, or even a tie. They wouldn't let him in without
e, even though he was Barrymore. The captain had to lend
m a tie. They gave us the best table, however, right down in
ont, and brought a bucket of champagne in his honor.

We were enjoying ourselves thoroughly watching the show when the master of ceremonies said: "Ladies and gentlemen, w are honored to have one of the great actors of our time in th audience. He is such a special person that we would like for hi to take a bow, and if he will come up on the stage, we have special award for him."

The spotlight came on our table and Barrymore got up an bowed. The audience applauded wildly. He refused, howeve to go up on the stage. The audience kept applauding and woul not be put off. The master of ceremonies took him to the micr phone and made some poor jokes about his private life. The aud ence lapped it up. They were seeing John Barrymore, whose nam was still a household word, though the days of his greatness we over, and he had become a caricature of his former self.

Finally, the master of ceremonies said: "Mr. Barrymore, t highest honor we can pay you is to let you dance a waltz with t most beautiful Earl Carroll girl." I could see that Barrymore w very uncomfortable. He suffered terribly from gout and cou hardly walk.

The master of ceremonies made a sign and out from the win walked one of the ugliest, most clownish apparitions ever see She had painted black teeth, a knock-kneed walk, and had put a fright wig. The audience roared, two thousand five hundre people laughing.

Decker, Fowler and I thought of going up on the stage and ta ing our friend away, stopping him from making a fool of himse But Barrymore signaled the orchestra to begin the waltz and we up to the woman who, by this time, was clowning for the bene of the audience. I don't know what he said to her, but she look at him rather peculiarly and straightened up. He put his ar around her, took her hand and led her in the waltz.

She was transformed; nothing for her existed but Barrymo You could see that she wished she could wipe away the make and take off the wig. The audience was laughing; they st thought it was funny, but they also began to sense that somethi remarkable was happening on stage. This strange, macabre dan was going on. It was like watching something terribly person happening before your eyes.

Finally, the music stopped. Barrymore looked at this lady, bent over and kissed her hand as if she were the Queen of England. He thanked her for the dance and watched her as she proudly walked off. There was a hush in the audience. He went over to the microphone, looked around the quiet room, and spoke: "As for you, ladies and gentlemen, you can all go fuck yourselves." There was stunned silence as he walked off the stage, and then, two thousand five hundred people stood up and cheered.

Robert Edmund Jones, the great set designer, once wrote that only a bad actor wonders where his light is; a good actor carries his light inside him. Jack carried the light inside him. Life had not been kind to him because he had no faith. This man who was adulated, who was worshiped by millions of women, who had the greatest talent, believed in nothing. He didn't believe in love and yet he yearned for love; I never saw a man in my life need love as much as that man. He was capable of giving it but he was not capable of receiving. I sometimes wonder if the Greeks translated the Hebrew script correctly when they wrote: "It is more blessed to give than to receive." The ability to receive gracefully is rare. The inability to accept love is to me the original sin, sadder than all others.

One of the reasons Barrymore accepted me was because he saw that I wanted nothing from him but to be found worthy by him.

After work Jack would invite me up to the house, where I met his cronies, among them Gene Fowler, W. C. Fields and John Decker. They were all to have a profound effect on my life.

John Decker was a man with enormous talent as a painter. He laughed at all Hollywood "art" collectors. He thought they were stupid shits who merely collected paintings as status symbols. To prove it, he painted a Rouault which he sold to Billy Rose for fifteen thousand dollars. That was a great joke. He also used to paint satirical paintings, like W. C. Fields dressed as Queen Victoria. His whole life was devoted to making a joke of everything. I bought several paintings of Decker's; they have faded because even then he cheated, he used special chemicals that made the paints dry too fast. But Dave Chasen, Artie Shaw, Billy Rose, Errol Flynn all bought his paintings, not because they were great, but because they were in vogue.

One of the most beautiful moments I ever experienced in m
life was around that period. A group of us were sitting in Barry
more's "dressing room" at his home. Somehow he got onto th
subject of favorite passages in literature. Everyone in that roor
had experienced success, except myself, and they all knew the emp
tiness of success without love. John Decker quoted Baudelaire
W. C. Fields pantomimed, Roland Young recited Shakespear
very succinct and funny. But it was all sad in a way, because the
were negating love.

When everybody insisted it was Barrymore's turn, he recite
T. S. Eliot. It was strange to see this man, who was saturated i
alcohol, sitting there in the armchair in dim light, suddenly begi
to talk and become the center of the world.

> *No! I am not Prince Hamlet, nor was meant to be;*
> *Am an attendant lord, one that will do*
> *To swell a progress, start a scene or two,*
> *Advise the prince; no doubt, an easy tool,*
> *Deferential, glad to be of use,*
> *Politic, cautious, and meticulous;*
> *Full of high sentence, but a bit obtuse;*
> *At times, indeed, almost ridiculous —*
> *Almost, at times, the Fool.*

He had summed up what he felt about himself. He had just d
vorced his fourth wife and he was sixty, with a great past bu
very little future. There was a long silence after he finished.

I was the only man who hadn't recited; undoubtedly, some (
them wondered what the hell I was doing in such an august gath
ering. They may have felt I was there only because of the gene
osity and benevolence of Emperor John. They started kidding m
and began clapping in rhythm.

Barrymore looked at me as if to say: Have the courage to stan
up among these monsters.

It was the most frightening audience I have ever faced; the
were all drunk, or close to it. I don't know what made me choo
what I did. I recited the Gettysburg Address. When I had fi
ished I felt I had made the wrong choice. Instead, I should hav
made them laugh. I heard John Decker say, "Oh, shit," and W. (

Fields made some derisive kind of gesture as if I had just spoken about the Holy Trinity at a Jewish wedding.

Then Gene Fowler said, "Well, those are pretty goddamned good words, aren't they, Jack?" And I looked over and Jack had tears in his eyes. I felt as if I was waiting for my reviews to come in. Jack said, "The only trouble is that the little shit believes it; he believes in those fucking words." There was another hush before he said, "Well, kid, I hope they don't disillusion you."

As I bade him good-night at the door of his Tower Road home, we stood on the lawn and looked at the sea of lights down below. He had been very quiet on the drive home. He seemed very pensive now as he looked at the never-never land below us known as Hollywood. I wondered what the great man was thinking, what forgotten dreams and pains the panorama below conjured up in his mind.

I turned to leave. I felt he wanted to be alone. As I started to drive away, he called over his shoulder: "Don't forget, kid, anybody can make shit out of beauty; it takes great courage to make beauty out of shit."

I left him standing silhouetted against the lights below. On the way to Sunset Boulevard, I pondered the statement.

Katie had resigned herself to my relationship with that cynical, riotous, drinking group. She admired John Decker's great talent as a painter but felt he spent more time in hiding it rather than developing it. John Barrymore was obviously living a travesty of his former self; only Gene Fowler seemed to be respectful of his responsibility as a writer-artist. Later, he was to write two magnificent books about the group. One was called *Good night, Sweet Prince* and the other, *Minutes of the Last Meeting*.

My wife was concerned that I was idealizing their offhand attitude toward life. I didn't tell her of my own fears that I might end up a lonely man, sitting on top of a hill looking down on a diadem of broken dreams. I would do everything in my power never to give up the hope that I could find happiness with my wife. We tried, God knows, we both tried. It wasn't only the ghosts that wouldn't let me rest, but the living as well.

One night, after months of seeing no one, because of my mad
ness to create a life that was ours and ours alone, Katie asked m
if she could have a party at our house. She would invite a fe
select friends that she was sure I'd be "comfortable" with.

The night of the party she was in great spirits. It was the firs
time she had entertained anyone since our wedding.

Most of the guests were girls she'd gone to school with, an
their husbands. Very few of them had anything to do with th
so-called Hollywood set, which I'd learned to dread.

While I tried to play the host and passed the drinks around th
group, I saw two women looking at my collection of books.

"My, so many books," said one.

"Yes," said the other, "Katie was always a great reader."

"Maybe they're his," suggested the first.

The other giggled. "Darling, have you taken a good look a
him? He's nothing but a stud. I don't think he can read."

I rushed into the kitchen and told Katie to throw her frienc
out of the house.

"What happened?" she begged.

"Fuck 'em. They think I'm just a dumb Mexican. I don't war
them around."

I told her of the conversation I'd overheard.

"But, dear, Shirley's always been a bitch. I'll tell her to leav
but the rest are nice people."

"No, goddamnit, they're all laughing at me. If you don't thro
them out, I will."

I don't know what she said to them. I disappeared into th
bedroom and was listening to *La Bohème*. After a while, Kati
came in and sat down. She was crying.

"Dear, we can't go on like this. You're bound to run into sill
people; you can't go on hating everyone. When I met you I fe
in love with you because you were so full of hope and love. I'
never met anyone that believed so in life."

"Yes," I shouted, "and you changed it all."

It was inevitable that I blamed her for all my failures. My care
had been reduced to playing third-rate gangster parts, Mexica
bandits and poor Indians who were always getting the shit kicke
out of them by the big strong white man. I knew I was a long wa
from defeating the ghosts.

One day, I walked into the office of the head of the studio and asked to be released from my contract. I told him that I was unhappy with my roles. He must have sensed there was more to it than the usual actor complaining about his career.

"Tony, I promise to try to find better parts for you."

"No, sir, I don't want to stay here."

"Why? We believe in you, I believe you have a fine future ahead of you."

I finally blurted it out. "I'll never be anything but de Mille's son-in-law at this studio. It's destroying me. I can't act worth a shit anymore. I have to go out and prove that I can stand on my own feet."

He looked at me for a long time. He, too, had a son working at the studio, going through the motions of being a producer. Everyone, including himself, knew he'd never make it. He picked up the phone and called the studio lawyer.

"Bill, Tony Quinn is in my office. He wants his release from us. I think he should have it."

He hung up the phone and held out his hand. "Good luck, Tony. I don't want to let you go but you're right; it would be a tough fight here for you. But it's going to be just as tough elsewhere. I hope you win."

I broke the news to Katie that night that she was married to an unemployed actor. Our small savings would only carry us a few weeks. Now she would be put to the test. She didn't seem bothered by it.

"Whatever you want to do is fine with me. Come on, dear, dinner is ready."

# 22

'LOOK, DOCTOR, I make it sound like I spent the first few years of my life with my wife shitting razor blades. I mean, you're a doctor and I sit here and tell you about my sickness. After all, if you go to a dentist you only tell the sonofabitch about your toothache. But it wasn't all pain and torture. I was in love with that beautiful girl. She was strong as hell, riding along somehow, taking all the punches. We had a great deal in common. We had the same love for walking in the hills and mountains, for spending long hours by the sea. I taught her to read all the books I had loved. She in turn introduced me to authors I'd never heard of. She was thrilled with my knowledge of painting and devoured books on the subject. We became involved with the same courses. We knew moments of great peace and unforgettable beauty."

"But . . . ?" asked the doctor.

"But — at the very moment when I'd begin to feel the serenity and happiness, the little sonofabitch would come and prick all the balloons."

"Did Katie know about the boy?"

"At first she'd tried to make peace with him. God knows she tried, but he wouldn't have anything to do with her. She knew he wanted to destroy us so she began to fight back. The more she struck out at him, the more tortured I became.

"One day, we had been on a long drive through the hills behind Santa Barbara, where she'd gone to school. Peculiarly enough, it was the same district where my family and I had picked fruit when we'd first come to California. The lovely rolling hills reminded her of the time when she'd gone out horseback riding with her school chums. The same terrain reminded me of the indignity of earning a living on your knees.

"I had taken a side road off the main highway and found myself driving over some freshly planted fields. From a farmhouse nearby I saw a woman start across the field, screaming obscenities at me for ruining her neat furrows. She reminded me of all the boss's wives I'd ever known. Though I had been wrong in driving across the fields, I felt the woman's anger was unwarranted. I started to get out of the car to answer her.

"Katie pulled at my jacket. 'Please, dear, we're in the wrong. Don't be Mexican; be Irish.'

" 'What the hell does that mean?' I asked angrily.

" 'I mean, charm her, don't fight her.'

"As I got out of the car, I faced the woman and her fury. 'Oh madam, forgive me; please forgive my stupidity. The truth of the matter is I was so enthralled by the beauty of the terrain that I missed the road. My wife and I are looking for a farm to buy, and when we saw your charming house my wife let out a scream — "There it is, exactly the house we are looking for." '

"The woman looked agape, first at me and then over toward my wife, sitting in the car. Then she turned and saw the tire tracks that had destroyed her beautiful, neat field.

" 'Tomorrow,' I jumped in, 'I will send some workmen to hoe and replant the field.'

" 'What's your name?' she asked, beginning to soften.

" 'Anthony Quinn,' I smiled.

" 'Could it be that you're Irish?' she asked, with a faint brogue.

"I nodded. 'My grandfather was from Cork.'

" 'Was he now?' she smiled. 'Me and my husband come from Killarney.'

" 'Is that a fact?'

" 'Well,' she said finally, 'won't you and you dear wife come to the house and join us for a spot of tea?'

"During tea, the lady scoffed at my offer to have her field fixed. She assured us that she had three very able-bodied Mexicans working for her who would fix it in no time. Katie shot me a warning glance and I made no comment. She promised us that if she ever thought of selling we would be the first to hear about it. As we left her house, she said that she was sure that I could charm a snake, like all good Irishmen."

The doctor enjoyed the story. "Is it true, Tony? I mean, are there moments when you can tell that you're being Mexican or Irish?"

"Yes."

"Which is easier to live with?"

"The Irish, but then nobody ever called me a dirty mick. I never had to take a beating because I was Irish. I only had the shit kicked out of me because I was Mexican. So I decided to be it most of the time."

"What do you suppose your life would have been like if you'd spent more time charming your way through life, rather than fighting it the way you do?"

"Christ only knows. Anyway, it had all been decided back there

293

when I was a kid and fought against the Irish kids on the banks of the Los Angeles River, on the side of the Mexican boys."

"Do you ever wonder about your Irish parentage?"

"Yes, often. I have a picture of my grandfather. He's a blond version of my father. When I was a kid I would stare at him for hours. I wanted to love him so much. I made up all sorts of stories about him, then I'd stop myself because I wondered if he could love his dark grandson."

"And now?"

"I love him very much, but I'm still afraid. I wonder if he approves of me."

"Don't you think he would be proud of all you've done?"

I laughed. "Doctor, the kid doesn't think I've done a damn thing. I don't know if Father and my grandfather would agree with him."

"What about your mother's father? How do you feel about him?"

"Fuck him. He's one ghost I've killed and buried. He didn't have the balls to acknowledge his responsibility."

The doctor made an imaginary cross in the air. "One down, and how many ghosts to go?"

"An army."

"Don't you feel we're getting rid of some of them?"

"Yes, some of them have lost by default. They've died on me."

The doctor started to tidy up his desk. I got up to put my jacket on. "When are you supposed to leave for Europe to start your new picture?"

"In a week or ten days."

"Well, we have to win the war soon, don't we? Where the hell do we find the bomb to blow up all the ghosts?"

As we headed down the hall, the doctor repeated that we'd have to work hard. He felt it would be dangerous for me to go to Europe in the middle of therapy. He explained that there were postoperative complications that could develop from mental therapy, just like those from any major operation. He walked me to my car. "The man you're going to play, Paul Gauguin, was a driven man himself, wasn't he?"

"Yes, poor bastard; but at least he made it."

"Did he think he'd made it?"

"No, I guess not. They'd kicked the hell out of him in Paris. They thought he was just another of the wild bunch that came to be known as the Fauves. Then his wife and his kids thought he was crazy. So I doubt he felt he'd made it."

The doctor nodded, patted me on the back, and said we'd meet next day.

# 23

KATIE AND I sat in a corner booth of a fashionable restaurant that jutted out over the sea. Out beyond the waves I could see the bright lights and activity of the amusement park. It was a warm, pleasant summer night and I could hear the distant squeals as the roller coaster started its breathtaking descent. The lights from the restaurant lighted a path over the waves as they crashed into the pilings of the pier.

We were just finishing our coffee. During dinner we had talked of everything except the issue that hung heavy over us. In a few days I'd be leaving for three or four months in Europe, alone, and in spite of my gut-searching with the psychiatrist we were no nearer the answer.

Katie's face had changed through the years. Her beautiful eyes still had the sparkle that I had seen back there during our youth, but they seemed to constantly be in search of nonexistent angels. It had always amazed me how much she resembled my grandmother as a young woman. Even Katie's mouth, which had once been the full mouth of expectant youth, was now set in resignation to a life she had not bargained for.

In the last few months our social life, which had never been overactive, had come to a complete halt. All of my evenings had been taken with the doctor. Many times after my sessions with him I'd come home to find that Katie had gone to sleep. During the day, I'd be busy at the studio with script conferences and wardrobe fittings. Whenever we did manage to spend time together during the weekends, I would catch her watching me out of the corner of her eye, no doubt looking for signs that I was on the way to finding an answer for our life. She, too, was looking. Her bedroom was decorated completely different from the rest of the house. It was almost monastic. She had very few paintings on the walls. Those she had selected were pictures of saints and philosophers. On her night table beside her narrow bed she had photographs of the children and me when we'd all been young. The books beside her bed also were evidence of the world she'd retreated to; Gandhi, Krishnamurti and endless books on Moral Rearmament.

Now, over coffee, she tentatively asked if I felt any better after all my sessions with the doctor. I told her the joke of the man who went to a psychiatrist because he had no control over his bowels. After months of psychiatric treatment someone asked him if he felt any better and he'd said: "No, I still shit in my pants but at least I understand why."

Katie laughed politely. I pointed out that though I understood many things about myself, it had not lessened much of the pain.

"Do you think I'm still totally to blame for your . . . ?" she hesitated.

"Insanity?" I laughed.

"Sickness, or whatever you call it."

"No, it's all messed up with my mother's marriage to Frank Bowles, my father's death, Grandmother, being Irish-Mexican, my ridiculous desire to be someone, the ghosts — but it's mostly the boy."

I could see her wince. She knew the danger of that terrain. She had learned to skirt the subject.

"Really, Tony," she sighed, "doesn't it seem ridiculous to put yourself and all the people you love through hell because of a twelve-year-old boy? How can you allow him to rule you? My God, you have kids of your own now; would you let them tell you how to live?"

I stared out at the tide coming in. I watched the waves as they beat against the web of pilings.

" 'And a child shall lead them . . .' " I quoted.

Katie laughed. "Certainly you don't think that boy has any similarity to the Bible?"

"Why not? He believed it. He tried to live by it. Why can't he be right? From what I've seen, age does not necessarily mean wisdom. Maybe children are closer to the truth."

I could see that she was getting annoyed, so I called for the check. On the way home very little was said. Once in the house she kissed me on the cheek and wished me a good night's sleep. As I was getting into bed, she came to the doorway.

"Tony, I can no longer fight for the boy's approval. I frankly don't give a damn about him. I only pray for my children's approval and God's. If after these sessions you can't make peace with our lives, I'd rather you found it somewhere else. It's been a long fight and I've found I can't win it. Good-night, dear."

An ultimatum. Do it, or else. She didn't have to remind me of the stakes. I knew what they were. But an ultimatum was like driving me into a corner. Life was already claustrophobic enough. I turned the light off and went to sleep alone in my room.

I dreamt my father, the boy and I were running down a long endless sandy slope. We were all laughing and happy being together. My father, with his long legs, always seemed to run faster and leap farther than the kid and I. The kid stumbled along, sinking occasionally into the soft sand. I was having a lot of trouble keeping up with them. My father would stop every now and then to see how we were doing. Then he'd turn and keep on leaping down the steep hillside. The desertlike land stretched out endlessly ahead of us. It was a terrain I'd never seen before. The earth was hard and caked as if it had never seen a drop of water. In the far distance I could see the mountains and some gathering clouds.

All of a sudden, a warm hot wind came up the valley. My father seemed to enjoy fighting against it. He bent his head and kept running toward the cliffs in the distance. The boy followed him laughing all the time. I felt the hot wind parching my throat. My lungs felt as if they would burst. I knew that if I didn't keep running I would be left alone in that vast empty expanse.

In the distance I saw a big, dark cloud hugging the caked earth. Then I felt the first stinging pellets of the sandstorm. The sand began to whirl all around us. We were engulfed by the dark brown choking dust.

I could see my father and the boy in the middle of it. My father had taken the boy's hand so the wind wouldn't carry him away. They called to me, but the wind and the sand were seeping into every pore of me. I was suffocating and couldn't reach them. Finally, my father led us to a narrow opening of canyon by the side of a mountain. The tall cliffs on each side protected us from the whirling storm.

To my father and the boy it was all a great game. They scampered up into the dark canyon. I tried to catch my breath, and ran after them. Suddenly, the canyon came to a dead end. The huge cliffs all around us were unscalable. My father seemed unperturbed. He smiled, as if to say, well, here we are, the three of us. I saw that the boy had the same look on his face. They were both staring at me as if they expected me to say something. I didn't know what to say to them. At first, running down the hill, I had felt so light. I had been delighted to be included in their game; then, in the desert storm, I'd been afraid they'd leave me behind. Now, as they stared at me, I began to feel like an outsider.

I was about to tell them that I was part of them, when I heard the deep roar overhead. We all looked up. There on top of the cliff, silhouetted against the sky, was a black panther. She snarled at us as if we were intruders in her lair. Then she was joined by another and another and another, until the rim of the canyon seemed to be ringed with big black angry cats. The canyon reverberated with the growl from their throats.

I saw the leader take a leap. For an interminable moment she seemed to be stretched out there in space like a still photograph one sees among those pictures taken by white hunters in Africa. Then I realized that it was the signal for all the cats to jump on us. My father grabbed one of the cats and began wrestling with it. They didn't really seem to be fighting; somehow they seemed like two figures wrestling in the throes of passion. The boy ran to the side of the cliff and wedged himself in a crevice, where the cats tried in vain to reach him with their huge paws. I found myself on the floor with a huge sleek animal snarling and clawing at me. I reached out to protect myself and found myself fighting for my life. I hung onto the coarse black hair. I wrapped my legs around her, feeling that as long as I could hold on she wouldn't be able to bite my neck. I was growing weaker and I made a desperate grab for her throat.

I heard her scream. I woke up and I was on the floor. I was hoking my wife!

During my dream I had apparently screamed and Katie had ushed into the room. She had found me groaning and obviously n great pain. She had tried to shake me awake when I had rabbed her by the throat, thinking she was the black cat about o devour me.

When I came to I took Katie in my arms and tried to explain he dream. But she was in tears. Not only had I scared her to death but I had almost choked the life out of her. I picked her up and tried to put her to bed. She jumped out of my arms.

"Leave me alone," she screamed. "Don't touch me. I can't live ike this. I won't live like this. You're crazy . . . you're crazy!"

She left me there in the dark. She was right. We couldn't go on ike that.

# 24

WAITED for the doctor to stop pacing. I saw him stop and traighten a Chinese print on the wall. I had run out of words. Now it was his turn. I expected him to pick up the phone any econd and call for the paddy wagon boys to come and put me in a straitjacket. I would almost have welcomed it.

"Tony," he said, sitting down beside me, "are you capable of killing someone?"

"We're all capable of killing, Doctor. Remember, I told you the tory once: when I was nine years old I almost killed a man who was molesting my little sister."

"And yet you told me about the time when you couldn't throw he right hand at that black boy you were fighting."

"That was different."

"Do you like to hunt?"

"No, I can't stand to kill animals."

"Yet, you feel you could kill human beings?"

"One says 'I'll kill you' in anger, and one almost convinces one self that one can do it. It's easy to talk about killing ghosts. I don' know, Doc. I suppose when it really comes down to it, I wouldn' be able to kill another human being."

The doctor nodded. "In the dream you just told me about, you were very happy cavorting down the hill beside your father and the boy."

"Ecstatic. It's the only time I feel complete, when the three o us are together."

"Does that have anything to do with your early religious up bringing?"

"You mean the Father, the Son, and the Holy Ghost?"

"Exactly."

"Oh, come on, Doctor," I said, reaching for a cigarette. "I have no illusions about being God. I'm not that crazy!"

"But aren't we all part of God? Isn't God us? Isn't that basically what religion wants us to feel? That we are all gods within God Aren't we supposed to strive for His attributes, His goodness, Hi understanding, His love? If He is the Father and the Son and the Holy Ghost, then aren't we also striving for the same entity?"

I took a long puff. "Doctor, you've certainly changed since first came and sat here that first day. I thought you were strictl Freudian; there's a little bit of Jung creeping in."

He waved that chiding remark aside. "We've discussed deatl before, Tony. I hope we've made some inroads into the acceptanc of the life cycle. One is born and one dies."

"To an extent. I think of it as a chemical change, but for th purpose of discussion let's say I will go along with the terminol ogy."

"Have you accepted your son's death by now?"

I jumped to my feet. "No, that is one subject I will not discuss That is one subject I told you I'd never talk about. I will no accept his death. As long as I am alive, as long as I breathe, a long as I can hear and see and touch, he will breathe, see an hear and feel everything with me. I couldn't face life without him I can live without the boy if I have to, but I refuse and canno live without my son!"

I started for the door. The doctor stepped in front of me. "Al right, Tony, we won't discuss it. But you have just said somethin

300

ery important. You *can* live without the boy. He *is* the cause of
a lot of your pain. He has put all the people who loved you
through hell. He will never let you be. As long as you keep humoring him and acknowledging him, he is going to make un-
realistic demands on you. To you he is very real. He has a
corporeal existence. To me he is a ghost. He is a memory we all
carry of our youth. We all have dreams that never came true, but
we can't let them haunt us. You are not a young man. You have
done more than millions of human beings who have existed before you. Your life has not been worthless; you've given many
people a great deal of pleasure, and perhaps you even lighted the
way for others. It is time for you to enjoy the fruits of all your
labor. The boy won't let you. I am not a violent man. I even worry
about killing a fly, but in all consciousness I say — it's time to kill
the boy."

# 25

DROVE THE CAR like a fury. I paid no attention to stoplights or
traffic. The streets and buildings were one big blur as I headed
down Sunset Boulevard and into the section known as Belvedere.
I was not merely driving down crowded streets, I was hurtling
through time and space. I had to go back, far back, and still
farther — through pain. Instead of scenery and buildings passing
outside the car window, it was years flying by. I couldn't stop to
look or acknowledge any of it. My mood had become one big mad
scream: "Kill him! Kill the sonofabitch before he kills me!" I felt
like a man sinking under an anesthetic, gasping for air. I was in
the center of a big tidal wave and being engulfed.

I found myself leaning against the clapboard house at the bottom of the ravine, trying to catch by breath. I had no idea how I'd
gotten there. I tried to remember, then slowly it started to come
back. Yes, I had parked the car somewhere near Brooklyn and
Rowan, where I had hoped to surprise the boy. When I'd seen

that he wasn't there, I'd run like a maniac toward the house where he lived.

My lungs felt as if they'd burst like a toy balloon. I could hear a man's voice inside the house. I recognized it as my father's. I was terrified to look through the window. What would I see? Maybe my mother had been right. Why does one look into the past? What goddamned answers does one hope to find? Why not just look at the now?

"Manuela," I heard my father's big voice call out, "Where's my son, Tony?"

I knew then the scene that was going to be played out. It was one I had run over and over in my feverish brain, like a broken down projector that keeps repeating the same images on the screen.

I finally made myself look through the window. I knew every detail. I had seen it hundreds of times. The old familiar flicker of the kerosene lamp. The young, thirty-year-old man who was my father sitting at the table. The two women, my mother — God she looked young! — and my grandmother, hovering over him serving him dinner. Next to him, propped up on some pillows, was my sister at the age of seven. Standing beside my father was the boy. His shirt was a mess and his hair uncombed. I saw the brown bag of grapes in the center of the table. The boy looked at the floor, listening to his father's long harangue.

"Manuela, today when I got off the streetcar I looked all over for my son. He wasn't at his usual corner. Instead, I was met by a dirty little Mexican with his shirt hanging out and a dirty face. The boy kept insisting he was my son but I said, 'No, you can't fool me; my son is never dirty. My son springs from kings in Ireland on his father's side and from emperors on his mother's side, and he never forgets it. My son walks like a prince no matter if he is selling newspapers or shining shoes. His poverty is only temporary; his royal spirit is eternal.' "

I saw the boy's lips start to quiver. The one thing he wanted most in life was his father's approval and now that was being denied.

The boy's grandmother stepped in and took the boy by the arm. "Go and wash up, Antonio."

She led him out the back door, where the faucet was.

302

In spite of the pain of recalling the scene, I knew it was the wrong time for sentiment. I had come to do the deed and would not be put off.

I started around the house toward the back, already planning how I'd have to cover the boy's mouth so he couldn't call for help. Then I'd drag him down the arroyo and bash his brains in.

Then I heard my grandmother open the back door and hand the boy a tattered towel and a clean shirt. As I peeked cautiously around the corner, I saw Grandmother standing beside him as he combed his hair in front of the cracked mirror that hung over the faucet.

"What happened?" she asked him in a soft consoling voice.

The boy explained, trying to hold back the tears, that he and Carlos Ramirez had had to fight off some boys who wanted to steal his paper corner from him. Just then his father had descended from the streetcar and he'd had no time to tidy up.

The woman nodded and led the now clean boy back into the room. The father looked up and saw them enter. He got up and with a big smile on his face, said:

"Hey, Elephant, where have you been?"

The boy didn't know what to answer. "I'm sorry I'm late, Papa," he murmured.

"Son," said the father, putting his arm around the boy, "I was just telling the women you weren't at your usual corner when I got off the streetcar. Right?"

"That's right, Papa, I wasn't there."

The man let out a big laugh. "Of course not. That boy was not my son. Come on, sit down and have some dinner."

As they both sat down, the father pretended to see the paper bag in the center of the table for the first time.

"And what do we have here?"

"Some grapes, Papa. They are the first of the season."

The man took the bag and opened it as if he were opening a bag of precious jewels. He took the grapes and held them up in the air triumphantly.

"Manuela, Mother," he called, "look what our son has brought. Aren't they the most beautiful grapes you've ever seen in your life?"

303

The boy dug into his plate happily. He smiled for the firs<
time.

I felt so silly, so ridiculous, skulking outside in the dark wait
ing for the boy, but I knew he'd eventually come out.

After the boy had finished dinner and the man had shared th<
grapes with the family, the boy's mother reminded him that h<
had to go to his music lesson. The boy went and pulled th<
saxophone case out from under the army cot where he slept, anc
started out the front door.

I saw the boy hesitate at the bottom of the steps. Had he guessec
that I was hiding behind the wheelbarrow in the center of th<
rose garden Grandmother had planted?

The boy's father came to the front door. His big frame fillec
the doorway.

"Elephant," he called after the boy.

The boy was hoping his father would ask him to cancel th<
music lesson.

"Yes, Papa?"

"Hurry back, son. Maybe we'll play some cards or checkers."

"Yes, Papa. I'll be right back."

The boy started for the street, lugging the big case.

The father was still watching his son disappear in the night. I
couldn't leave my hiding place. When the man finally turned bacl
into the house, I ran after the boy.

The boy had taken a shortcut up the steep incline that led to
Brooklyn Avenue. He turned at the top when he heard my foot
steps.

I heard the saxophone hit the hillside and clatter down th<
ravine. The boy knew that I could cut him off if he headed bacl
toward the house. He started running across the street.

I ran after him. I'd forgotten how fast the little bastard was
I saw him start to clamber up the fence of the Belvedere Junio
High playground across the street. The fence was over six fee
high, and he was having difficulty climbing on the slippery wire

Just as I reached up for him and made a grab at his shirt, h<
jumped to the other side. I heard my pants tear as I vaulted th<
fence. I couldn't have cared less. I couldn't let the boy out of m<
sight.

He was running across the open soccer field. I made a desperat<

304

lying tackle at him and managed to grab his leg and trip him. Before he could recover, I was on top of him.

I had him by the throat. The boy clutched at my hands. He was fighting like a tiger.

I'd forgotten that he was used to the rough-and-tumble of street fighting, where no rules existed. I almost screamed in pain as I felt his knee butt me hard in the groin, but I knew that if I let him go I'd never be able to catch him again. I was too old to keep on running after him forever.

I hung on desperately. Soon my weight was too much for him. We seemed to be struggling there in the dark for hours, and now we were both spent.

I held onto him, as I tried to catch my breath. "I'm . . . I'm going to kill you, you little sonofabitch!"

As I reached for his throat and felt his body go soft in my hands, I was amazed by the feel of his skin. He reminded me of my own sons and the wonder of the feel of their skin.

God, oh God! I couldn't bring myself to close my hands on his throat. My fingers wouldn't respond. They seemed ossified, paralyzed.

I pulled my hands away and sat down beside him.

The boy lay on the ground, watching me.

"Kid," I said, after the heaving in my chest had subsided, "I don't want to kill you. But I will, unless you promise to lay off."

"Man, for years you've blamed me for all the shit you put yourself through. Have you really asked yourself how much of it is me and how much of it is you?"

"The doctor said —" I started feebly.

"Fuck the doctor. This is you and me talking. He only hears what you tell him. You're one of the great dodgers of all time. I don't listen to the words, I listen to what you are leaving out."

"No, now don't start it all up again. You have driven me up a wall. Nothing that I ever did pleased you."

"So why should you worry? Who the hell am I? I'm just a little eleven-year-old Mexican kid. What the hell would I know about your Beverly Hills, Paris, London and Costa Brava jet-set crowd? Why do you want my approval, as long as you have theirs? All you have to do is give big fancy parties in your house or yacht, and you've got it made."

"But that's not what I want, either."

"What do you want?"

I could feel his eyes piercing me in the dark. I couldn't bring myself to tell him I wanted his love. I didn't want to beg.

"I want him to approve of me. I want the old man to approve of me."

"He's tough. You want to be loaded with that royal shit story? He'll never approve of you unless you walk like a prince."

"What about you?"

"Me?" he asked softly. I could feel him trying to give me an honest answer. "I'm stuck with it. I have to believe him. He's my father. I've seen him take on big cats. I've seen him work like a common peon for me. I've watched him walk through shit and still glitter as if he were made of gold. I'll never meet another man like him. I'm stuck, mister."

I knew what he meant. We were both stuck.

"Have I ever pleased you?" I asked helplessly, as I had asked so many times before.

"A couple of times — when you dared. When you weren't thinking of protecting the things. When 'it' became more important than the approval of the cunts and the phony characters you thought were class."

I knew we were on dangerous terrain. I tried to change the subject, but he kept on.

"God, all those cows! That tall drink of water from London you brought down here once to show her how far you'd climbed in the world. That movie queen you almost committed suicide over."

"You were there?"

"Who the hell do you think pushed the gun aside? Did you think we'd all worked like sonsofbitches in the hot sun so that you'd end up putting a bullet in your head over a big-busted B-picture queen?"

"Come on now —" I started.

"No, let's have it out. Maybe the doctor is right, maybe you have to kill me — because I'm going to keep reminding you that you're never going to find monogamy going from bed to bed."

"Suppose I promise that I'll —"

"No, it's too late with her. I know you blame me for that going wrong."

I stood up. "Don't tell me you weren't."

"Not all of it. In the beginning, yes. Later it was you."

I could feel my anger rising again. It was no use. I couldn't reason with him.

He got up slowly.

We stood there, waiting for each other to make the first move. I knew that if he started to run, I'd lose him in the dark. I lowered my voice as if approaching a dangerous animal.

"I won't take the blame for her. We're both guilty."

The boy started to move away from me cautiously.

"Come on, boy, don't start it all over again. I don't want to chase you."

I held up my hands to prove that I didn't intend to get into another death struggle with him. He wouldn't believe me, and kept backing away.

"Your wife is right, you know; you are crazy — you are capable of murder."

The reminder of that painful incident infuriated me. I moved toward him menacingly. He turned and ran for the fence. I saw him lean down and pick up a piece of abandoned lead pipe. He waved it over his head. I stopped in my tracks.

"You'd kill *me*, wouldn't you?" I asked in surprise.

He clutched at the pipe. "Don't try me. If you think *I'm* going to let *you* kill *me*, you're out of your mind."

I had reached an impasse. How the hell do you kill a ghost? What weapons do you use? I looked up at the starry sky for an answer. I heard no voice from Heaven.

The boy stood there with the pipe, ready for action. It was no use. I knew I had lost. I turned and started across the fence. The boy started after me.

"Hey — hey, mister, where you going?"

"To hell with you, kid. There are more ways than one to kill you. As far as I'm concerned I'll just turn you off. You're just another ghost."

"You'll never make it, old man. My father and I will haunt you for the rest of your life. We're not going to let you rest, no matter what you do. You can surround yourself with all the things and the crap, you will never enjoy them. No matter how many beds you hop into hoping to feel loved, you're not going to find it."

I knew he was right. Walking away was not going to accomplish a damned thing. I knew the answer. It was so simple, but my pride wouldn't let me. I couldn't beg the little sonofabitch and yet I knew it was the only thing that would calm my feverish brain. I wanted the boy to love me, or at the least, to stop rejecting me. The boy guessed it.

"Man, I don't want to hurt you. I know all you've done. I know about all the shit you've had to take. I know the times you've stood up to be counted, honest I do. But you can't run away now and pretend a whole life never happened. You can't pretend Sylvia or Father or Mother or any of us never existed." I turned on him. "You mean you all want your pound of flesh?"

"No, man, we're not your agents; we won't be content with ten percent, you stupid idiot," he shouted angrily. "We did it all because we loved you. We want the best for you. All we demand in return is that you give us your best."

The fact that he'd said he loved me brought mist to my eyes. If only he hadn't said it in anger like that, everything might have been solved right there and then.

"You knew when you came here you wouldn't be able to kill me," he continued. "It would be like killing yourself. You came down here to make a deal, right?"

"Boy, I'm damned tired. I'd like to rest for a change. It's been a long haul. So I didn't find the streets paved with gold; I didn't find that miracle for you, but I've done my best."

"No, mister, you've been just another movie actor with the hot wants. There are bigger things in life. More important things."

"Like what?"

"Like knowing that nobody in the world has it made until everybody gets a fair shake."

"Kid, I'm not ever going to be any kind of a God. You're right, I'm just an actor. For better or worse I've tried to say it all with the tools I had. I know how you look down your nose at everything I do. Maybe it would have been a better life as an architect, but already they've started to tear down Frank Lloyd Wright's buildings as antiquated. The literary sharks have begun to tear to pieces all the work Hemingway left behind. Our hero Thomas

Wolfe is now considered an overblown windbag. It's all changing. There *are* no permanent truths. Acting may not be the most noble profession in the world, but it's the only one that was open to me. And believe me, kid, a lot of us go way out on the limb trying to grapple with the truth. And truth is a double-edged sword. You have to handle it with great care or you can cut off your balls."

I turned away and headed for the fence without looking back. As I vaulted over it I heard the kid laughing. "Hey, you're still in pretty good shape for an old man."

I paid no attention to him as I headed for my car, over by the lumberyard. I could hear his footsteps behind me. I walked down the dark alley and saw the familiar black convertible waiting for me. The boy stood silently by as I turned the key and heard the deep purr of the engine.

"Nice car, mister."

I leaned out the window. "Yes, it is, boy, and I've earned it by the sweat of my groin. I've taken more beatings for it than all the punches thrown at me at those smokers. But you know what?"

"What?"

"I'd give it all up if I could come up with one undying statement."

The boy smiled. "Like the ocean is too small to quench my thirst?"

"No, that one just drove us nuts. I mean something people could live by in peace without all the hot wants."

"It's very simple, man. It has to do with love."

I nodded. "And that, young man, is the hardest word to deal with. *That* you can't demand or buy or make a deal for. It just has to *be* — like faith."

I threw the car into gear and started to pull away. The boy ran beside the car.

"Hey, take me with you."

"Where do you want to go?" I asked.

"Everywhere," he said, running beside the car. "Anywhere. We'll find it together."

"You want too much, kid. When you reach my age the legs begin to go. I can't get you what you want."

"How do you know what I really want?"

Something in his voice made me stop the car. I studied his face, and the high Indian cheekbones and the tousled hair coming down over the forehead. "What is it you really want?"

He looked directly into my eyes. I felt I was seeing myself for the first time. "I want you to love me, to accept me. I don't want to be a ghost, I want to be part of you."

I reached over and pulled the handle of the car door. "Get in."

He jumped into the car and sat down beside me. As I started the car up again, down the gutted alley, I saw the boy reach out and touch the rich black leather on the dashboard.

"Where shall we head for?" I asked him, as we turned into Brooklyn Avenue.

"When was the last time you were in the desert?"

"About a year ago. The Jordanian desert."

"How was it?"

"I felt God was there."

I didn't have to go into details. He understood. Perhaps he'd been there with me on that afternoon when I'd gotten lost among the sand dunes and felt for a few frightening moments the full meaning of eternity.

He smiled. "Let's head for the desert, man. Let's see if God is there."

I turned right down the dark boulevard. As we passed the boy's house I could see the kerosene lamp still burning. The boy remembered that the saxophone case was still lying down there in the ditch. I was beginning to read his mind.

"Forget the sax, kid. You'll never be a Rudy Vallee."

I revved the car engine and sped along the empty avenue. Through the rearview mirror I could see the streetlights flickering in the distance. I could have sworn I saw a big enormous black cat sniffing at the pavement where my father had died. I thought I saw it start to run after the car, then it was swallowed up in the dark night.

I looked at the boy beside me. He had gone to sleep. I reached over and caressed his unkempt head. There was a smile on his face.

When we reached the desert I saw the first flicker of dawn over the Sierra mountain range. The boy woke up as the car came to a halt on top of a bluff. Down below, the multicolored desert stretched out for miles and miles. There was no sign of life.

I jumped out of the car and started down a long sandy hill, hoping to get to the floor of the desert and watch the sun flood the baked earth with its light. The boy ran past me, his little legs churning up the sand.

When we got to the hard bottom of the desert, the sun made its majestic appearance over the ridge.

I knelt down before the awesome power of the birth of a new day and asked God to light the way. When I finished I looked up and saw the boy standing beside me.

"Anybody that can still be brought to his knees by the miracle of a new day can't be all bad, mister."

"Yeah," I had to agree, "I feel better."

"Say it, man."

"Say what?"

"Love," he said simply.

I tried to get the word out but it wouldn't come.

"L . . . ," I started, but the doctor had been right; there was something caught in my throat. I had to disgorge it before I could say the word.

I felt my body begin to heave and the dam of tears came pouring out. When the tears were done I tried to articulate the word tentatively. At first it came out as a hoarse whisper — "L . . . ove" — then clear and louder — "Love" — "LOVE."

The canyons all around me reverberated with the only answer to all pain — "L O V E !"

The boy was suddenly gone. But I knew I'd never again be alone.

I shouted out joyously, just for the hell of it — "L O V E !"